ENGLISH FOR LAW STUDENTS

With a foreword by
Professor Vijay K Bhatia

City University of Hong Kong

ENGLISH FOR LAW STUDENTS

C VAN DER WALT

Academic Support Services, University of Stellenbosch
BA Hons (English) PU
Hons (Applied Linguistics) PU
MA PU for CHE
D Litt University of Pretoria

A G NIENABER

Senior Lecturer in Law, University of Pretoria
Advocate of the High Court of South Africa
BA Hons (English) University of the Witwatersrand
LLM University of Pretoria

First Edition 1997
Second Impression 1999
Third Impression 2001
Second Edition 2002
Second Impression 2004
Third Impression 2005
Fourth Impression 2006
Fifth Impression 2007
Sixth Reprinted 2007

© Juta & Co, Ltd
PO Box 24299, Lansdowne 7779

First edition edited by Dr W. McKay
Page design by Jo Goodwill
Cover design by Pencil Box
Typesetting by Mckore Graphics

ISBN 0 7021 5928 X

Printed by Shumani Printers

FOREWORD
TO THE FIRST EDITION

Of all the specialist disciplines within English for Specific Purposes, it is English for Law which has been given very little attention. In the last few years, there have been several expressions of general concern for a significant level of decline in the standards of legal expression, including those from the UK, the USA, Australia and a number of other Commonwealth countries, but efforts to repair this damage have been few and far between. There are several reasons for such neglect.

Although legal language has almost universally been acknowledged as problematic as far as its construction, interpretation and use is concerned, attempts to introduce reforms in legislation and other genres of legal language have always met with resistance from the professional legal communities. Like many other disciplinary cultures, legal professionals also like to maintain the integrity of the specialist genres they tend to use for the achievement of their professional goals.

Secondly, as is generally the case with most professional uses of language, legal genres have always been considered the privileged concerns of the legal discourse community and therefore beyond the reach of a wide majority of English language teachers. In the context of legal education, therefore, language training has always been considered the responsibility of the legal experts rather than that of the language teacher. However, most legal educators have neither the time nor the expertise in language teaching to train their students in the intricacies of legal communication, with the result that most of these apprentice legal scholars have generally been left on their own to learn the use of legal expression at work. In most cases, it is like learning surgery from experience, which can be very difficult for the surgeon and equally hard on the patient.

Thirdly, although legal language has long been the focus of attention in philosophy and sociology, in linguistics and discourse studies, it has attracted attention only recently. In fact, the field of discourse and text analysis itself is of very recent origin. Any principled and pedagogically effective approach to specialist language teaching requires a considerable research effort in the analysis of legal genres and a period of sustained interest in the subject discipline.

Finally, unlike the sciences, law has never been regarded as a universal discipline. Since there are a variety of legal systems in use in different countries, one tends to assume that linguistic as well as discoursal requirements will necessarily operate quite differently across national boundaries, and hence English for law courses have been assumed to be unlikely to travel from one country to another or from one legal system to another. This assumption makes English for Law a somewhat less attractive commercial proposition than, for example, English for Science and Technology, or even for Business and Economics. To some extent this may be true, but it is equally likely that it may not be so. Linguistic research in discourse and genre analysis in the last few years indicates that in spite of the variation in legal systems in different countries, there can still be a considerable common linguistic ground to motivate a more or less common and yet flexible approach to English for law.

In this context, the volume of teaching materials put together by C VAN DER WALT and A G NIENABER (two of the main interested participants, an English and a law teacher) is an extremely significant development. Although, in an area like this, it is important to combine expertise from the subject discipline with that in applied linguistics, it is by no means an easily accessible option. It can be even more difficult than trying to find a team of perfect dancing partners, who are expected to perform their role harmoniously without getting in each other's way. The authors of this book have combined their expertise in the areas of English and Law, with their experience of teaching students who are not first language users of English to cope with their studies in the specialist discipline, to produce a very useful and effective set of teaching materials to help English for Law teachers to train apprentice law graduates.

The authors are not new to the field of English for Academic Legal Purposes. They have completed and published several studies in the field and this set of materials is based on a comprehensive investigation of the language needs of law graduates, which they have published in various legal and other journals. This certainly is one of the many strengths of the volume. Many of the early ESP materials published in the seventies and some published more recently have failed to make an impact, partly because of the lack of either a research basis in terms of a rigorous analysis of the learners' needs or an understanding of the nature of the specialist use of language being taught. This volume has plenty of evidence to support the claim that the authors have done their homework carefully and are well acquainted with the realities of the classroom in legal contexts. The materials have been based on a systematic study of their students' use of English in academic legal settings.

One of the most interesting and insightful strategies the authors have used to their advantage is in the teaching of grammar. Unlike many other ESP textbook writers who either ignore grammar completely or incorporate features of general grammar as part of their materials, Van der Walt and Nienaber have used specifically problematic and relevant features of the syntax of law for an 'incidental' discourse-based teaching of grammar. This approach makes teaching of grammar not only interesting but most relevant too. Syntax has such an important role to play in legal expression that any neglect on the part of the language teacher can have disastrous consequences. On the other hand, the use of syntax in legal language is highly complex and specialised, so any account of general grammar can be misleading, inadequate and pedagogically ineffective, and of course, boring. So the key to the teaching of grammar in English for Law courses is to make it **specific** (on the basis of analytical investigation), **relevant** (as a result of ethnographic and textual analyses of learners' difficulties) and **motivating** (by using ESP methodology, which is explanatory and interesting). The authors have made a good attempt to incorporate all these into a pedagogically economical and effective set of materials. Although the book has been written for a specific audience, in a number of ways, especially in terms of the general approach and the nature of exercises, the materials can usefully be adapted for undergraduate level academic pro-grammes in other parts of the English speaking world.

Another interesting aspect of the book is that it has been designed to be used either independently as a course book, or as a flexible set of materials, which can be supplemented by the practising teacher. In either case, the authors recommend an approach which takes advantage of the expertise of the subject teacher in an effort which could be regarded as a close approximation of what has been regarded as a fairly well-established ESP methodological innovation in the form of team-teaching.

I feel that it is a very useful addition to the field of English for Law, which has long been waiting for such a break-through in terms of teaching materials. The teachers of English who have an interest and an obligation to train prospective legal professionals will find it a very useful addition to their collection of teaching materials.

Professor Vijay K Bhatia
17 August 1997
Department of English
City University of Hong Kong
Hong Kong

FOREWORD
FOR LECTURERS

BACKGROUND

The approach, design and content of this book are based on four years of empirical research that included performance analyses of student writing in law subjects, a needs analysis conducted among undergraduate law students at three different universities and numerous interviews with law students and their lecturers in law faculties and in departments of English. The full report was published in the law journal *De Jure* (Vol 1, 1996, pp 71–88) under the title, 'The language needs of undergraduate law students: A report on empirical investigations.'

This second edition incorporates suggestions from lecturers who use the book. We also included a number of new exercises. The two revision units have been substituted in their entirety.

THE STRUCTURE OF THE COURSE

The book has fourteen units and two revision units in the form of one-hour tests. At the start we provide practice in those study skills that students will need right from the first day of formal study. Each unit is divided into three main sections: section A is concerned mainly with the development of reading skills, section B focuses on functional grammar activities above sentence level and section C develops study and communication skills in an integrated fashion. At the back of this book we provide a list which details the development of skills (in all three sections) from the first to the last unit.

We cover the grammatical points that **law** students find most problematic (as is evident from performance analyses of their writing). In our view students need to become autonomous learners, capable of using grammars and dictionaries to continue the learning process outside the classroom. For this reason we offer some explanation of grammatical terms and rules. We do not follow traditional grading conventions (for example from 'simple' to 'complex' tenses) but deal with features of grammar as they appear in reading texts and according to the demands of the sections on integrated skills.

SCHEDULING THE WORK

At a rate of two periods (of one hour each) per week, the course could be completed in a single semester. When we tried out our material in real life, we barely succeeded in completing Section A of a single unit in an hour with a big class (more than 100 students). If lecturers should include additional reading, oral, grammar and writing activities, this expands the book into a full year course. For example, you could add listening comprehension activities to enhance the note-making skills described in the first five units.

FEEDBACK ON EXERCISES

One of the most important comments on the first edition related to the amount of feedback we included at the back of the book. Many lecturers complained that they could not use the exercises because of the readily available feedback. For this reason we removed this section of the book and it is now available on disk from the publishers.

COOPERATION BETWEEN FACULTIES

We designed the units in such a way that they may also be used for self-study. Obviously students will gain the maximum benefit from group discussions and detailed feedback from tutors. Similarly, close cooperation between the law faculty and language lecturers will lead to the development of exercises and tests which are most pertinent to the students' needs. The revision units offer examples of the types of questions that could be set for tests and examinations. We did not include questions that require practice in argumentative writing in the revision units because they are difficult to self-evaluate. Lecturers should devise their own tests.

Clearly, students will not be able to acquire all the language skills they need to be successful in a single year. We propose that students be given continuous guidance in the form of extended writing tasks. For example, after students have finished their compulsory language course, they will have to write assignments and research papers in advanced law courses. The first drafts of assignments could be edited for errors by the students with the assistance of the language specialist, making the acquisition of language skills an on-going process. This implies close cooperation between the language specialist and lecturers in the law faculty.

Our hope is that teaching from this book will give you as much pleasure as we had in writing it!

The authors, 2002

FOREWORD
FOR STUDENTS

This book was written for all students who study law in English, whether they are first-language speakers of English or students who use English as an additional language. We studied the type of errors law students make in their writing and we asked them to tell us what they expect from a language course. On the basis of their responses, needs and problems we designed this course.

The purpose of this book is not to teach you law, but to develop skills which will help you to read, study and write successfully in your law subjects. You will encounter subjects with which you may not be familiar yet, but this should not deter you from applying and developing reading, writing and thinking skills on such material. We use extracts from law textbooks, cases and legislation and you should use your knowledge of the law in class discussions and writing activities. You will need to enter into a partnership with your language lecturer so that she helps you with reading and communication problems while you provide the legal know-how.

We hope that through this book, you will become more aware of the role of language in law studies.

The authors, 2002

CONTENTS

UNIT 14:
Advanced Research in Law Subjects

ACKNOWLEDGEMENTS

We would like to acknowledge the help and support of lecturers and students in departments of English and faculties of law at Vista University (Mamelodi Campus), University of Pretoria, the University of South Africa and Potchefstroom University for CHE. Students who answered question-naires should take credit not only for assisting us, but also for helping future generations of students.

We would like to thank Prof André van der Walt of the law faculty of the University of Stellenbosch for reading the final manuscript and for making suggestions regarding the content and the pedagogical design of the course. We would also like to thank Dr Walter McKay for editing the manuscript at very short notice. Any errors remaining are ours alone.

Permission has been sought to reproduce material from D R White (ed) *Trials and Tribulations: An Anthology of Appealing Legal Humour* 1989 Highland Park: Catbird Press.

Permission has been granted to reproduce extracts from the following publications:
- S A Strauss *Doctor, Patient and the Law* 1991 Pretoria: JL van Schaik (pp 126–128)
- Dick Usher 'Plain words' *Fair Lady* (17 May 1995)
- J P Naudé *Butterworths Forms and Precedents* Vol 6 Part 2: 44 1994. 'Marriage and settlement contracts' Durban: Butterworths
- Jordaan, Louise, 1993.'*Mens rea* – common purpose – dissociation from – *S v Singo* 1993 1 SACR 226 (A) *Codicillus* 34(2): 75–76
- Ehrenbeck, Mirelle 1995 Constitutional law – Human rights – Right of access to state information – Police docket – *Khala v Minister of Safety and Security* 1994 4 SA 218 WLD *Codicillus* 36 (1): 72–73
- Roos, Annelies, 1994. Law of delict – Defamation Defences – Onus of proof – *Neethling v Du Preez and Others*; *Neethling v The Weekly Mail and Others* 1994 1 SA 708 (A) Codicillus 35 (2): 102–104
- G Block *Effective Legal Writing* Fourth Edition 1992 New York: Founda-tion Press, Inc
- E Campbell, E J Tooher & L P York *Legal Research: Materials and Methods* Fourth Edition 1988 North Ryde: The Law Book Company (pp 271–272)

- H C Bosman *Cold Stone Jug* 1999 Cape Town: Human & Rousseau (pp 101–102)
- W le Roux 'Something as strange as the African veld': Herman Charles Bosman, story telling and democratic citizenship *Codicillus* 41(2): 7–21.
- Barry Ronge 2000 *Filthy Lucre*. Sunday Times Magazine
- Beeld (for the article on Rastafarians in Unit 8)
- Natal Witness (for the article on Rastafarians in Unit 8)

UNIT 1
INTRODUCTION TO ENGLISH FOR LAW STUDENTS

A READING
Beginner's guide for law students by D Kleyn and F Viljoen (1995:1,2)

B LANGUAGE FOCUS
1 WORD FORMATION
2 ADJECTIVES
3 ADJECTIVE BUILD-UP
4 NOMINALIZATION

C INTEGRATED SKILLS
1 DRAWING UP A SCHEDULE OF WORK FOR THE ACADEMIC YEAR
2 NOTE-MAKING SKILLS: STAYING ORGANIZED
3 CORRESPONDING WITH INSTITUTIONS OF LEARNING
4 STUDY NOTE

This unit introduces you to the language of the law: we talk about tertiary education in general, law studies in particular, and the way in which language pervades and determines academic study at tertiary level. We touch on the use of dictionaries and the formation of words. To help you plan your studies we discuss the drafting and use of study programmes and how to write formal letters to tertiary institutions of learning.

A READING

In this section of each unit you will be asked to **skimread**, **scan** or to read **closely** or **carefully**.

- To **skimread** means to read quickly, usually focusing on headings, the first and last lines of paragraphs and words that are underlined or

1

emphasized in **bold** print. The purpose of this type of reading is to get the **gist** or a global impression of a text.

- To **scan** is to look at the page, searching for specific information. For example, if you are looking for a report on your soccer team's weekend match you will scan the sports pages for a photo or a heading that indicates such a report.
- To do **close reading** or to read carefully is self-explanatory. Such reading will take time, you will probably have to read the same text more than once, focusing on main and supporting ideas.

Before you read the text below, think about **study** at **tertiary level** (colleges, technikons, universities). Which of the following beliefs about tertiary education best reflects your own ideas on the topic?

- Being a student is simply a stage of life during which all young people experiment with outlandish ideas in the safety of an environment where they cannot do any real harm.
- A student is a type of apprentice, preparing to practice a specific trade or profession.
- It is not so important that students learn something at the various institutions; they must enjoy the time spent there and get rid of all their youthful irresponsibility. There will be enough time for the harsh realities of life later on.
- Tertiary education is the gateway to a better life. No matter what somebody studies, she is sure to be a better person and worthy of a high salary.
- An institution of tertiary education is a place where students learn to think creatively and form their own opinions while they prepare themselves for an occupation or profession.

What do your friends think? Perhaps you prefer a combination of these ideas? One's view of university or college education depends to a large extent on the culture of a country. We, the authors of this book, like the last option and for this reason we wrote the book. We hope to challenge you to think about certain matters while helping you to develop the language skills you need in your law studies and in law-related professions.

Skimread the following extract from the introduction to *Beginner's guide for law students* by Kleyn and Viljoen (1995:1,2, see 4 *Study note* at the end of this unit). Your lecturer can time you or you can time yourself: you should not take more than one minute.

2

INTRODUCTION

Studying at university differs from that at school. The university student has to **master** a huge mass of study material in a short period of time. She must be able to **evaluate** critically and be able to **apply** knowledge to facts.

This applies particularly to the study of law. Law is part of our everyday   5
experience, so it is more accessible than the study fields of, say, engineering or medicine. No student of average intelligence, therefore, needs to be overwhelmed by the study of law. However, our everyday world is governed by a multitude of legal rules. The most striking feature of studying law is the **volume** of material that has to be absorbed. Students are required to understand   10
and apply rules and principles and be able to criticise them. A meaningless repetition of facts is neither required nor expected.

Although you are required to learn a lot about law, no lawyer will ever know the law in its entirety. You will learn certain **skills**. After the completion of your studies, you must have acquired the **techniques** and knowledge to   15
find the law on any topic. These tools are dealt with in chapters 4 and 19.

Success lies in **dedication and discipline**. The most important hint to a student is to remain involved with the subject continuously. We recommend involvement in three phases:

⇒ **Before a lecture or tutorial class:** prepare.   20
⇒ **During a lecture or tutorial class:** listen and make notes.
⇒ **After a lecture or tutorial class:** revise and assimilate all the
    information.

Study methods differ from student to student and depend on each student's **personality**. It will also differ from **study field** to study field. No single   25
method can, for instance, be used consistently in both legal philosophy and criminal procedure. Individual **lecturers** may also have their own requirements. You will have to adapt to these. The **method of examination** (such as an open-book test) may also require a different study method. The guidelines here are, therefore, not directives, but suggestions. They are   30
provided to help you find your own style and study method through experimentation.

Give brief answers to the following questions without going back to the text:

1   Which of the five views of tertiary education (mentioned above) do Kleyn and Viljoen hold?

2   According to the extract, what is the most striking feature of studying law?

3   Which characteristics, according to the authors, will lead to success in the study of law?

4   In one sentence state the point the authors make in the last paragraph.

5   What is the purpose of the words printed in **bold**?

6   What is the purpose of the arrows in lines 20–23 of the extract?

Read the passage again, more carefully this time. You should not take more than a minute and a half. Check and revise your answers to the questions above.

Two law subjects are mentioned in the last paragraph of the extract: legal philosophy and criminal procedure. Which law subjects will you follow this year? On a clean sheet of paper, write them down and add the course codes and the lecturer(s) responsible for each course. If necessary, divide the page in order to list first and second semester subjects.

Put this list of subjects where you can see it every day because it is important to keep the different subjects and their lecturers separate in your mind. We will return to this list later in the unit.

WORDS AND THEIR MEANINGS

Which of the following words do you think are important for an understanding of the extract (underline your choices):

evaluate	accessible
overwhelmed	multitude
entirety	dedication
consistently	directives

Re-read the sentences in which these words appear and write down what you think they mean. Even if you do not know exactly, try to guess the meaning from the **context** (the text that surrounds the word). For example:

> *directives*: The context of this word is the sentence in which it appears (line 30): 'The guidelines here are, therefore, not directives, but suggestions' (Kleyn and Viljoen 1995:1,2).

4

The 'not ... but ...' words in the sentence tell you that *directives* is opposite in meaning to *suggestions*. When you make a suggestion, you advise or propose a specific course of action that another person may follow or ignore. The opposite of *suggestion* is a more binding proposal, more along the lines of an order or instruction. Therefore, a *directive* is like an order or an instruction. As you can see, you can get some idea of the meaning of a word by looking at the word in its context.

Not every word in a text is vital for your understanding of the text. Consult with your lecturer or your study group and decide whether you agree with us that the following words are **not** crucial to the understanding of the extract from Kleyn and Viljoen:

> accessible, multitude, consistently, directives

Why are these words not so important? If you read the sentences in which they appear you will see that you can understand, more or less, what the writer wants to say even if you omit those words. If we re-write the sentences in which *accessible* and *multitude* appear, leaving out the phrases in which these words appear, they read:

> Law is part of our everyday experience. No student of average intelligence, therefore, needs to be overwhelmed by the study of law. However, our everyday world is governed by legal rules. The most striking feature of studying law is the **volume** of material that has to be absorbed.

Note that our version is not as clear in meaning as the original. We want to make the point that you can get to the general meaning of a text without understanding every single word, because the author usually gives us more than a single clue to the meaning of the text.

DICTIONARY EXERCISE

Dictionaries are a necessity for students in arts and law faculties. Moreover, one kind of dictionary is not enough. If you study through a language that is not your first language you need **four** different types of dictionaries:

- a bilingual dictionary, with your first language and the language of learning in both directions, for example, English to Sesotho and Sesotho to English.

- a dictionary of the language of learning, that is, a dictionary of, for example, English that explains words in English (a monolingual dictionary).
- a thesaurus, which is a dictionary that groups together words with more or less the same meaning.
- a law dictionary, preferably one that includes a section explaining Latin and technical terms.

This may seem over-ambitious, especially if your law books already are quite expensive, but dictionaries are an investment. You could consider buying a bilingual and an explanatory dictionary first and using library copies of the others, until you are able to buy them as well.

You need a **bilingual** dictionary to check for the meaning of words used in lectures and textbooks and to translate terms from your first language when you write assignments.

You need an '**explanatory**' or **monolingual** dictionary to check on derivations of words and their spelling. A bilingual dictionary will give you the spelling of *focus*, but it will not tell you (as a monolingual dictionary does) that the past tense form is *focused* (with one *s*) and that the word can be used with the prepositions *on* after a verb and *in/ out of* after a noun. Some dictionaries of this kind also give examples of sentences in which the words appear.

A **thesaurus** is indispensable for writing assignments and essays. It helps you to find the right word. One can usually look up, for example, an English word for a Sesotho word, but it may not be quite the right word in the context of your writing. A thesaurus gives you a list of *synonyms* (words that mean more or less the same) from which you can choose the word most suited to the context of your writing. This process works on the basis that users recognize the appropriate word mainly because they have seen it used previously in the texts that they read.

Finally, a **law dictionary** will become increasingly important as you continue your studies, especially if you come across very specialized legal and Latin terms that are not usually included in ordinary dictionaries.

Those of you who are fortunate enough to work with word-processing programmes that include spell-checkers and dictionaries will probably only need a bilingual and a law dictionary.

1   Study the following synonyms for *evaluate*:
    assess, calculate, estimate, gauge, judge, rate, reckon, value

Re-read line 3 in the extract from *Beginner's guide for law students* and decide which of the above synonyms can be used instead of *evaluate* without changing the meaning of the original sentence.

2   Which synonym is the basic form or stem of the word *evaluate*?

The meaning of a word can often be derived (obtained or acquired) by going back to its most basic form: its stem. One builds words by adding to the stem. Use an ordinary dictionary or a thesaurus and find the stem of the following words:

striking   entirety

3   Your ability to use a dictionary with ease and efficiency depends to a large extent on your knowledge of the alphabet. See how quickly you can arrange the following words in alphabetical order:
    try, trial, ticket, transfer, trail, title, tried, trustee, tuition, title registration, tutorial, two, transit, transference, transferee, tout, time-share, trust

4   You will need the same skill to draw up a list of sources when you hand in an assignment or dissertation. See how quickly you can arrange the following authors in alphabetical order:

Joubert, M   Albrecht, L.
Martins, de L.S.   Albrechtsoon, J.S.
Van Eck, J.J.   Van Wyk, A.M.
Mongane, W.S.   Van der Westhuizen, M
Williams, A.J.   Mokoena, D.B.
Rashid, A.   Mokwena, R.
Rasheed, M.   Radebe, N.

Consult your lecturer to check that you have followed your institution's **bibliographical style** (the way in which sources are listed). Each institution, and sometimes each faculty, has its own style. For example, surnames that start with 'Van' are sometimes not listed under 'V, but under the first letter of the last part of the surname. In the above examples 'Van Eck' would then be listed under 'E' and 'Van Wyk' under 'W'.

B LANGUAGE FOCUS

It is useful, particularly in an academic situation, to know how words are formed and what their function is in a sentence. In the above examples we said that the meanings of words can be **derived** by looking at their stems, for example *evaluate* can be traced back to *value*. Let us assume that you still do not know what *evaluate* means. You know it has something to do with *value*, which is a more familiar word. But you can get even closer to the meaning if you know the function of the word in the sentence. Is the word a *verb* or a *noun*? Does it describe another verb or noun? If you know that it is a verb, then *evaluate* is something that a person (in this case a student) does.

If you have forgotten what the following terms mean, ask your lecturer to explain or look them up in a dictionary or grammar book:

noun   verb
adjective   adverb

We think that it is important for you to know these terms because they can help you to study from grammar books and dictionaries without the aid of a teacher.

The extract from *Beginner's guide for law students*, line 3, reads: 'She must be able to evaluate critically' (Kleyn and Viljoen 1995:1). We know that *evaluate* functions as a verb and means something along the lines of *to value*. With this knowledge we can read the first paragraph again and, because of the context, we can guess that *evaluate* must mean something along the lines of 'The student will have to value critically a huge mass of study material'. Competent users of English (not necessarily first-language speakers), know the 'tricks' of getting meaning from a text because they know they will not always have time to look up words. They can also use this knowledge to make new words, for example, *evaluation* from *evaluate*.

1   WORD FORMATION

Look at the following words and complete the table by giving the function of the word (noun, adjective, verb or adverb) and making a new word that belongs to the word class given in brackets:

WORDS	FUNCTION	NEW WORD
For example		
study	verb or noun	adjective: studious
critically		(verb)
average		(verb)
absorb		(adjective)
completion		(adverb)
prepare		(noun)
consistently		(noun)
adapt		(noun)
revise		(noun)
procedure		(adjective)

legal		(noun)
criminal		(noun × 3)
directive		(verb)
individual		(adverb)
different		(noun)

2 ADJECTIVES

Negative forms of adjectives can sometimes cause spelling problems, for example

legal becomes *illegal*
material becomes *immaterial*
reconcilable becomes *irreconcilable*

Write down the negative form of the adjectives in the following legal phrases. They do not necessarily start with 'i-', as in the examples.

a) (retrievable) breakdown of marriage
b) (fair) labour practice
c) (literate) person
d) in an (official) capacity
e) (perfect) title
f) (tenable) argument
g) (effective) government
h) (lawful) assembly
i) (sane) person
j) (admissible) evidence
k) (proper) conduct
1) (solvent) estate
m) (limited) funding
n) (visible) exports
o) (revocable) trust

3 ADJECTIVE BUILD-UP

The use of several adjectives to describe one noun may create problems. Block (1992:91, see 4 *Study note*) calls this 'adjective build-up'. For example:

• small claims court cases
• failed juvenile delinquency rehabilitation programmes
• annual executive committee meeting

It is not always possible to avoid a string of adjectives and in descriptive language use we find sentences like:

9

- a fancy red woollen cardigan
- brand new Italian leather sandals

As a general rule a more neutral adjective follows one which expresses a personal point of view, as in **failed** *juvenile delinquency rehabilitation programmes* and *a **fancy** red woollen cardigan*. In the case of descriptive language, grammar books suggest that adjectives are listed according to the rule **size – age – colour – origin – material – noun.**

However, in the case of law texts it might be better to eliminate some of the adjectives in the following ways:

- make verbs and adverbs of nouns and adjectives:
    annual executive committee meeting
        becomes
    ... the executive committee that meets annually ...

    failed juvenile delinquency rehabilitation programmes
        becomes
    ... programmes to rehabilitate juvenile delinquents failed ...

- change the word order:
    small claims court cases
        becomes
    ... cases brought before the small claims court ...

As you can see, each of the examples makes a sentence in itself, and the problem of adjective build-up can be avoided by making an extra sentence or phrase.

Try to improve the following phrases by eliminating adjective build-up:

a) absent, tax-evading farmer syndrome
b) inter-regional traffic regulation ordinances
c) small craft industry insurance
d) third international public sector industrial enterprise show
e) unemployment compensation fund statistics

4 NOMINALIZATION

Writers of law books are often accused of overusing **nominalization**, that is, they use **nouns** where they could use an active verb, adverb or adjective with only one noun. (**Nouns** are words that **name** things. If you change a verb to a noun, you **nominalize** the verb.) The above examples of adjective build-up also illustrate nominalization, because nouns are used to describe nouns, and verbs and adjectives are avoided.

Compare sentences (a) and (b):

a) The defendant was found guilty of the acceptance and use of drugs and the court put emphasis on the importance of juvenile rehabilitation.
b) The court found the defendant guilty of accepting and using drugs and emphasized the importance of juvenile rehabilitation.

Which sentence is an example of excessive **nominalization**?

If you thought (a), you are right. Although this sentence is not incorrect, it is clumsy. Nominalization often requires the author to repeat *of* in sentence (a): 'guilty **of** the acceptance and use **of** ...'. The sentence is also longer than it needs to be: sentence (a) is 23 words, sentence (b) only 18.

Nominalization is often caused by the use of 'vague verbs', like *put, make, have, give* and *is*. In sentence (a) above, the writer uses a 'vague verb' when writing: '... the court *put* emphasis on' instead of the appropriate verb '... the court **emphasized** ...' as in (b). Look at the following sentences:

- they *have* doubts about the reliability of ...
- the court *made* a decision to ...
- the judge *is* of the opinion that ...
- the lawyer *gives* advice on ...

All of these sentences can be shortened by making a verb of the noun that follows the vague verb, as in the example *the court emphasizes*. Try to change the above sentences in the same way.

Try your hand at the following sentences by substituting vague verbs and nominalizations with simpler and more direct language.

c) An important source for lawyers is the *Lawyers' Journal*. In the index reference is made to the most important judgments of each quarter.
d) The judge put into doubt the wisdom of the establishment of children's courts.
e) The rules of the interpretation of statutes put emphasis on the establishment of clear and unambiguous meaning.

C INTEGRATED SKILLS

1 DRAWING UP A SCHEDULE OF WORK FOR THE ACADEMIC YEAR

In the extract from the *Beginner's guide for law students* (Kleyn and Viljoen 1995:1,2) that you read at the beginning of this unit, the authors warn that 'the most striking feature of studying law is the **volume** of material that has to be absorbed' (1995:1). Under the heading *Preparing for tests and examinations* they say the following (Kleyn and Viljoen 1995:5):

> First ascertain the **scope** of the work for the test or exam. The starting point for any preparation is the **syllabus**. Begin by giving yourself an overview of the terrain covered for the test or exam. You can do this by making a list of **subjects (a subject index)**. This serves as a framework of the course material and will show you where the detail that you are going to study fits in. Such a list of subjects is usually set out in the syllabus of the course. You can use that as a starting point but you must draft a list yourself that you can fully understand. You should **memorise** this list of subjects to enable you to recall the overall picture easily.

In the first part of this unit you drew up a list of subjects you will study this year. You need to use this list to plan your work so that you have an overview of what lies ahead. Put up this schedule of work where you can see it every day, in front of your desk or on the refrigerator door if necessary! Doing so is useful for at least two reasons:

- You maintain an overview of the year's work, which gives you a sense of control.
- You make a mental note of the dates on which you have to write tests and/or hand in assignments, so that you (hopefully!) do not realize afterwards with a shock that you had to write a test or hand in an assignment the day before.

To draw up a schedule of work you need:

- A year planner, or a big calender where you can see the whole year at a glance. You could also draw up such a calender on an A3 page (double A4 size). There must be enough space for each day so that you can write down the names of subjects and other necessary detail.
- The names and codes of subjects.
- Course outlines and/or tutorial letters which list the dates for assignments, tests and examinations.

12

- Highlighters or pens in two colours (one of which should be red or bright pink).

Before you fill in details of academic work on the schedule, indicate holidays, birthdays and other times when you know you probably will not be able to study. Think about your own study patterns:

- Does noise distract you?
- Do you study in one place or all over your room or house?
- What is your study style:
  - pressure-driven, studying right through the night?
  - you study until late and arrive just in time for the test?
  - you go to sleep early and get up at 03h00 to study?
  - you study for days and then you 'let the stuff settle' (that is, you do not look at the material) for a day before the test?

Your own personal learning style will determine how much time you allow to prepare for assignments, tests and examinations.

Circumstances beyond your control may also influence your study patterns. You must be realistic when you plan your studies. If you live in a hostel or a commune or close to a noisy street and you know that you only concentrate when there is peace and quiet, you should consider studying in a library or late at night and early in the mornings.

The most important point about studying is that you must do a little every day. Students at residential universities think that they are studying when they listen to lectures, but it is only **afterwards**, when you go back to your notes on the lecture and you integrate them with the textbook and with previous knowledge, that you are really studying. There must be time for this every day, except weekends and holidays, when you might need to do catching up!

Scan your timetable for test and examination dates and note in bright red or pink the days and **times** when each subject is written. Throughout the year you might have to add dates on which assignments have to be handed in.

Those of you who study at a **distance education institution** (and more than 50% of all South African students do!) will need to note the due dates for assignments. You also need to take into account the time it takes for your assignment to get to your lecturers. If you know that the postal service from your area could be slow, you need to allow two weeks for your assignment to be received on time. Distance education institutions often put a stamp on assignments to indicate the day on which they were

13

received, so this might be an indication of the time it takes your assignment to reach its destination. The time it takes for your assignment to reach its destination is important information because it means that you cannot work on your assignment up until the day on which it is due. Your planning will have to take the delay into account, so that your calender might look like this (a fragment):

MARCH		APRIL	
1		1	*Post Ass. 3 PRV !!!*
2	*Post Ass. 1 PRV !!!*	2	
3		3	
4		4	
5		5	
6	*Post Ass. 2 PRV !!!*	6	
7		7	*DUE: Ass. 2 PRV*
8	*DUE: Ass. 1 PRV*	8	
9		9	

Unfortunately, you hardly ever enrol for only one subject. If you have to submit assignments for different subjects on the same day or within a day of each other, you will have to plan your study time accordingly. This is obviously also true for the writing of tests and examinations. Your programme might then look like this:

MARCH		APRIL	
1		1	*Post Ass. 3 PRV !!!*
2	*Post Ass. 1 PRV !!!*	2	*DUE: Ass. 2 SUC*
3		3	*DUE: Ass. 2 PRV*
4		4	
5	*Post Ass. 2 SUC !!*	5	*DUE: Ass. 1 LMT*
6	*Post Ass. 2 PRV !!!*	6	
7		7	
8	*DUE: Ass. 1 PRV*	8	*DUE: Ass. 3 PRV*
9	*Post Ass. 1 LMT !!!*	9	

You need to look carefully at the study material and the prescribed text-books. These will give you an idea of the amount of work involved. Once you start studying you will quickly realize that, because of the nature of a specific subject, the lecturer and your own circumstances and limitations, you will need to spend more time on some subjects than on others. Therefore you may have to adapt your planning continuously.

2 NOTE-MAKING SKILLS: STAYING ORGANIZED

In the rush of moving from one class to another and making proper notes it is easy to get bits of paper confused, or to write notes on the back of a page on which you wrote the notes of another subject. You could carry separate files or notebooks for each subject, but if you also want to take your textbooks along, you could have a very heavy bag! You might consider taking a writing pad; one of those that are glued at the top with holes punched in the left-hand side of the page. When you get to a class, take care that you

- always start on a new page;
- always write on only one side of the page (that way you can add notes later on the back of the page);
- make a wide margin on the left or right-hand side of the page, so that you can add notes to your own notes;
- put the date at the top of the page with the name of the subject or lecturer.

The last point is important, especially at the beginning of your courses, because you could become confused over the subject content when you are not yet familiar with it. The suggestion is that you leave the files for the various courses at home and file your notes at the end of the day. At that stage you should also look at your notes and try to integrate them with the relevant textbook and cases. If you are asked to prepare material for a specific subject, you can do this on your note pad and add the class notes to the same page.

3 CORRESPONDING WITH INSTITUTIONS OF LEARNING

a) Writing semi-formal letters

Students who study at distance education institutions often find it necessary to write letters or send faxes to either administrative personnel or to lecturers responsible for their courses. The guidelines provided below are also relevant for letters and faxes written in the business world.

Although students at **residential** institutions for tertiary education prob-ably do not need to write semi-formal letters, they might also benefit from this section because the format of a semi-formal letter and of a facsimile (fax) will be useful in their professions.

In all correspondence with an educational institution you need to ask yourself the following:

- To whom should the letter be addressed?

If names and addresses are not individually listed in your study materials you should address problems with registration, fees, and material that you did not receive, to **The Registrar**. You could elaborate on this by writing 'The Registrar (Finance)' or 'The Registrar (Registration)' or 'The Registrar (Examinations)'. Even if the person in charge of examinations is not a registrar, the institution's internal postal system will be able to send your letter to the right department or section. You should address problems that you have with your courses, such as aspects of the work you do not understand, to the lecturer responsible for the course. This person will be named in your tutorial matter.

- Do you have your student number at hand?

You **must** mention your student number in all correspondence with the educational institution.

Your letter should follow this format:

---

8 Behring Street
5093 Hopetown
22 March 1997

The Registrar (Finance)
Ambition College
PO Box 789
1001 Glitter City

Dear Madam

NON-PAYMENT OF FEES: STUDENT 571109

I would like to draw your attention to the fact that . . . .
. . . .

Yours faithfully

F Radebe

F Radebe (Ms)

Note:

- You need to give the date.
- You must provide a short subject line, either in capitals or underlined (**not both**) that states the subject of the letter. **The subject line should include your student number**.
- If you do not know the person's name, you write 'Dear Sir' or 'Dear Madam' or 'Dear Sir/ Madam'.
- If you start with 'Dear Sir' you should end with 'Yours faithfully', although this is not a hard and fast rule.
- You should try to use phrases like 'I *would* like ...' or I *would* appreciate ...' or '*Could* you ...'.
- If your letter is handwritten, you should both sign and print your name.

A letter to the lecturer responsible for a course in which you have certain problems, could look like this:

---

8 Behring Street
5093 Hopetown
22 March 1997

Professor R Driven
Department of Private Law
Ambition College
PO Box 789
1001 Clitter City

Dear Professor Driven

LATE SUBMISSION OF ASSIGNMENT 2: STUDENT 571109

I would like to apologize . . . .
. . . .
Yours sincerely

F Radebe

F Radebe

Note:

- In this case you know the name of the recipient (Prof Driven) and therefore your letter ends with 'Yours sincerely'. This formulation is used increasingly for all kinds of letters.
- Make sure that you also include the name of the department in which the lecturer is teaching.

17

The conventions for semi-formal letters change continuously. You should check with your lecturer that she or he agrees with the abovementioned format.

b) Writing and sending facsimiles (faxes)

Not all institutions allow students to send them faxes, because they are expensive to **receive**. You should first find out whether it is permitted.

Faxes come in different shapes and formats, but the following information must be provided on the first page:

- You must say **for whom** the fax is meant and **from whom** it is sent.
- The institution and fax number of both these persons must be given.
- A date must be given.
- You must say how many pages you are sending.

If you are writing your own fax you could use the following as a guideline:

```
FAX TO:    Mr D Mpinda            FROM:    Ms F Radebe
           Department of Mercantile Law    Harvard S. School
           Ambition College               Hopetown
           Fax (322) 456789               Fax (2332) 5324
           Tel (322) 456788               Tel (2332) 5325


Dear Mr Mpinda

Request for assistance Assignment 3: student 571109

I would like to enquire about the reference to . . . . . . . . . . . . . . . . . .
. . . . . . . . . . . . . . . . . . . . . . . . . . . . . . . . . . . . . . . . . . . . . . . . .

Yours sincerely

F Radebe
_____
F Radebe


FAX OF 1 PAGE OF WHICH THIS IS PAGE 1
```

Note:
- The format is similar to that of a semi-formal letter, although you do not need to give a full postal address.
- You still need to give your student number.

- Pages must be numbered and you must state how many pages there are, in case one page does not go through.
- It is wise to provide a telephone number as well so that the recipient can let you know immediately if the faxing process has been interrupted in some way or if a page did not go through.

Once more you should consult with your lecturer as to whether the above format cannot be substituted by, for example, printed cover pages.

c) Communicating with lecturers by e-mail

Although e-mail is generally regarded as an informal means of communication, you still need to be considerate and polite when you communicate with your lecturers. Depending on the degree of formality in your relationship with specific lecturers, you can start off the message with 'Dear Prof So-and-so' or 'Hallo Sam'. The most important part of your message is the subject line, where you need to give your lecturer enough information to be able to place you and your request in the appropriate context. No lecturer is going to be able to place a request such as the following:

From:	203487KgaboM
To:	Prof G Siyabonga
Subject:	Help!

Hi Prof

I cannot find the court case for next week's class? Where is it?

Bye,
M

You need to tell the lecturer which course you're taking, what the problem is and how it occurred. If this is a problem that affects the whole class, it is much better if the class representative writes on behalf of everybody.

> **From:** 203487KgaboM
> **To:** Prof G Siyabonga
> **Subject:** Private Law 101: availability of court case for 13 August class
>
> Dear Professor Siyabonga
>
> The library seems to have lost the court case *Tshabalala v Natal Law Society* that you want us to prepare for next week's class at 11 o'clock. I'm writing on behalf of several students who are struggling to get hold of the case. Mr Smith, the subject librarian, says it must be lost. Could you help us?
>
> Regards
> Maki Kgabo

If you made an arrangement with your lecturer to submit assignments by e-mail, it will help her or him to give your file a name that links it to you. Imagine the confusion if the lecturer has to rename 150 files that have all been named 'assignment1.doc'. Add your name, the course code and number of the assignment (where applicable), for example: 'Kgabo PPL223 Ass1.doc'. It's probably best to arrange with your lecturer about the naming of electronic assignments.

4 STUDY NOTE

The way in which we refer to other books or sources is the **reference style** that is used in arts and education faculties all over the world. This book is about the **language** of the law and therefore uses the preferred style of language departments. When we quote or cite from 'Smith (1988:23)' it means that the author is Smith, the book or article was published in 1988 and the specific quotation is from page 23. The assumption is that if you need more details about the publication, you can page to the section called *Bibliography* or *References* where all the authors and sources referred to, are listed alphabetically with the date of publication right after the name.

Note well that this style of reference differs from the style followed in law schools and faculties. Their style of reference is discussed in unit 14.

UNIT 2
DIVISIONS AND SUBJECTS
IN THE STUDY OF LAW

A   READING

Beginner's guide for law students by D Kleyn and F Viljoen (1995:98, 101, 102)

B   LANGUAGE FOCUS
1   MORE GRAMMATICAL TERMS
2   COMPLETE AND INCOMPLETE SENTENCES
3   ASKING QUESTIONS, MAKING REQUESTS

C   INTEGRATED SKILLS
1   NOTE-MAKING SKILLS: DEVISING A SYSTEM OF ABBREVIATIONS
2   DIAGRAMMATIC REPRESENTATIONS OF A TEXT
3   FINDING INFORMATION
4   STUDY NOTES

The purpose of this unit is to provide you with an overview of the different branches of the law and to situate the subjects you are studying within that structure. We look at ways in which knowledge can be structured by means of a diagram (a diagrammatic representation) and at how such a diagram can help you to maintain an overview of your studies. This unit continues the work done in unit 1 by looking at the formation of words and sentences again and we introduce more tools of grammar for you to use in your studies. We develop the discussion on note-making and, finally, we focus on finding the main sources for your law studies in the library.

A READING

Refer to the list of subjects that you made in unit 1 and think about the work you have done in each subject up to now. They all may seem to be concerned with vastly different things, but do some seem to deal with similar topics? Have you heard a lecturer say, 'You will learn more about this matter in Subject X'? If you have, these subjects are probably related in some way.

Look at the following list and try to link groups of subjects that seem to go together:

commercial law	law of succession
family law	property law
law of contract	company law
constitutional law	human rights law

Study the following diagram from *Beginner's guide for law students* (Kleyn and Viljoen 1995:98)

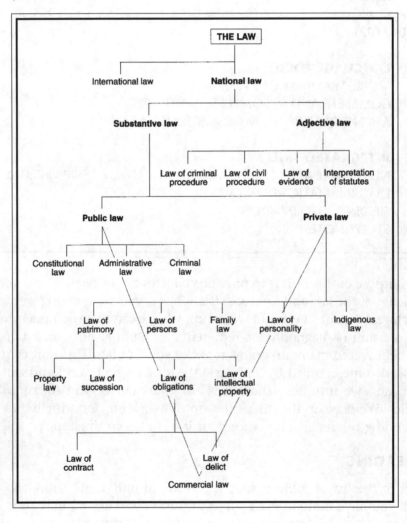

Look closely at the headings of the different divisions of the law and at the words printed in **bold**. Answer the following questions briefly in consultation with your lecturer or other students. In these questions the knowledge that you already have of the law is not as important as your ability to make sense of the information provided in the diagram.

1 What is the purpose of this diagram?
2 Why is *National law* printed in bold and in a bigger script than *International law*?
3 Which seem to be the four largest divisions under *National law* and how do you know that these are the largest?
4 What do you think is the meaning of the two diagonal lines that run from the headings *Public law* and *Private law* to meet in one point *Commercial law* at the bottom of the diagram?
5 Try to guess what is dealt with in each of the 19 subdivisions of national (that is, South African) law.

With this diagram in mind, read the following description carefully (Kleyn and Viljoen 1955:101, 102). Take your time and re-read it, if necessary.

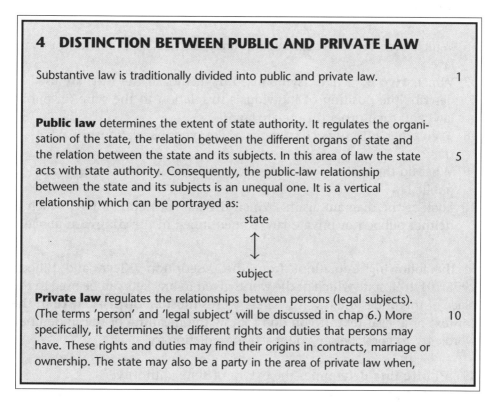

4 DISTINCTION BETWEEN PUBLIC AND PRIVATE LAW

Substantive law is traditionally divided into public and private law.   1

Public law determines the extent of state authority. It regulates the organisation of the state, the relation between the different organs of state and
the relation between the state and its subjects. In this area of law the state   5
acts with state authority. Consequently, the public-law relationship
between the state and its subjects is an unequal one. It is a vertical
relationship which can be portrayed as:

state

↕

subject

Private law regulates the relationships between persons (legal subjects).
(The terms 'person' and 'legal subject' will be discussed in chap 6.) More   10
specifically, it determines the different rights and duties that persons may
have. These rights and duties may find their origins in contracts, marriage or
ownership. The state may also be a party in the area of private law when,

---

for example, it enters into a contract with an individual. But in this instance
the state does not act with state authority; it is in the same position as any   15
other person. The private-law relationship is therefore an equal one. It can
be portrayed as a horizontal relationship:

person   ←——→   person
(legal subject)   (legal subject)

When a person wants to enforce her rights against another, the provisions
of the law of civil procedure apply.

The distinction between public and private law is often artificial and   20
unrealistic. Often the state, with state authority, encroaches upon the area
of private law, for example, when the state through legislation dictates
certain contractual relationships between employer and employee. But
the basic distinction between public and private law is important in order
to understand the functioning of substantive law in general.   25

Try to answer questions 6–9 in two minutes without looking at the
description.

6 Which **two** types of relationship are governed by public and private
   law?
7 Which **two** adjectives (symbolized by arrows in the text) are used to
   describe the position of individuals in relation to the state (in public
   law) and each other (in private law)?
8 **Two** other adjectives characterize these types of relationship: what are
   they?
9 What do the authors conclude about the division between private and
   public law?
10 Look at the diagram again. Which division of national law, which is
   neither public nor private law, is mentioned in the **diagram** above?

In the following quotations from the description (Kleyn and Viljoen
1995:101,102) state which of the words given in brackets can be used in the
place of the underlined words. These words must be **appropriate** in the
context of a legal text. If you don't know the meaning of the underlined
words, try to guess before you reach for a dictionary!

11 '**Public law** determines the <u>extent</u> of state authority.'
   (expanse, scope, reach, amount)

12 'It can be <u>portrayed</u> as a horizontal relationship.'
(painted, drawn, depicted, described)
13 'These rights and duties may find their <u>origin</u> in contracts, marriage or ownership.'
(source, basis, cause)
14 'When a person wants to <u>enforce</u> her rights against another, the provisions of the law of civil procedure apply.'
(implement, apply, carry out, administer)
15 'The distinction between public and private law is often <u>artificial</u> and <u>unrealistic</u>.'
(superficial and unreasonable, forced and impractical, synthetic and foolish)
16 'Often the state, with state authority, <u>encroaches</u> upon the area of private law,...'
(trespass, invade, intrude, infringe)

Did you find more than one appropriate word in some cases? If you and your fellow students could not agree, your lecturer will be able to help. Did you find words that could **not** be substituted? One such case is *enforce*, which, as it is used in sentence 14, is **a fixed legal expression** with hardly any synonyms.

Look at the relationship between sentences in this extract. Within a paragraph the authors make a general statement followed by a clarification, in which the authors explain or give examples. We can say the authors move from a general to a more specific point.

17 In line 3 it is stated: '**Public law** determines the extent of state authority. It regulates the organisation of the state, the relation between the different organs of state and the relation between the state and its subjects.' The sentence starting with *Public law* is an opening statement followed by more specific detail. Read the extract again and find another example of a statement which is clarified in more detail.
18 Find two examples of statements followed by a clarification **in the form of an example**.

Did you notice that explanations or clarifications are often introduced by words such as *specifically* (line 11) and *for example* (lines 14 and 22)? Opening statements can be followed by detailed explanation, examples, qualifications and/ or conditions. In lines 13 and 14 the statement, 'The state may also be a party in the area of private law' is explained by means of an example, 'when, **for example**, it enters into a contract with an individual' followed by a qualification, '**But** in this instance...'.

25

Qualifications and conditions are usually introduced by words such as *but, however* and *if.*

19 Can you find another example of an opening statement followed by an **example** and a **qualification** in the above extract?

It is important that you should be aware of this kind of organization of knowledge: statement followed by clarification and/ or specification and/ or qualification. Your study of law will often require you to look at the way in which *general* rules (expressed as statements) are applied in *specific* examples and the relevant **qualifications** or **conditions**. You can also imitate this pattern when you write: a general statement with its clarification, example and qualifications will form **one paragraph**. When you move on to the next general statement, you have to start a new paragraph, as Kleyn and Viljoen did in the passage above. In B LANGUAGE FOCUS (below) more will be said about statements and unit 5 will continue the discussion of main ideas and the formation of paragraphs.

WORDS AND THEIR MEANINGS

The following words appear in the extract *Distinction between public and private law* (Kleyn and Viljoen 1995:101, 102). Re-arrange them in groups of words that are more or less similar in meaning and/ or that belong in the same context. For example *division* and *distinction* are synonymous in the context of the extract. Use your knowledge of the function of words (verbs or nouns) as a guide, that is, nouns belong with nouns, verbs with verbs and so on.

person	regulates	relation
contract	individual	
relationship	dictates	provisions
acts	determines	
subject	party	rights and duties

In the sentences below some of the words in the list above are used again, but their original function has been changed, that is, verbs are used as nouns, nouns as adjectives, and so on. See how quickly you can find the correct form of the words **and check your spelling**!

1 The parties in this case are under (contract) obligation to inform each other of a change of address.
2 The minister announced (regulate) measures until such time as legislation has been (act) by parliament.

3   Under the general's (dictate) rule the citizens of the country were (subject) to countless house-to-house searches.

4   The contract can be (individual) to (provision) for the (person) needs of each consumer.

B LANGUAGE FOCUS

1 MORE GRAMMATICAL TERMS

In unit 1 we reviewed the main functions of words in sentences: nouns and adjectives, verbs and adverbs. Study the following brief explanation of pronouns and participles because you need to know these terms for the discussion that follows. Ask your lecturer or refer to a grammar book if you feel you need more guidance.

a)   When you want to avoid using a specific noun repeatedly, you can make use of *pronouns*, words that stand in the place of, or refer to, a noun. For example:

When a person wants to enforce *her* rights...
        instead of
When a person wants to enforce a person's rights...

Pronouns used most often are:
he, she, it, they, him, her, its, their

There are two important points you need to remember about the use of pronouns:

•   The pronoun must agree with the noun; that is, you must take into account whether the noun is singular or plural, and whether it is male or female. Students often use the singular pronoun *it* when the noun is plural, for example:

There are many problems and we must solve it as soon as possible.

It is used to refer to *problems*, and the sentence should read:

There are many problems and we must solve them as soon as possible.

You also need to take care not to confuse *she, he, her* and *him*. This problem is dealt with in unit 4.

•   The second important point is that you should try to put the pronoun as close as possible to the noun to which it refers. Look at the following sentence:

I 'phoned my brother while he was visiting our father and he said ...

27

Does the *he* refer to the brother or the father? You need to rewrite the sentence to make the reference clear.

Can you rewrite the following sentences to make them less ambiguous?

1. The students had to buy the textbooks in February but *it* was out of stock.
2. The court decided on the merits of the case that *it* has to refer it to the Constitutional Court.
3. Students who help in the Legal Aid Clinic provide a service to people and *they* learn what justice in action means.
4. If you do your assignments on a regular basis and attend the necessary classes they will give you enough marks in case you cannot write the examination.
5. The judge examined the facts and told the defendants that they were insufficiently prepared.

b) *Participles* are forms of the verb that can function as adjectives or nouns and they appear as *present participles* and *past participles*. For example:

Studying is time-consuming. (The **present** participle of the verb *study*, which is *studying*, acts as a noun because it takes the verb *is*.)

The **determining** factor in this case is... (The **present** participle of the verb *determine*, which is *determining*, acts as an adjective that describes the noun *factor*.)

The **detained** prisoner asked to see her lawyer. (The **past** participle of the verb *detain*, which is *detained*, acts as an adjective that describes the noun prisoner.)

As you can see the **present** participle is formed by the **present** tense form of the verb with -*ing* added and the **past** participle is the so-called *third column* form of the verb. (If you weren't taught the different 'columns' of verbs at school, ask your lecturer about this, or refer to a grammar book.) These participles appear without the verb forms that we usually find with -*ing* (such as, *is going*) and the *third column verb* (**have** *written*). Therefore they cannot be regarded as full or main verbs and are usually followed by another verb (the main verb). A phrase, such as *Hoping to see you* ..., lacks a full or main verb. By adding a main verb you create a proper sentence: *Hoping to see you* **is** *the only thing that keeps me alive.*

Study the following extract from an ante-nuptial contract and say whether each underlined word is a present or past participle.

Ante-nuptial contract <u>including</u> accrual <u>sharing</u>

Be it hereby made known

THAT on the 6th day of April 1980 before me John Lawyer, notary public, <u>sworn</u> and <u>admitted</u>, <u>practising</u> at Potchefstroom, and in the presence of the <u>subscribed</u> witnesses, personally appeared

A J Citizen ('the <u>Intended</u> Husband')
and
C Everywoman ('the <u>Intended</u> Wife')

(Adapted from Naudé 1994:45.)

*"It won't take long. I just wanted my attorneys
to go over the exact wording of the ceremony."*

As you can see participles appear quite often in formal legal texts. It is extremely important that you note the function of participles: they have the form of a verb but are not 'pure' verbs. Therefore it is necessary to add a 'main' verb to indicate the action in the sentence, as in the contract above:

> The intended husband and intended wife personally **appeared** before the notary public.

In this long and involved sentence the past participle *intended* acts as an adjective (to describe the future husband and wife) so there has to be a main verb (*appeared*) to say what they are actually doing.

29

2 COMPLETE AND INCOMPLETE SENTENCES

Study the following 'sentences' and indicate those that you think are not full or complete sentences.

a) The distinction between public and private law which is artificial.
b) For example, you cannot drive without a licence.
c) Public law, which regulates the organisation of the state, the relation between the different organs of the state and the relation between the state and its subjects.
d) Hoping that this law will come into effect as soon as possible.
e) Under the provisions of this act three subsections that deal with contraventions of state authority.

Check your responses with your lecturer and with other students and try to improve the sentences you identified as 'incomplete' in some way.

Sentence (a) above could be the start of a sentence but it is not complete because there is no main verb. You have probably heard your teachers and lecturers ask, 'Where is the verb? A sentence must have a verb!' You can keep on adding nouns and adjectives to a sentence, but without a verb, it is not a sentence. For example

> The law of criminal procedure in the South African situation, with the exception of the TBVC regions and notwithstanding the favourable political climate, ...

This is still not a sentence. Just as in the above example of an ante-nuptial contract, you need to add a main verb which states what the law of criminal procedure **does** or **is**. For example,

> The law of criminal procedure in the South African situation, with the exception of the TBVC regions and notwithstanding the favourable political climate, **is** in crisis.

A sentence has to have a *subject* (a thing, person or idea that determines the action or the verb in the sentence) and a *main verb*. The subject is often a noun or a word or words which function as nouns and this subject determines the form of the main verb. In the example above the subject is *The law of criminal procedure* and the main verb: *is*. In sentence (e) above there is neither a subject nor a main verb. To make it a full sentence you could insert 'we find' or 'there are':

Under the provisions of this act **there are** three subsections . . .

You could also add another verb after *three subsections*:
Under the provisions of this acts three subjections **are included** . . .

Study the following sentences and in each case underline the subject with a wavy line and the main verb with a straight line. Look out for past and present participles: they cannot be the main verb!

a) The contract was signed on a fixed date.
b) The partners, agreeing to set aside their grievances, shook hands on the deal.
c) Accepting that the contract was null and void, the parties decided to settle the matter out of court.
d) The deceased wife left her money in trust for her five-year old daughter.

And now for a really difficult example!

e) "In determining the accrual of the estate of the Intended Husband at the dissolution of the intended marriage, there shall be left out of account the assets set out below, as well as any other assets acquired directly or indirectly by virtue of the possession or former possession of such assets, it being recorded that the value of such assets has been ignored for the purpose of arriving at the net commencement value of the Intended Husband's estate" (Naudé 1994:45).

When you write assignments and answers in tests and examinations you should edit your work and make sure that you do not leave sentences incomplete. In assignments and test answers lecturers often come across very long sentences without a main verb. This happens because students put the subject at the beginning of a sentence and then they get so involved in the rest of the sentence that they forget to end it properly. You will be able to correct this if you read your answers again. However, there is usually so little time for revision and editing in tests and examinations that it is better to **prevent** incomplete sentences by keeping your sentences short.

3 ASKING QUESTIONS, MAKING REQUESTS

Many students, especially if they are not first-language speakers of English, find it difficult to ask questions during lectures and seminars. (See 4 STUDY NOTE 1.) The following phrases are used to make requests in a classroom situation:

31

- 'Excuse me sir/ madam/ Prof More...'
- I don't understand the meaning of ....'
- 'Could you repeat...' (Do not expect lecturers to repeat sentences so that you can copy down every word. See *Note-making* below.)
- 'Yesterday you said X, but now you say Y, could you explain why X and not Y?' or 'The textbook says X but you say Y. Which one should we follow?' or 'Do you think the textbook is wrong?'

You may also find yourself in a situation where you have to request something, either for the class or for yourself. The relationship between a lecturer and students is usually a semi-formal one, but the situation or context will determine your language use. You may, for example, **request** a favour or a compromise:

'Could we rewrite the test that most of us failed?'

However, you can use the same form to **demand** that the lecturer not infringe upon your rights:

'Could you refrain from using sexist/racist language in class?'

The word *demand* is a very strong word and should not be used when you are merely *requesting* something.

Look at the following requests and rank them from semi-formal, everyday requests to very formal requests. Use numbers from 1 to 7, with 1 representing the least formal and 7 the most formal request. Give requests that are more or less at the same level of formality the same number.

- ☐ I would like to ask, as spokesperson for the whole class, if we could rewrite the semester test that the majority of the class failed last week.

- ☐ Please close the door sir, we're freezing in here!

- ☐ Could you allow the class representative to make a brief announcement at the beginning of the next period?

- ☐ Do you know at what time the semester test starts?

- ☐ Can you warn us when there is only 10 minutes left before the end of the test?

32

☐ I would appreciate it if you could ignore my poor performance on the previous semester test and only take the better test into account for my year mark. I was very ill when we wrote the first test...

☐ Do we have to prepare for multiple-choice questions?

NOTE:

Remember that the formality of a request depends on a variety of factors and the relative status of lecturer and student is not the most important factor. The seriousness of a situation could require the use of very formal structures such as *could* and *would* and the obligation to explain *why* the request is made. Inappropriate language might sabotage the request or demand. Note too that formal requests such as '*Could* you ...?' and 'I *would* appreciate it if you *could/ would...*' are forms that you will need to use outside institutions of tertiary education. In business and law practice these forms of request are generally accepted as appropriate in a professional situation, particularly in written language.

C INTEGRATED SKILLS

1 NOTE-MAKING SKILLS: DEVISING A SYSTEM OF ABBREVIATIONS

Whether you are making notes on something you are reading or of a lecture, you need to develop skills to reflect the content of the text you are reading or hearing. Lectures are particularly troublesome because you cannot go back to them to check that you interpreted the meaning correctly, unless you tape-record your lectures. In this unit we want to focus on one way in which you can make the writing task a little easier, which is to use abbreviations.

Abbreviations of ordinary words can be found everywhere:

- eg = for example
- ff = following
- p = page
- NB = very important or note well
- etc = etcetera

Dictionaries usually list conventional abbreviations. Take a look at the lists provided in your own dictionaries and decide which examples may be useful.

33

You also need to develop a personal set of abbreviations for your subjects. Here are some suggestions as to how you can do this:

- Invent abbreviations for the subjects you will be taking, for example, *Fam* for family law, *Rom* for Roman-Dutch law, *Suc* for law of succession and so on.
- Skimread the first few pages of the textbooks of these subjects and see if you can find the terms that are being referred to repeatedly. In family law one would expect words like *family, parents, children, marriage, birth, illegitimacy* and so on to appear quite often. On the basis of the textbook and your first few lectures you should be able to predict the frequency of such terms so that you can create abbreviations for the most frequently-used ones.
- Make capitals and lower case letters work for you; *Fam* could refer to family law and *fam* to family. Similarly *Suc* could refer to the law of succession, *suc* to succession and *sucd* to succeed.
- Use one letter for terms that you will encounter in all your subjects (these are just suggestions!):
  C for court, *LC* for lower court, *CAC* for court of appeal, *HC* for high court, *CC* for constitutional court
  c for case
  A for appellant, *a* for act, *adv* for advocate
  D for defendant
  J for judge
- When you are in a lecture and you cannot keep up, use SMS techniques: leave out the vowels of words, except where they are at the beginning of words. U shld b abl 2 mk sns of yr nts aftrwrds!
- Find abbreviations for fixed phrases like 'of the' (*o/t*), 'for the' (*f/t*), 'in the' (*i/t*) and so on. You could also use *2* for 'to' and *4* for 'for'.
- Instead of writing down words that show the links in an argument, you could use signs and numbers. The steps in an argument can be numbered or indicated with a dash (–) for each successive step. You could also use mathematical signs like:
  + for *and*,
  = for *is*, or *same as*
  → ← for *next* and *back*
  ∴ for *thus* or *therefore*.
- Instead of writing down the full title of a statute you could write *Act 20/95* or the main word of the title: *Sectional Titles Act*. In the same way you could use the name of the first party in a court case to refer to it, for example, the *Gadamska case*.

The most important point about abbreviations is that you must be able to make sense of them for a long time afterwards. You should go through your notes on the same day that you heard the lecture so that you can clarify and elaborate on points that you scribbled in a hurry. You should also find out from your various lecturers how they want you to refer to legislation and court cases in assignments, tests and examinations. If you use an abbreviated form in your notes but they want more detail in assignments and tests, you should take care to add the detail to your notes after the lecture by checking in your textbook or in the library.

2 DIAGRAMMATIC REPRESENTATIONS OF A TEXT

The diagram and arrows in the extract that you read under A READING (from *Beginner's guide for law students* by Kleyn and Viljoen 1995) are attempts to give structure to very complex material. Such diagrams reduce and simplify subject content to provide readers with an overview of topics discussed previously or with a framework for a discussion that follows the diagram.

You can also make use of this technique to summarize your work and there are many ways to do this. Kleyn and Viljoen's diagram (1995:98) can be called a **linear**, **top-down representation** or a **tree diagram**. Linear diagrams can also be bottom-up and/or from left to right, depending on the material. Their main function is to show which parts in the structure come first, have the most authority or are the most inclusive, and how these parts branch off into other structures. The image of a tree is useful here: there is a main stem, fed by different roots and branching out in various directions; the thicker roots and branches (main sections) have off-shoots (subsections) which, in turn, have smaller off-shoots (sub-subsections).

The structure of institutions such as a state department or parliament is often portrayed in a linear, top-down fashion to indicate a **hierarchy** or ranking, with the most powerful person or body at the top and the least powerful at the bottom. Such a diagram also indicates to the people in the organisation who is responsible for what, and who can be called upon to listen to grievances, suggestions for improvement, appeals for salary increases and so on.

In Kleyn and Viljoen's diagram (1995:98) where the different divisions of the law are shown, we are not really talking about a hierarchy, but rather about a main stem (The Law) with two big branches, international and national law. However, there are many different ways in which a system such as the law can be represented.

35

A circular representation could be used to indicate that international law is the all-inclusive term within which national law functions, in the same way that national law includes substantive law. For example:

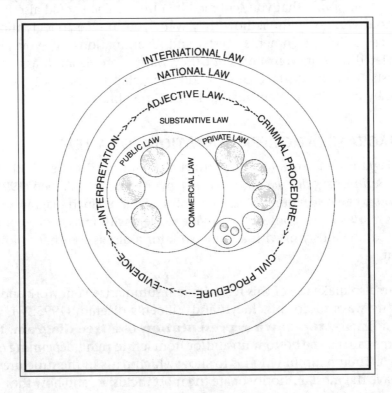

Another circular representation could be that of a machine with inter-locking gears and an engine. Substantive law is 'driven' (like the cogs in a wheel) by adjective law, for example:

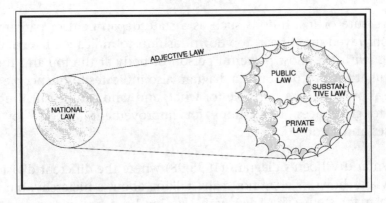

You could also use what is known as a spidergram (more about this in unit 5), where a central concept grows legs like a spider:

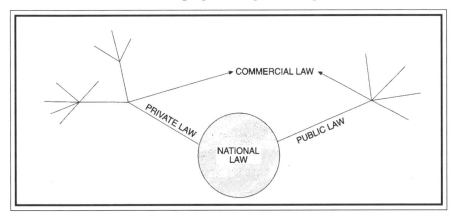

The nature of the material and even the way in which you look at the material will dictate the structure into which you fit it. A linear representation could suggest that divisions are clear-cut and easily separable. Kleyn and Viljoen (1995:101,102) state explicitly that the divisions are not always applicable (lines 20-25) and that they are traditional (line 1). This implies that the diagram is an **aid** towards a basic understanding of the divisions of the law and not a detailed and clear-cut reflection of them.

NOTE:

It is important to realize that diagrams can never clearly represent abstract concepts, but that they are tools which textbook writers use to structure your understanding of the material. You must, therefore, read the explanation of a diagram so that you understand the conditions under which it has validity.

When you use diagrams to summarize and remember abstract concepts, you should use the appropriate diagram. The examples of circular diagrams and spidergrams can, in some cases, be regarded as inappropriate. One could object to a circular diagram with bigger and smaller circles because international law does not enclose or encompass national law. Such a diagram might be better suited to illustrate the interaction of groups within a larger association, for example different electoral districts within provinces. The image of the engine can be said to be too mechanical; the law is not a machine and one division does not necessarily 'start' or 'drive' another. Such a diagram may be more useful to illustrate cause and effect, for example, the different actions set in motion when a person fails to pay an instalment on her mortgage. A spidergram might be better suited to simpler material, for example, the smaller number of subdivisions of private law could be accommodated in a spidergram.

Page through your textbooks, study material, newspapers and magazines and study the diagrams (if any) that are used. Do you think the diagrams are appropriate? Can they be improved?

Study the following attempt to put the divisions of South African law in a diagram. If you like it, try to complete it. If you don't, say why you think the diagram is inappropriate and suggest changes or improvements.

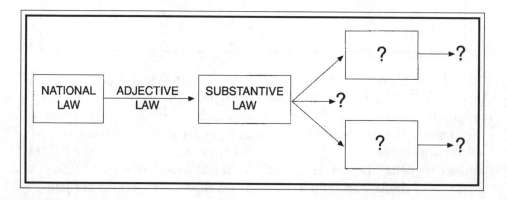

3 FINDING INFORMATION

Your main sources of information during your undergraduate years are your lecturers and textbooks, but they are not always sufficient. Lecturers and textbooks refer to other sources, mainly cases, casebooks and journals, which must be consulted in the library. Some people claim that law students make more use of the library's photocopying machines than its books — we hope this is not true!

Some institutions organize study tours through their library; find out if this is the case at your institution and take such a tour as soon as possible. If you are a student at a distance education institution, read through your study material carefully to see how you can make use of a centralized library and find out how well-stocked your local library is. You might even want to join a local educational institution's library, which should be possible if you show them your student card. All students who study away from home and who need to do the inevitable holiday assignment at home should join their local library, even if they use only the dictionaries and take advantage of the peace and quiet for study purposes.

Go through the following list and tick if your answer to each question is 'yes'. If you cannot tick a particular item, you need to take action as soon as possible!

- Do you know where your institution's library is?
- Do you know if you need a special card or your student card to use the library?
- Do you know how many books you can take out at a time and what the lending period is?
- Does the library use a card catalogue or a computerized catalogue or both? (A catalogue is a system which tells you which books the library has and where they are shelved.)
- Can you use the catalogue system?
- Do you know if there is a special subject advisor for law students?
- Do you know where the law books are shelved?
- Do you know where to find South African court cases?
- Do you know where to find law journals?
- Do you know where to find books, articles or photocopied cases reserved by the lecturer for law students?

THE GOLDEN LIBRARY RULE

If you want to find a specific book, case, act or journal article, **you should have as much information as possible about it**.

As soon as you have your library/student card you need to find out how to access information. Libraries use different cataloguing systems, so you need to ask a librarian to show you how to use the system in your institution's library.

a) Finding books in a library

If you want to find a book you should **at least** have the initials and surname of the author (spelt absolutely correctly) and a main word in the title of the book, or the full title of the book and the author's surname. Most libraries follow a system whereby you can search for a book by using either its title or the surname of the author. If you have both, you make things much easier for yourself.

Study the title pages of books which appear on the next page. Write down the following information about each book:

> The author or editor, the title, the year of publication and the place of publication.

LAND REFORM AND THE FUTURE
OF LANDOWNERSHIP
IN SOUTH AFRICA

PAPERS READ AT A SEMINAR
PRESENTED BY THE DEPARTMENT OF PRIVATE LAW
OF THE UNIVERSITY OF SOUTH AFRICA
ON 2 NOVEMBER 1990
Edited and introduced by

AJ VAN DER WALT

B Jur Hons(BA) LLB LLM LLD
Professor in the Department of Private Law
University of South Africa

Juta & Co, Ltd

T H E
S T R U G G L E   F O R
H U M A N   R I G H T S

An International and South African Perspective

by

Lorenzo S Togni

B.Soc Sc (Hons), M. Pub Ad (UCT), D. Phil (UNISA)

Juta & Co, Ltd

You will see that the year of publication is not mentioned. Many books provide that detail on a page facing or following the title page, next to a sign that indicates the owner of copyright on the book: ©. This is the person or institution that will take you to court if you photocopy the whole book or substantial parts of it without their permission!

In the first title page provided above there is an **editor** instead of a single author. This means that the book contains a selection of writings by different authors and that one person (the editor) took the responsibility to collect the various papers, edit them and publish them in one book. It is important to note whether a book has an author or editor(s) because an edited book might be catalogued differently. Some libraries do not catalogue books under the name(s) of the editor(s), but under the names of the different authors, or they catalogue the book under its title if there are more than two editors. The golden rule applies here as well; if you have all the information the librarian will be able to find the book because she will know what the cataloguing policy is.

Page through one of your law textbooks and see if you can find the following:

- A table of contents
- An index
- A glossary (see 4 STUDY NOTE 2)
- A list of cases referred to in the book.
- A list of statutes referred to in the book.
- A bibliography

If you do not know what these terms mean, look them up in a dictionary or ask your lecturer. You will often be referred to these sections in textbooks and it is important that you know where to look for an index or a glossary and what its function is.

b) Finding cases in the library

If you want to find a South African case which was reported after 1947, you need to know the name or **heading** of the case and the year in which it was reported. Reported cases are published together, in one volume, every three months, so there is reference in the heading of the case to the year and the quarter in which it was published. For example, 1992(l) would refer to a case published in the first three months of 1992. Each volume of cases has an index in which cases are listed alphabetically as to the heading of the case, that is, according to the name of the first party in the heading.

In many instances your lecturer might ask the library to make three or four photocopies of a specific case and **reserve** these for students' use. Respect this rule and photocopy from the reserved copies, because it ruins a whole volume of reported cases if four or five hundred students photocopy from the same book!

If you want to find a South African case that was published **before** 1947, you need to know in which **province** of the then South African Union the case was decided. Your lecturer will give you very specific indications and you will need to ask the librarian to help you. More is said about finding cases in unit 3.

c) Finding legislation in the library

Legislation is shelved in different ways by different libraries. Some collect the legislation published in the Government Gazette of a specific year and at the end of the year bind everything in a volume with the relevant year on the back. You therefore need to know the year in which an act was promulgated in order to locate it.

Statutes are also collected in loose-leaf format, that is in files from which acts can be removed and replaced. The first volume of such a series usually contains a chronological table of statutes followed by an alphabetical index of the titles of the acts. The acts are then grouped according to the specific areas of the law to which they are relevant, for example, acts that legislate labour issues will be shelved under 'L', those that legislate property under 'P', and so on. The subjects are usually indicated in the alphabetical index of the first volume.

d) Finding journal articles in the library

In the case of academic articles published in law journals the name of the author and the title of the article are important, but you need not know the precise details. If you know, for example, that Hlope published something on property, you will find the article if you know the **name** of the journal, its **volume** and **number** and the **year of publication**, for example, *South African Law Journal*, 1989, volume 70 number 3. Some journals include an index of all the articles published in a specific year in the last issue of that year, so if you know the year, you can still find the article. However, not all journals have such an index, so you have to remember the golden library rule!

In law textbooks references to journals are often to abbreviations of the titles. What follows is a list of some of the most important South African law journals as they are abbreviated.

Try to find the full title of the following journals:
- CILSA
- SALJ
- THRHR
- TRW
- TSAR
- SAJHR

You might also encounter the abbreviation *LAWSA*; find out to which publication this refers and of what help it might be to you.

e) More information in your library

You need to know about at least three more important sources of information in a library: a *micro-fiche*, a CD-Rom system and the Internet.

Micro-fiche is French for 'very small card' and indicates a fairly old-fashioned system whereby a great amount of information is reduced to fit onto a small 'card'. To retrieve the information the card is placed under an 'eye' which enlarges it on a screen so that you can read it. Types of information stored in this way are newspaper articles and academic theses and dissertations. Some libraries have either part of or their whole cataloguing system on *micro-fiche*. You will need a librarian to show you how to use this system. It takes quite a lot of practice to manipulate and use the cards.

CD-ROM (Compact Disk Read Only Memory) is used to store a mass of information on discs that look exactly like music CDs. They operate in the same way, that is, you put a CD onto a type of turntable and the information is displayed on your computer screen. Of particular importance for law students is the fact that Juta, a South African publishing firm, has transferred all South African cases and legislation onto CD-ROM, known as JUTASTAT. You should find out if your library subscribes to this service which is updated every year. You can also make printouts of information on CD-ROM for study purposes.

The *Internet* and *World Wide Web* are rich sources of information if you use them wisely. Your lecturers will probably refer you to specific sites where you can find cases of the Supreme Court of Appeal, the Constitutional Court and Land Claims Court from 1994 onwards. New decisions appear on the Internet long before they are available in print. You should also find out from the library to which electronic academic journals they subscribe because you will be able to access these journals for research assignments.

Useful sites for court decisions are

- Constitutional Court decisions: www.concourt.gov.za
- Supreme Court of Appeal:
  wwwserver.law.wits.ac.za/scrtappeal.scaindex.html OR
  www.uovs.ac.za/Faculties/law/supreme.htm
- Land Claims court: wwwserver.law.wits.ac.za/lcc

South African legislation can be found at www.acts.co.za

Useful sites for comparative law links can be found at the website of the Australasian Legal Information Institute (www.austlii.edu.au) and at the Cornell Law School Legal Information Institute (www.law.cornell.edu).

4 STUDY NOTE 1

If you have problems with question forms you need to discuss this with your lecturer or look up the section in a grammar book. It is important that you understand the use of structures such as

- *Do you understand...*
- *Did you know...*

and so on.

STUDY NOTE 2

Not many lawbooks will have a glossary. It is used in books which attempt to explain technical terms to lay people, usually as a list of terms with explanations at the back of a book. An example is *You and the small claims court* by S A Strauss, a book that explains legal procedures to the ordinary public.

UNIT 3
READING THE JUDGMENT
IN A SOUTH AFRICAN
COURT CASE

A   READING
Tshabalala v Natal Law Society 1996 4 SA 150 (N)

B   LANGUAGE FOCUS
1   RELATIVE CLAUSES
2   CONNECTORS
3   COMPLEX SENTENCES

C   INTEGRATED SKILLS
1   MAKING NOTES WHILE LISTENING TO LECTURES
2   SUMMARIZING A CASE
3   STUDY NOTES

In this unit we look at the judgment in a court case and how one goes about reading such a judgment. We examine main ideas and arguments and continue to look at note-making skills — this time we look at making notes while listening to lectures. In the language section we study the use of complex sentences, connectors and the use of *who, which* and *that*. Finally we look at how one summarizes a case.

A   READING

1   Why do you think are some judgments published in the law reports? What does the word *precedent* signify in this regard?

2 Make a list of some of the words that you think you might find in a judgment.

WORDS AND THEIR MEANINGS

3 Did your list include any of the following words? Work with a fellow student and supply brief descriptions for each of these words:

- plaintiff
- applicant
- appellant
- to dismiss an appeal
- to deliver judgment
- the decision confirmed
- entitled to
- conceded

- defendant
- respondent
- held (to hold)
- to deny an application
- to award damages
- the court *a quo*
- reciprocal obligation
- *obiter dictum*

4 What information does the title of the case provide? Do you understand the abbreviations:
- v?
- LTD?
- JA?
- AJA?
- JP?
- QC?

Now read through the text of the following case carefully and then attempt to answer the questions that follow:

TSHABALALA v NATAL LAW SOCIETY

NATAL PROVINCIAL DIVISION

HOWARD JP and LEVINSOHN J

1995 November 10   Case No 2107/95

*Attorney—Candidate attorney—Irregular service—Relief in terms of
s 13(2) of Attorneys Act 53 of 1979—Court not empowered to
regularise service which was not performed under articles or
contract of service as defined in s 1 of Act.*
*Statute—Interpretation of—Change of expression—Effect—Employment
of different language to express substantially same idea
irrelevant—Mere fact that Legislature more economical in use
of language not signifying change of intention.*

TSHABALALA v NATAL LAW SOCIETY

HOWARD JP   1996 (4) SA 150   NPD

Section 13(2) of the Attorneys Act 53 of 1979 does not empower the Court to
  regularise service by a 'candidate attorney' which was not performed under articles
  of clerkship or a contract of service as defined in s 1 of the Act. The language of the
  subsection is clear and unequivocal: it is irregular service as a candidate attorney
  that the Court may regularise, not irregular service generally. (At 1520/D4)/E.)
Ex parte Edwards and Another 1996 (1) SA 451 (C) not approved and not followed.
The fact that the Legislature, in re-enacting a statutory provision, employed different
  language to express substantially the same idea (*in casu* in s 13(2) of Act 53 of 1979
  which was a re-enactment of s 19(1) of the Attorneys, Notaries and Conveyancers
  Admission Act 23 of 1934) is irrelevant. The mere fact that the Legislature has been
  more economical in its use of language does not signify a change of intention. (At
  153G–H.)
The following decided cases were cited in the judgment of the Court
  Bosman v Prokureursorde van Transvaal 1984 (2) SA 633 (T)
  Ex parte Edwards and Another 1995 (1) SA 451 (C)
  Ex parte Singer: Law Society, Transvaal, Intervening 1984 (2) SA 757 (A)
The following statutes were considered by the Court:
  The Attorneys Act 53 of 1979, ss 1, 13(2): see *Juta's Statutes of South Africa 1995*
  vol 5 at 3–101 and 3–106
The Attorneys, Notaries and Conveyancers Admission Act 23 of 1934, s 19(1).

   Application for an order declaring that certain service by the applicant was regular
service as a candidate attorney. The facts appear from the
judgment of Howard JP.
    D J Shaw QC for the applicant.
    C P Hunt for the respondent.

Howard JP: At the conclusion of the appointment we dismissed this
application with costs. These are our reasons for doing so.
   During the period from 1 July 1994 to 10 July 1995, the applicant was
employed as a 'candidate attorney' by Shepstone & Wylie, a firm of
attorneys. This period of service was not rendered under articles of
clerkship as defined in s 1 of the Attorneys Act 53 of 1979, but pursuant
to a letter of appointment which did not bind her to serve any particular
attorney for any specified period in accordance with the Act. The letter
of appointment stipulated that:
    'As soon as possible after your arrival at the firm you will sign a contract of articles
of clerkship which will govern your and your principal's specific professional
obligations.'
It was not until 11 July 1995 that the applicant entered into articles. In
terms thereof she bound herself to serve a partner of the firm as a
candidate attorney for a period of two years from 1 July 1995 to 10 July
1997. The stipulated period was two years because the applicant had
become entitled to be admitted as an advocate, as envisaged by s 2(1)(b)
of the Attorneys Act. She became qualified to be admitted as an advocate
during June 1995 when the Minister of Justice, acting in terms of s 2 of
the Recognition of Foreign Legal Qualifications and Practice Act 114 of

TSHABALALA v NATAL LAW SOCIETY

HOWARD JP   1996 (4) SA 150   NPD

of 1993 (as amended by the Recognition of Foreign Legal Qualifications
and Practice Amendment Act 10 of 1995), exempted her from the
requirement referred to in s 3(2)(a)(i) of the Admission of Advocates
Act 74 of 1964. By virtue of the provisions of s 9(l)(a) of Act 114 of
1993 she was thereupon deemed to have satisfied the requirements
referred to in s 3(2)(a)(i) of Act 74 of 1964.

The applicant applied for an order that for the purpose of her admission
as an attorney the period of service from I July 1994 to 10 July 1995,
when she was employed pursuant to the letter of appointment, is to be
regarded as having been served under articles of clerkship duly registered
in terms of the Attorneys Act. Counsel for the applicant, Mr *Shaw*,
submitted that the Court could grant an order to this effect by virtue
of the provisions of s 13(2) of the Attorneys Act, which reads:

'If any person has not served regularly as a candidate attorney, the Court, if satisfied
that such irregular service was occasioned by sufficient cause, that such service is
substantially equivalent to regular service, and that the society concerned has had
due notice of the application, may permit such person, on such conditions as it
may deem fit, to apply for admission as an attorney as if he had served regularly
under articles or a contract of service.'

I accept for the purposes of this judgment that the applicant's failure to
perform the service in question under articles was occasioned by sufficient
cause, and that such service was substantially equivalent to regular service
under articles. The only question for decision is whether s 13(2) empowers the
Court to regularise service which was not performed under articles or a contract
of service as defined in s 1. In my view, it manifestly does not. The language of
the subsection is clear and unequivocal: it is irregular service as a candidate
attorney that the Court may regularise, not irregular service generally. If there
were any doubt about this a reference to the (signed) Afrikaans text would
dispel it. That provides:

'Indien iemand nie gereeld diens as kandidaat-prokureur verrig het nie, kan die
Hof. . . .'

Section 1 provides that in this Act, unless the context otherwise indicates,
'candidate attorney'

'means any person bound to serve under articles of clerkship or to perform
community service under a contract of service'.

It follows that irregular service as a candidate attorney, within the
meaning of s 13(2), is irregular service under articles or a contract of
service as defined.

This was the construction placed on s 13(2) by the Full Bench of the
Transvaal Provincial Division in *Bosman v Prokureursorde van Transvaal*

TSHABALALA v NATAL LAW SOCIETY

HOWARD JP   1996 (4) SA 150   NPD

1984 (2) SA 633, and again in *Ex parte Singer: Law Society, Transvaal, Intervening* which was confirmed on appeal and reported in 1984 (2) SA 757 (A). When these cases were decided the English text of s 13 was the same as it is now, save that it referred to irregular service as 'an articled clerk' ('klerk onder 'n leerkontrak' in the Afrikaans text).

In contending for a different construction, Mr *Shaw* was constrained to rely solely on the judgment of Farlam J (Van Niekerk J concurring) in *Ex parte Edwards and Another* 1995 (1) SA 451 (C). In that case the applicants sought an order in terms of s 13(2) to regularise service which was not rendered under articles. Counsel for the Law Society submitted that on the plain wording of s 13(2) an applicant seeking relief thereunder must have served, albeit irregularly, as a candidate attorney, ie under articles. Farlam J rejected this submission for reasons which appear at 454B–H:

'I do not agree with Mr *Binns-Ward's* submission that the wording of s 13(2) of the Act is "plain". In my view, it is ambiguous, the ambiguity flowing from the fact that it is not clear what words are governed by the word "not": do those words include the words "as a candidate attorney" or does the word "not" only govern the words "served regularly" so that only a candidate attorney can apply for relief under the section?

In answering this question it is helpful to refer—as Mr Viljoen who appeared together with Mr Van Eeden for applicants urged us to do—to s 19(l) of the previous Act, the Attorneys, Notaries and Conveyancers Admission Act 23 of 1934, which section was the predecessor of s 13(2) of the present Act. Section 19(l) of Act 23 of 1934 read:

"Where *any person articled to an attorney* has not served under such articles strictly in accordance with the provisions of this Act, the Court, upon being satisfied that such irregular service was occasioned by sufficient cause, and that such service although irregular, is substantially equivalent to regular service, and that the law society concerned has had due notice of the application, may, subject to the provisions of clause 6 of the First Schedule, permit such person, upon such conditions as it may deem fit, to present (if otherwise qualified) his petition for admission as an attorney in the same manner as if the service in question had been regular and in conformity with the provisions of this Act."

(The emphasis is mine.)

The equivalent of the words I have emphasised in s 13(2) of the present Act is the expression "any person". As was said by the Appellate Division in *Port Elizabeth Municipal Council v Port Elizabeth Electric Tramway Co Ltd* 1947 (2) SA 1269 (A) at 1279:

"In the construction of statutes a deliberate change of expression is *prima facie* taken to import a change of intention."

TSHABALALA v NATAL LAW SOCIETY

HOWARD JP   1996 (4) SA 150   NPD

The change of wording in the present case is, in my view, a strong indication that Parliament did not intend s 13(2) of the present Act to be limited in its operation to service by persons already articled.'

I find myself in respectful but total disagreement with these views. The perceived ambiguity does not exist. The meaning is the same whether the word 'not' governs the entire phrase 'served regularly as a candidate attorney' or only the words 'served regularly'. Either way, it is service as a candidate attorney that is postulated. The word 'not' obviously governs the entire phrase, but unless one ignores the words 'as a candidate attorney' s 13(2) cannot be construed to cover irregular service by persons other than candidate attorneys.

If my interpretation of s 13(2) is correct, the fact that the Legislature employed different language to express substantially the same idea in s 19(1) of Act 23 of 1934 is irrelevant. The mere fact that the Legislature has been more economical in its use of language does not signify a change of intention.

In any event, I consider that we are bound by the judgment of the Appellate Division in Singer's case *supra* to hold that s 13(2) is limited in its operation to irregular service under valid articles (or a valid service contract in the case of a candidate attorney performing community service). *Ex parte Edwards and Another* (*supra*) Farlam J purported to distinguish Singer's case on the following basis (at 455):

'I do not find the case Mr *Binns-Ward* cited by way of analogy, *Ex parte Singer: Law Society, Transvaal, Intervening* (*supra*), of any assistance in the present matter. It was a case of legal disqualification. I can readily understand how it is that a person who is not legally qualified to enter into a contract of articles cannot be heard to say that his service was substantially equivalent to regular service. But considerations of that kind do not arise here. Both first and second applicant were legally qualified to enter into a contract of articles, as a principal and as a clerk respectively.'

As Mr *Shaw* observed, the learned Judge might usefully have added that, although qualified to do so, the first and second applicants never did enter into a contract of articles. In Singer's case the irregular service was rendered pursuant to articles which were null and void because the applicant entered into them at a time when he was still enrolled as an advocate. The Court held that s 13(2) could not be invoked to regularise this service, not simply because the applicant was not legally qualified to enter into the articles, but because the service was

'wholly ineffectual, having been rendered pursuant to a "contract" which was void and therefore unproductive of legal consequences'.

TSHABALALA v NATAL LAW SOCIETY

HOWARD JP   1996 (4) SA 150   NPD

In other words, the service was not service under articles. *A fortiori*, where no articles are entered into, purported service as a candidate attorney is not service under articles.

In my respectful opinion, the case of *Ex parte Edwards and Another* (*supra*) was wrongly decided and should not be followed.

Levinsohn J concurred

Applicant's Attorneys: *Shepstone & Wylie*, Durban. Respondent's Attorneys: *Von Klemperer, Davis & Harrison Inc*, Pietermaritzburg.

Tshabalala v Natal Law Society 1996 4 SA 150 (N)

A case reported in the law reports always contains certain key elements:

- the name of the case
- the court by which the case was heard
- the name(s) of the judge(s)
- the date(s) of the hearing
- key concepts of the case in telegram style
- the headnote containing the facts and legal principle decided in the case
- what the case is about (what kind of case it is)
- the names of the legal representatives for the different parties
- the date on which judgment was given
- the facts of the case
- the law applicable to the facts of the case
- analysis of authorities (legislation, precedent and legal writing)

When the case is heard before a court of first instance (the court where the case is heard first, before the case can go on appeal) the following is also included:

- *obiter dicta* (remarks made in passing — optional)
- the order (decision, including the order for costs)
- the names of the attorneys in the case

When the case is heard on appeal:

- *obiter dicta* (optional)
- the order of the court of first instance
- the order of the court in the appeal
- the names of the attorneys in the case

51

5   Glance through the text and try to find these key elements, so that you
    can see exactly how the material is organised.

6   Look at the development of the text.
    – Why does the case start by stating the key principles decided in the
      case?
    – What do the first five words of the telegram-style summary of the key
      principles tell us?
    – What does *Cur adv vult* mean?

7   Scan the text to find four Latin terms. Work with a friend, use your law
    dictionary and write down the meaning of these words. Why are these
    terms written in italics?

8   Reread the text, this time with more care. Why does the judge start his
    judgment by giving a history of the facts of the case?

9   Does the court allow or dismiss the application?

B LANGUAGE FOCUS

In unit 2 we studied complete and incomplete sentences closely. In this
unit we examine the structure of complex sentences.

1 WHO, WHICH or THAT?

Read the following sentence and choose the right word from the alternatives in brackets:

I'm looking for the books (that/ which/ who) have been prescribed for
Private Law 101.

Are you sure of the answer? Many people don't know when to use *that*,
which and *who*. These words (called *relative pronouns*) tell you more about
the noun.

See if you can formulate the rule by studying the following sentences:

• I spoke to the judge *who* gave judgment in the controversial abortion
  case.
• The car *that* caused the accident drove away.
• South Africa is a country *where* the rights of citizens are protected by a
  Bill of Rights.
• Have you seen the attorney *whose* client slapped him in the face?

The following scheme may make it easier for you to remember the grammatical rules:

WHEN TALKING ABOUT	USE CLAUSE WITH PRONOUN
people	who
things	which, that
places	where
possession	whose

It is important that you place the relative pronouns as close as possible to the noun, otherwise the meaning may not be clear. For example, in the following sentence it is not clear to which noun *that* refers:

> There are a number of books in the library *that* deal with this subject.

Do the books or the library deal with the subject? When your sentences get longer and more complicated, it is even more important to put the relative pronoun right next to the noun.

In a few of the following sentences the relative pronouns (who, which, that) have been used **incorrectly**. State why you think the sentence is wrong and correct it.

a) The child that appeared in court is my niece.
b) That is the murderer which killed the woman.
c) I am going to consult with a lawyer that is a specialist in divorce settlements.
d) This is the hotel where the man was shot who abused his children.
e) I studied every case which I could lay my hands on.
f) Have you met the lawyer whom is going to defend you?
g) That is the man whose advocate I am.

Very few people still use the form *whom*. But for those of you who want to sound very learned, the following may be useful. *Whom* is used only for a person, when that person is the indirect object of the verb, for example:

> I gave the book to *him*.
> The man to *whom* I gave the book is my cousin.

The use of words like *to*, *from*, *for* and *at* usually indicate that the relative pronoun will be *whom*.

Work with a partner and try to find relative pronouns in the court case you have just read.

53

2 CONNECTORS

Connectors are words like *and, so, but, because,* and *further,* that are used to join or connect different pieces or sections of sentences. They show the relation between what the writer said before and what she will say next.

Connectors are often used in legal texts. Learning to understand these words will help you to follow arguments in legal texts, and will help you to understand complex sentences.

a) Give a brief explanation of the meaning and use of the following connectors, using a dictionary for words that you are unfamiliar with:
   thus, but, therefore, for, however, further.

for example:
   therefore: for that reason, consequently (meaning)
                    to give logical consequence (use)
   however: by contrast, on the other hand (meaning)
                    to show contrast with something that was
                    said before (use)

b) How do these words function in the court case that you have just read?
c) Use your dictionary and write down the **meaning** and **function** of the words printed in bold:

   In any event, I consider that we are bound by the judgment of the Appellate Division.

   It follows that irregular service as a candidate attorney, within the meaning of s 13(2), is irregular service under articles or a contract of service as defined.

   This period was not rendered under articles of clerkship, **but** pursuant to a letter of appointment.

3 COMPLEX SENTENCES

The use of long, complex sentences, typical of legal English, makes text-books and court cases difficult to read.

- As a general rule, if you have difficulty understanding a sentence, read it twice.
- If you still have difficulty, try this technique:

Think about the global meaning of the sentence:

a) What are the main points?
b) What other information is important?

Divide the sentence into short phrases. Study each phrase:

- for content — what information does it give us?
- for function — what is its relation or connection to the rest of the sentence?

Study the following example:

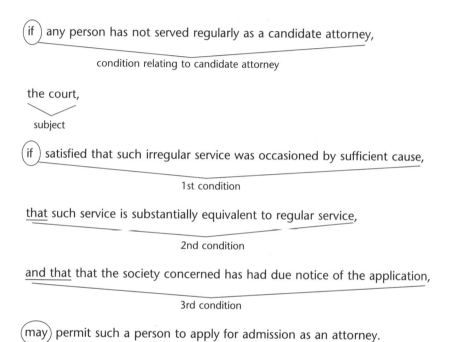

At first, this technique of breaking up a sentence into shorter segments may be time-consuming, but with practice, you will soon be able to mark the divisions directly on the text and analyze the meaning and importance of each short phrase in your head.

- Practise this technique on the sentence marked 'A' in the reading text.

C INTEGRATED SKILLS

In this section we examine how you should make notes of lectures and how you should summarize a case. In unit 4 we will look at how you make notes when you are reading a textbook or court case.

55

1 MAKING NOTES WHILE LISTENING TO LECTURES

The most logical prerequisite for note-making is class attendance. Be sure that you attend classes regularly, as it is often difficult to decipher other students' illegible and inferior notes. By listening to a lecture and making notes, you already prepare yourself for the examination because the act of writing aids understanding.

Always make sure that you have some idea of what the lecture is about before you start making notes. A good lecturer will give you some indication of the range of the work that he or she will cover in the course of a lecture. In this way you will be able to refer to relevant pages in the textbook or a case so that you can check your notes later and eliminate irrelevant detail, as well as determine the most important ideas of the lecture.

Many students think that good notes are notes in which they have written down everything the lecturer said. This is not at all true. It is doubtful whether anyone is able to write down a lecture word for word, and the aim of note-making while listening to a lecture should rather be to make a separate and individual summary of a lecture so that you make sense for yourself out of what you hear.

You should also start devising your own set of abbreviations for words that you will use often in your notes. It serves no purpose to write out words that are often used, such as defendant, judge, court, property, case, etc. Rather use abbreviations for these words, but make sure that you use them consistently so that you don't later forget what a certain abbreviation means.

Keep class notes on one particular subject together so that you will be able to find them easily when you have to integrate them with work you have to do for assignments, tests and the examination. Try to keep your notes in the sequence in which you took them. This can be done by each time writing the date and subject at the top of the page on which you make your notes.

SOMETHING TO DO:

Make notes when you listen to your next law lecture (students who study by means of correspondence and who therefore do not attend class could take notes in a meeting at the office or when listening to a programme on the radio).

a) Decide whether you made good notes by evaluating them against the following criteria:

- use of abbreviations
- whether you are able to use the notes to determine the main ideas of the lecture
- whether your notes are an individual summary in which you make sense of what was said, or whether they are merely disjointed phrases that you caught while trying to take down every word the lecturer said
- whether you have managed to include all the important points of the lecture
- the legibility of your notes

b) Decide on a law class that most of you attend. Bring your notes on that class to your English class and compare your notes with one another.

Another hint: When a lecturer indicates during a lecture that certain work is important, mark that section of the work in some way (red pen, for example). Lecturers are seldom able to resist the temptation to reveal possible examination questions in class. Another good reason for attending classes!

2 SUMMARIZING A CASE

Another important skill that you need to acquire when you embark on a study of the law is the writing of a summary. We summarize cases so that we may arrive at the essence of those cases. For example, we need to understand how a certain case alters or contributes to the legal position regarding a certain issue.

When we summarize something we condense it so that only the most important point or idea remains. If we can use the well-known metaphor — to summarize is to take the flesh of a text away so that only the bare bones remain.

When you make summaries of court cases you should make them so that you can refer back to the summary to refresh your memory about the relevant facts of the case and the legal principle laid down in the case. All other superfluous and irrelevant material such as minute factual detail, should be left out. The following is an example of how one should summarise a case:

57

Tshabalala v Natal Law Society (N)

Facts:

Appl employed as 'candidate attorney' from 1 Jul 94 to
10 Jul 95. Service not under article of clerkship as
def in s 1 of the Attorneys Act 53 of 1979, but
pursuant to a letter of appointment. Appl applied for order
that for purposes of her admission as an attorney the period
not rendered under articles is to be regarded as having been
served under articles of clerkship by virtue of s 13(2) of
the Attorneys Act.

Legal question:

Whether s 13(2) empowers the Court to regularise service
not performed under articles as def in s 1.

Finding:

No.

Reasons for finding: (Ratio decidendi)

The language of the subsection is clear and unequivocal: it is
regular service as a candidate attorney that the Court may
regularise and not irregular service generally.

In the following few exercises we are going to apply what you have learnt.

Study the case of *Van der Westhuizen v Van der Westhuizen and Another* 1996 2 SA 850 (C) carefully and then carry out the instructions that follow.

VAN DER WESTHUIZEN v VAN DER WESTHUIZEN AND ANOTHER 1996 (2) SA 850 (C)

CAPE PROVINCIAL DIVISION

KING J

1996 March 28   Case No 9181/95

Husband and wife—Marriage—Delicts—Action for damages for adultary, alienation of affection, loss of consortium and contumelia— Damages—Measure of—Although society may view adultery with less disapprobation than in past, marriage remains cornerstone of society—Different degrees of reprehensibility in such deficit— Plaintiff experiencing disintegration of her marriage, hostility of her husband and hurt and humiliation of woman whose marriage violated in most grievous manner—Award of R20 000 damages for disgraceful case of conscious and deliberate desecration of marriage relationship.

It may be that society views with less disapprobation than in the past the commission of adultery, 'the act of violating the bed of a married person'. There are, it must be recognised, degrees of reprehensibility in the delict of violating the marriage relationship, ranging from the isolated, chance encounter to the sustained, continuing invasion of the sanctity of the marriage relationship. (At 852B-C/D.) Marriage remains the cornerstone, the basic structure of our society. The law recognises this and the Court must apply the law. (At 852I/J.)

The Court, in an action for damages against the woman (the second defendant) who had committed adultery with the plaintiff's husband, held that the plaintiff had undoubtedly suffered from the second defendant's delict. The plaintiff had experienced the disintegration of her marriage, the hostility of her husband and the hurt and humiliation of a woman whose marriage had been violated in the most grievous manner. The Court described the matter as a disgraceful case of conscious and deliberate desecration of the marriage relationship, necessitating an award of damages which would reflect the serious nature of the second defendant's misconduct. The Court accordingly awarded the plaintiff R20 000 damages for adultery, alienation of affection, loss of *consortium* and *contumelia*. (At 862I, 852J-BWA and 853B.)

Unopposed civil trial in an action for damages for adultery, alienation of affection, loss of *consortium* and *contumelia*. The facts appear from the reasons for judgment.

L G *Troskie* for the plaintiff.

No appearance for the second defendant.

VAN DER WESTHUIZEN v VAN DER WESTHUIZEN AND ANOTHER 1996 (2) SA 850 (C)
KING J   1996 (2) SA 850   CPD

King J: The plaintiff has instituted action against her husband, the first defendant, for divorce, and relief ancillary thereto; the action is pending. Joined in the action as the second defendant is the woman who the plaintiff avers committed adultery with the first defendant.

The second defendant gave notice of intention to defend, but did not persist therein and was barred. The action against her proceeded on an undefended basis.

The plaintiff testified that she and the first defendant had not lived together as man and wife since December 1994. It is common cause on the pleadings that they were married in 1990 and have a three-year-old daughter.

The parties' separation occurred as a result of proceedings brought by the plaintiff against the first defendant for the latter's removal from the common home 'after he brought his girlfriend (the second defendant) into the home and he became violent'.

The defendants met when the second defendant commenced employment as a receptionist in a company which the plaintiff described as 'our company' (ie that of herself and her husband). The second defendant's employment commenced in July 1992.

Early in 1993 the plaintiff discovered that the defendants were spending time together at the office after close of business. The first defendant started coming home later and later and his drinking became worse. On a Saturday night in August 1993 the plaintiff saw the defendants together at the Cape Town Waterfront and from then on the situation at the office became, in the plaintiff's words, 'markedly worse'; the plaintiff and the second defendant ceased speaking to each other.

The plaintiff testified that prior to the intervention of the second defendant, she and the first defendant had had a good marriage; they were very close, worked together, spent much time together and were very happy.

The relationship between the defendants continued and on 9 December 1994, at midnight, the first defendant brought the second defendant into the common home and they went together into a bedroom. Two days before this incident, the plaintiff had confronted her husband about his affair with the second defendant; his response was to dismiss the plaintiff from her employment. The defendants are now living together.

The plaintiff described the cause of her understandably injured feelings as the destruction of the marriage relationship and the hostility of her husband towards her, which included physical abuse. She testified that she found it

---

VAN DER WESTHUIZEN v VAN DER WESTHUIZEN AND ANOTHER 1996 (2) SA 850 (C)

KING J   1996 (2) SA 850   CPD

'very difficult to live with the fact that a receptionist whom I employed eventually ended up serving me coffee in the morning (ie at the office) after having had sex with my husband the night before and this went on for months on end and in a very aggravated state in the office where we weren't talking and the atmosphere was terrible and, secondly, for her to come into my home the way she did, I find that very hard to deal with'.

The plaintiff seeks damages in the sum of R25 500 made up as follows:

(a) damages for alienation of affection and *contumelia*   R8 500
(b) damages for adultery and *contumelia*   R8 500
(c) damages for loss of *consortium*, companionship and
    contumelia   R8 500

Now it may be that society views with less disapprobation than in the past the commission of adultery, 'the act of violating the bed of a married person' (*Johnson's Dictionary*). There are, one must recognise, degrees of reprehensibility, ranging, one supposes, from the isolated, chance encounter to the sustained continuing invasion of the sanctity of the marriage relationship.

In casu there is nothing which mitigates the second defendant's misconduct. There is much which counts in aggravation thereof; these latter factors may be briefly enumerated

(a) the second defendant was at all times aware of the fact that the plaintiff and the first defendant were married;
(b) it would furthermore have been apparent to the second defendant, who saw both of them daily, that their marriage was happy, and successful;
(c) the flaunting of the adulterous relationship was a cause of great humiliation to the plaintiff;
(d) that relationship continued unabated despite requests by the plaintiff that the participants desist;
(e) as a result of the relationship, the plaintiff lost her job and her husband became antagonistic and violent towards her;
(f) the second defendant actually moved into the common home after plaintiff had found the position to be intolerable and moved out;
(g) the second defendant acted throughout with complete insensitivity towards the plaintiff and with unconcern for her injured feelings.

In short one can hardly imagine a more callous disregard for the marriage relationship or a more blatant intrusion into a previously happy and fulfilled marriage.

61

VAN DER WESTHUIZEN v VAN DER WESTHUIZEN AND ANOTHER 1996 (2) SA 850 (C)
KING J   1996 (2) SA 850   CPD

Plaintiff's only recourse is to law; in this way she has sought to assuage the pain she has suffered and the indignity she has been subjected to. Plaintiff said in evidence that it was not
'the financial side altogether. I just felt I had to take some steps against what I had suffered.'
The plaintiff has undoubtedly suffered. She has experienced the disintegration of her marriage, the hostility of her husband and the hurt and humiliation of a woman whose marriage has been violated in the most grievous manner.

Marriage remains the cornerstone, the basic structure of our society. The law recognises this and the Court must apply the law. I regard this as a disgraceful case of conscious and deliberate desecration of the marriage relationship, necessitating an award of damages (I intend to award one lump sum) which will reflect the serious nature of the second defendant's misconduct.

This is an appropriate case for an award of costs on the Supreme Court scale.

It is ordered:
(a) The second defendant is to pay the plaintiff R20 000 as damages for adultery, alienation of affection, loss of *consortium* and *contumelia*;
(b) The second defendant is to pay the plaintiff's costs of suit.

Plaintiff's attorneys: *Miller, Gruss, Katz & Traub.*

Van der Westhuizen v Van der Westhuizen and Another 1996 2 SA 850 (C)

a) Identify and mark the key structural elements in the margin of the case. (These elements are mentioned in section A READING).
b) Imagine that you are reading this case while preparing for the examinations. Reread the case carefully, this time making notes as you read.
c) Identify the central ideas in the court's judgment.
d) Using the main ideas identified in (c), attempt to indicate how the judge's argument develops.
e) Write a summary of the case.

Read through the next case carefully and then answer the questions.

REGINA v. OJIBWAY*

BLUE, J.—This is an appeal by the Crown by way of the stated case
from a decision of the magistrate acquitting the accused of a charge
under the Small Birds Act, R.S.O., 1960, c.724, s.2. The facts are not in
dispute. Fred Ojibway, an Indian, was riding his pony through
Queen's Park on January 2, 1965. Being impoverished, and having   5
been forced to pledge his saddle, he substituted a downy pillow in
lieu of the said saddle. On this particular day the accused's misfortune
was further heightened by the circumstance of his pony breaking its
right foreleg. In accord with Indian custom, the accused then shot
the pony to relieve it of its awkwardness.   10

The accused was then charged with having breached the Small Birds
Act, s.2 of which states:

  2.   Anyone maiming, injuring or killing small birds is guilty
  of an offence and subject to a fine not in excess of two
  hundred dollars.   15

The learned magistrate acquitted the accused holding, in fact, that
he had killed his horse and not a small bird. With respect, I cannot agree.

In light of the section my course is quite clear. Section 1 defines
"bird" as a "two legged animal covered with feathers". There
can be no doubt that this case is covered by this section.   20

Counsel for the accused made several ingenious arguments to which,
in fairness, I must address myself. He submitted that the evidence
of the expert clearly concluded that the animal in question was a
pony and not a bird, but this is not the issue. We are not interested
in whether the animal in question is a bird or not in fact, but   25
whether it is one in law. Statutory interpretation has forced many
a horse to eat birdseed for the rest of its life.

Counsel also contended that the neighing noise emitted by the animal
could not possibly be produced by a bird. With respect, the sounds
emitted by an animal are irrelevant to its nature, for a bird is no less 30
a bird because it is silent.

63

Counsel for the accused also argued that since there was evidence to show accused had ridden the animal, this pointed to the fact that it could not be a bird but, was actually a pony. Obviously, this avoids the issue. The issue is not whether the animal was ridden or not, but whether it was shot or not, for to ride a pony or a bird is no offence at all. I believe counsel now sees his mistake. 35

Counsel contends that the iron shoes found on the animal decisively disqualify it from being a bird. I must inform counsel, however, that how an animal dresses is of no concern to this court. 40

Counsel relied on the decision in *Re Chicadee*, where he contends that in similar circumstances the accused was acquitted. However, this is a horse of a different colour. A close reading of that case indicates that the animal in question was not a small bird, but, in fact, a midget of a much larger species. Therefore, that case is inapplicable to our facts. 45

Counsel finally submits that the word "small" in the title Small Birds Act refers not to "Birds" but to "Act", making it the Small Act relating to Birds. With respect, counsel did not do his homework very well, for the Large Birds Act, R.S.O. 1960, c. 725, is just as small. If pressed, I need only refer to the Small Loans Act R.S.O. 1960, c. 727 which is twice as large as the Large Birds Act. 50

It remains then to state my reason for judgment which, simply, is as follows: Different things may take on the same meaning for different purposes. For the purposes of the Small Birds Act, all two-legged, feather-covered animals are birds. This, of course, does not imply that only two-legged animals qualify, for the legislative intent is to make two legs merely the minimum requirement. The statute therefore contemplated multi-legged animals with feathers as well. Counsel submits that having regard to the purpose of the statute only small animals "naturally covered" with feathers could have been contemplated. However, had this been the intention of the legislature, I am certain that the phrase "naturally covered," would have been expressly inserted just as "Long" was inserted in the Longshoreman's Act. 55 60

Therefore, a horse with feathers on its back must be held for the purposes of the Act to be a bird, and a *fortiori*, a pony with feathers on its back is a small bird. 65

> Counsel posed the following rhetorical question: If the pillow had
> been removed prior to the shooting, would the animal still be a bird?
> To this let me answer rhetorically: Is a bird any less of a bird without   70
> its feathers?
>
>   *Appeal allowed.*

H Pomerantz and S Breslin in D R White (ed)
Trials & tribulations: Appealing legal humor (1989) 211–213

a) What is the meaning of the following words/phrases?
    i)   acquitting (line 2)
    ii)   charge (line 2)
    iii)   dispute (line 4)
    iv)   impoverished (line 5)
    v)   pledge (line 6)
    vi)   downy pillow (line 6)
    vii)   *in lieu* (line 6)
    viii)   misfortune (line 7)
    ix)   breached (line 11)
    x)   ingenious (line 21)
    xi)   contended (line 28)
    xii)   neighing (line 28)
    xiii)   decisively (line 38)
    xiv)   legislative intent (line 56)
    xv)   contemplated (line 58)
    xvi)   *a fortiori* (line 66)
    xvii)   rhetorical (line 68)
b) Rewrite all the arguments put forward by counsel for the accused in
    your own words.
c) Rewrite S 2 of the Small Birds Act, R.S.0, 1960 (line 13) in your own
    words so that it is easier to understand.
d) Trace the argument Blue J uses to arrive at his judgment.
e) Do you think this is a 'real' case that actually came before the court?
    Why/why not? If we assume the case is not 'real' what do you think is
    the writer's purpose? (See unit 11 for **purpose**).

65

3 STUDY NOTES

a) Finding a court case in the library:

One of the South African series of law reports used most often is the *South African Law Reports*. Ask your librarian's advice on where to locate this series in your library.

When you are given a case to read you should take careful note of its reference. A typical reference for a case that appears in the *South African Law Reports* will look like this:

> *SUNSHINE RECORDS (PTY) LTD V FROHLING AND OTHERS 1990 (4) SA 782 (A).*

You will find this case in Volume 4 of the *South African Law Reports* of 1990 on page 782.

All South African law report references work on this principle — the name of the case is given first, followed by the year and volume, which are in turn followed by the page reference and jurisdiction. Criminal cases are found in the *South African Criminal Reports*. Constitutional cases are found in the *South African Law Reports, Butterworths Constitutional Law Reports, Butterworths General Reports* and *Juta's Constitutional Review*.

- See if you can work out where to find the following case in the *Butterworths Constitutional Law Reports*:

> *S v MAKHATINI 1995 (2) BCLR 226 (D).*

Do you perhaps know what the D in brackets after the case refers to?

It is also possible to locate cases which deal with a certain issue even though you do not know the names of these cases. To find such a case, look at the keyword index in the general index of the law reports. Ask your librarian how to use the 'Noter up' or the 'Table of Cases', in order to see whether a specific case is still authoritative. Refer back to Unit 2 Section C3 for Internet sites where you can find court decisions from 1994 onwards.

UNIT 4
DEALING WITH
TEXTBOOKS

A READING
Introduction to the Law of Property by A J Van der Walt and
G J Pienaar (1997:30–32)

B LANGUAGE FOCUS
1 PRONOUNS
2 CONDITIONALS

C INTEGRATED SKILLS
1 SUMMARIZING MATERIAL FROM TEXTBOOKS
2 NOTE-MAKING SKILLS: USING THE TEXTBOOK
3 MULTIPLE-CHOICE QUESTIONS

This unit provides an introduction to some of the concepts you will come
across in your study of property law. The reading material is an extract from
a property law textbook and we guide you to study the words and concepts
that appear in it. More note-making tips are given as well as exercises on
pronouns and conditionals. We discuss the writing of summaries and how
to tackle the much-hated multiple-choice questions.

A READING

The extract that follows is taken from the textbook *Introduction to the Law of
Property* by Van der Walt and Pienaar (1997:30–32). Go back to the diagram
that you studied in unit 2: where does property law fit in?

Answer the following before you read the extract.

- The heading of the extract below is *Property rights*. What do you expect will be discussed in a section on property **rights**?
- What kind of property do you own and what rights do you have regarding that property?
- Can you, for example, destroy your property? Can you sell it?

WORDS AND THEIR MEANINGS (1)

Before you read the extract below, you need to have some understanding of the terms used in it. Look up the following words in your English (monolingual) and law dictionaries, discuss them with your fellow students and write a brief explanation next to each word. Use your knowledge of the function of a word (noun or adjective) to guide you.

an asset	a corporeal thing	a delict
a movable thing	an immovable thing	immaterial goods
a creditor	a lease	a servitude
a bond		
to do something extensively		
the correlation between two things		

After you have written down your explanations, study the brief descriptions in the column below and write down a word (from the list above) that fits each description. Use the function of the words to guide you, that is, a verb will explain another verb, and so on. (Remember that these descriptions are **not** exact explanations.)

not physical, intangible	
an unlawful act that causes harm or damage to someone	
physical	
relationship	
transportable	
a right to use part of somebody else's property	
a person who is owed money	
comprehensively	
possessions	
a scheme to borrow money against a house or land	
something that is fixed	
the temporary lending of something against regular payments	

READING: PROPERTY RIGHTS

Read the first part of the extract up to line 42. See if you can read this in three minutes.

3.1 BACKGROUND

3.1.1 Property rights

The law of property deals with "property" in its widest sense, including all assets that form part of a person's patrimony or estate, or all of what is referred to in non-legal terminology as a person's "possessions". This includes rights in corporeal things (movable and immovable), rights in immaterial property and rights deriving from obligations such as contract or delict.

5

EXAMPLE

In the widest sense a person's property may include the following assets:

10

(a) A motor car (ownership, real right, corporeal movable thing)

(b) A house (ownership, real right, corporeal immovable thing)

(c) A flat in a sectional title scheme (ownership, real right, corporeal movable thing)

15

(d) A time-sharing interest in a shareblock scheme (shares, creditor's right, movable incorporeal thing)

(e) Shares in mining company (shares, creditor's right, movable incorporeal property)

20

(f) Short-term lease of an office suite (lease, creditor's right, movable incorporeal property)

(g) Registered long-term lease of a factory (registered lease, limited real right, immovable incorporeal property)

(h) Registered right of way over a neighbour's farm (servitude, limited real right, immovable incorporeal property)

25

(i) Mineral rights in the family farm (mineral rights, limited real right, immovable incorporeal property)

(j) Usufruct of implements in family farm (servitude, limited real right, movable incorporeal property)

30

(k) Registered bond over neighbour's farm for cash loan forwarded to neighbour (real security right, limited real right, immovable incorporeal property)

(l) Copyright to a book on the family history (immaterial property right)

35

(m) Right to a state pension and medical scheme to which the person contributed for ten years (creditor's right, incorporeal property)

All the rights mentioned above are property rights in the sense that   40
they form part of the person's estate, and therefore they are all important
for the law of property in the wide sense. In this sense all of them might
also qualify for the protection afforded to rights in property in terms of
section 25 of the *Constitution* of 1996. (The constitutional protection of
property rights is dealt with in chapters 23 and 24.)   45

The law of things, as it used to be defined traditionally in the narrower
sense, deals with only some of these rights, namely those that relate to
corporeal things. (You can refer back to chapter 2, where the characteristics
of things are discussed.) In this narrower sense "things" do not include
the rights mentioned under *(d), (e), (f), (l)* or *(m)* above, since *(d), (e), (f)*   50
and *(m)* are creditor's rights and *(l)* is an immaterial property right. Some
of these rights are traditionally dealt with in the law of contract and
immaterial property law respectively. In this narrower sense it was usually
said that the law of things is restricted to real rights pertaining to
corporeal things.   55

However, since the introduction of the *Constitution* of 1996 it has become
impossible to restrict the scope of the law of property in this way. Even
before the introduction of the *Constitution* in April 1994 some property
lawyers argued that there were many exceptions to the traditional rule
that the law of things related to corporeal things only, specifically with   60
reference to a number of property rights in so-called incorporeal things.
Furthermore, in 1994 it became necessary to extend the attention of
lawyers to all kinds of property that might be protected in terms of section
28 of the *Constitution*. For practical reasons some property rights cannot
be dealt with extensively in the law of property course at university, since   65
they are the object of specialised courses such as immaterial property law
or company law. However, the law of property course has to at least
recognize the fact that these rights are rights in property, and it has to
deal with all other property rights, including those that do not relate to
corporeal things.   70

In this book we use the term "law of property" and not "law of things",
because we deal with a number of rights that do not relate to corporeal
things. However, we will not deal with creditor's rights, corporate
property rights or immaterial property rights, since they are discussed in
other law courses.   75

There is one part of the law of property which does not deal with property
rights, but with property-related interests and relations (referred to as
unlawful property relations) that cannot qualify as rights. These areas of
the law of property are important because, even though the law does not
recognize them as rights, these property relations do have certain legal   80
implications. (This aspect is explained briefly in chapter 1, and dealt with
in chapters 12 to 15.)

One of the most interesting and troublesome aspects of the law of
property is the recognition and protection of customary property rights.

Traditionally these rights were not regarded as part of the law of property, 85
since they are unique rights created and developed in the sphere of
customary society. Due to the close corrrelaton between these rights and
the social position and status of their holders, they do not fit easily into the
western common-law picture of real rights, and consequently they were
traditionally neglected by property lawyers. However, in view of the   90
enormous socio-economic importance of these rights, especially with
regard to the occupation and use of land, it is necessary to take note of
their existence, and to understand their function within the broader
picture of the law of property. In view of the recognition of customary law
in the *Constitution* it is also important to understand the proper relation   95
between common-law and customary-law land rights. (Customary land
rights are discussed in chapter 21, and the implications of the *Constitution*
are discussed in chapters 23 and 24.

In conclusion it can be said that the law of property as discussed in this book is
concerned with real rights of corporeal things, as well as other property rights
not related to corporeal things, and customary property rights. It also includes a
number of property relations that are not regarded as rights.

(*Introduction to property law*, Van der Walt and Pienaar 1997:30-32)

Answer the following questions by referring to the lines you have just read.

1   In unit 2 you studied the divisions of the law. In line 2 of the passage
    above the words 'patrimony' and 'estate' are mentioned. How are these
    two terms linked to property law in the diagram in unit 2?
2   Find 4 synonyms in lines 1–5 for the concept *property*.
3   Which three types of property rights are distinguished in lines 1–5?
    (Quote a sentence from lines 1–5 and number the three types.)
4   Go back to the descriptions of words in *Words and their meanings* (1) and
    try to improve on them by linking an example (from lines 9–36) to a
    word, for example
        an *immovable* thing is something like a house, something that is not
        transportable

Skimread the rest of the extract (read the first and last lines of each
paragraph) in no more than one minute. Then answer the following
questions without looking at the extract.

5   Which one event changed the scope of the law of property?
6   Which term is preferred by the authors of this textbook: *law of things* or
    law of property?

71

7 Which aspect of the law of property do the authors of this textbook find both interesting and tough to handle?
8 What is *customary law*? (You might have to check the meaning of this term in your law dictionary, with fellow students or with a law lecturer.)

Read the extract again, this time with care. Go back to your answers above and check them against the passage, then answer the questions that follow.

9 The law of property was traditionally restricted to specific things. Quote a line from the passage that states what these things are.
10 How did the introduction of the Constitution contribute to a more comprehensive understanding of property law?
11 In what way can the term *law of property* be said to be more inclusive than the term *law of things*?
12 What reason is given in lines 64–70 for **not** including certain aspects of property rights in this textbook?
13 Which **two** reasons are given in lines 85–90 for the fact that customary property rights were neglected by property lawyers?
14 Which **two** reasons are given in lines 90–96 for including customary property rights in this textbook?
15 The authors conclude by saying which **four** aspects of property law are discussed in the book; which are they?

After you have checked your answers with your lecturer and your fellow students and you agree about the answers, rewrite your answers to questions 9 to 15 as a summary. Compare your summary with the text. Do you think your answer-notes can be regarded as an adequate summary of lines 46–103? Ask your lecturer to help you evaluate you summary.

The procedure you have just followed in reading this extract can be used to read the fairly complicated material you will come across in your law studies:

One: you scan the text for headings and subheadings.
Two: you skimread.
Three: you ask yourself, what is this about? That is, you try to formulate for yourself (write it down!) the general idea or **gist** of the text.
Four: you read again, confirming and improving your initial reaction
Five: you reread if necessary. This time you note statements with clarifications or qualifications and reasons.

Read **introductory** and **concluding paragraphs** with special care. Quite often the main point of a whole section is anticipated in the introduction and summarized in the concluding paragraph.

72

WORDS AND THEIR MEANINGS (2)

1   In unit 1 we discussed negative forms of adjectives. There are quite a number of such adjectives in the extract on property rights. See if you can write down the negative forms of the following adjectives without looking at the extract:
corporeal   material   movable
legal

Check your spelling!

2   Complete the table by following the example:

NOUN	ADJECTIVE	NEGATIVE ADJECTIVE
Example:		
constitution	constitutional	unconstitutional
limit		
tolerance		
practice		
difference		

Another type of word-formation that you will encounter in law textbooks is the use of the verb to form two nouns which refer to people, for example:

employ > employ*er* — employ*ee.*

The first noun indicates the **agent** and the second the **recipient** of a specific type of action, that is, an employ*er* gives work to (employs) an employ*ee*, who receives direction and compensation.

3   Try to form similar nouns with the following words. Use your dictionaries and take special care with spelling!
lease
pay
credit
debit
grant
legate

B LANGUAGE FOCUS

1 PRONOUNS

In unit 2 a brief explanation was given of the function of *pronouns*. A pronoun usually appears **after** the noun to which it refers, for example, *The owner cannot exercise **her** rights...*, where *her* is used in the place of, and to avoid repeating, *the owner.*

Choose from the following pronouns to fill the gaps in the sentences:

he, she, it, they, himself, herself, itself, themselves, his, her, its, their.

a) This course does not deal with creditor's rights, since _____ are dealt with in other courses.
b) The legislator has the right to exercise _____ powers and this includes the exercise of any discretion vested in _____.
c) The appellants had to avail _____ of the opportunity to show the court the effect of squatting on their land.
d) The court made _____ decision on the basis of the owner's inability to produce _____ bill of sale.
e) Economic, social and political changes forced the legislature to radically change _____ attitude towards the homeless.

NOTE:

It is extremely important that you distinguish between *he/his/him/himself* and *she/her/herself*, particularly in a law subject such as family law. If a general rule is described, you could use either *he* or *she*. In such a case these pronouns are called the *generic* he or she which means that the pronouns are used to refer to anybody, regardless of their gender. It is expected of textbook writers to use gender neutral language by using *he* and *she* alternately or *she/he, him/her* and *herself/himself* throughout the text. Some writers use only female pronouns to raise their readers' awareness of gender issues. However, in some cases it is extremely important that the reader knows whether the person referred to is male or female. Study the following extract from a student's answer in an examination:

'The **husband** decided to move out of the house and leave the **wife** with the children. **He** sold all **her** dresses in order to buy food.'

In this case the **wife** sold **her** dresses to feed **her**self and the children, but the student confused the pronouns **he** and **she** and the lecturer had no choice but to subtract marks, because she had no way of knowing if the student understood the case correctly! Can you see how important the correct pronoun is?

Read the following discussion of a case and substitute pronouns for the underlined nouns. Make sure that you know who is male and who is female!

f)   The facts of the case are as follows. M, a successful male nurse, married D, a surgeon, after <u>M and D</u> had signed a pre-nuptial contract. D had a successful practice which she had built up over three years, whereas M had just finished <u>M's</u> studies and had to pay back a big study loan. Three years after their marriage M had paid off a third of <u>M's</u> loan and D's practice had doubled <u>the practice's</u> income. M felt neglected and <u>M</u> started an affair with one of <u>M's</u> fellow nurses. D found out and <u>D</u> forced <u>M</u> to move out of <u>D and M's</u> house and instituted divorce proceedings. M now claims half of the value of D's practice and insists that <u>D</u> repays half of <u>M's</u> study loan.

Study the following extract from *Introduction to the law of property* by Van der Walt and Pienaar (1997:49) and say to which nouns the underlined pronouns refer.

g)

EXAMPLE

If you sell land that might perhaps have potential to be developed as a holiday resort at a later stage, you would like that potential to be reflected in the sale price. Normally <u>this</u> would be done by raising the price of the land by a certain amount, but if the purchaser is not convinced of the potential for development <u>she</u> might be unwilling to pay the higher price. An alternative would then be to sell the land for the normal price, excluding the possible potential for development, but to provide that the seller would be entitled to a share in the profit from such development, should it take place eventually. This provision for a share in the development profit would constitute a valid contract between the seller and the purchaser, but <u>it</u> would create contractual creditor's rights only, and these rights would be enforced against the purchaser only. If the purchaser sells the land to a new owner the contract would not be valid against <u>her</u> as <u>she</u> was not a party to the original contract. In order to secure the seller's right to receive part of the development profit against all later owners of the land the right has to be a real right which is registered against the title deed.

75

In the following sentences some pronouns have been used incorrectly. Decide which are wrong and improve the sentences.

h) In this case the court based their decision on a balance of convenience. The Mulder Company will suffer loss of market value of its property and it will not be able to meet their debts when they sell to Interstate Whitewashers. On the other hand, the interests of the general public and their right to information have to be considered.

i) The dentist is entitled to remove her equipment from the practice as long as she does not cause any damage.

j) Anybody could gain entry to the house and they could help themselves to its content.

k) The court examined the meaning of the word 'required' and decided that they had to be given a wider interpretation.

l) The ante-nuptial contract gave the wife control over her mother's business, but he could not manage the business without the expertise of his husband.

Note that some pronouns look as if they represent more than one person, but they take a singular verb, for example
   everybody, everyone, anyone, anybody
Sentence (j) above, for example, is wrong because *anybody* is followed by the pronouns *they* and *themselves*, whereas it should be followed by *he* or *she* and *herself* or *himself*.

m) Check your control of the use of these pronouns by correcting the following conversation. Use the lists above if you think there might be a more suitable pronoun, but do not add **nouns**. Take care — not all the sentences are incorrect!

   Simon and his friend Bongi are discussing current political changes.

   Simon: Not any of these political reforms amount to much and there are not exceptions!

   Bongi: There are not many people who will agree with you on that point!

   Simon: Yes, if all agreed with me, something might change, but any with a bit of money wants to cling to it desperately without consideration for the have-nots.

   Bongi: You're ignoring the fact that more optimism about the economy might persuade anyone to invest their money, but few people are so stupid as to let go of their money when there is not the slightest chance of getting many back.

2 CONDITIONALS

A sentence which expresses a condition usually starts with words that indicate the **speculative** nature of the message: *if, unless, suppose, on the condition that*. Somewhere in the sentence you will also find words that indicate uncertainty: *may/might, will/would, can/could, shall/should*. Such sentences have a very special place in law studies and it is extremely important that you understand both the **grammar** and the different **meanings** of such sentences. Can you explain how the following sentences differ in meaning?

Type A: If Simon *buys* the land, he *will* also *acquire* the mineral rights.

Type B: If Simon *bought* the land, he *would* also *acquire* the mineral rights.

Type C: If Simon *had bought* the land, he *would* also *have acquired* the mineral rights.

Do you agree that Type A **predicts** with relative certainty what will happen? In this case one could also use *When* in the place of *If* because Simon may still buy the land. In Types B and C *when* is inappropriate as explained below.

Type B is **speculation** about what might happen if something is done. You can imagine Simon's greedy grandchildren speculating on what might happen if he should decide to buy the land; there is a possibility that he might buy the land, but it is so remote that *when* cannot be used.

In *Type C* you can **imagine** Simon's grandchildren crying their eyes out because their grandfather had gone bankrupt before they could persuade him to buy the land; there is not the slightest possibility that this speculation can become a reality. The minute you can insert 'If **only** Simon had...', you know that the sentence speculates on something that cannot possibly happen anymore.

All three of these types of conditional play an important role in law studies. In the following discussion the **meaning** and **grammar** of all three types will be discussed in the context of law texts.

TYPE A

Use in law texts: The first type can be used to illustrate general rules of cause and effect:

77

'If the owner's entitlement to control is limited... he can still alienate the thing...' (From *Introduction to the law of property*, Van der Walt and Pienaar 1997:60).

Grammatical structure: This is usually:

If/When + present tense + future tense or can/ may

TYPE B

Use in law texts: The second type of conditional is used to speculate on possible courses of action and their consequences. This type of formulation is of particular importance when you are given problem questions to solve and you are asked to advise an imaginary client. You would then consider different courses of action: 'If he *did* this, then that *would happen*, if he *did* something else, then there *would* be a different result'. You are considering different moves and their consequences, as in a chess game, before you actually decide on a specific course of action.

Grammatical structure: This is usually:

If + past tense + could/ would/ should/ might

TYPE C

Use in law texts: The third type is used when lecturers want to point out what might have happened if a particular case had taken another turning. Lecturers do this to illustrate what various chains of cause and effect would look like in the context of a particular case: 'If the owner *had given* three months' notice of his intention to sell the flats, his tenants *would not have succeeded* with their action because their contract explicitly required prior notification of at least three months.' You could also be asked in an examination or test to say what would have happened if something else had happened so that the lecturer can test your knowledge of certain rules.

Grammatical structure: This is usually:

*If (only) + past perfect + could/ would/ should/ might **have***

Keep the explanations above in mind and find the correct form of the verbs in brackets.

a) If you (want) to raise a small loan, you (can) use your movable property to provide security. Simon was in a difficult position: if he (want) to raise a small loan, he (will) have to provide his birthday watch as security. But what (will) happen if he (lose) the bet and (can) not repay the loan?

b) "If you (grant) your neighbour the right to use an access road over your farm the neighbour (aquire) the right to a certain limited use of your property. (Van der Walt & Pienaar 1997:29).

c) In *Ex Parte Geldenhuys 1926 (O)* a husband and wife left in mutual will a piece of land to their children in undivided shares. The question is whether the children's rights are real or creditors's rights. If they (are/were) real rights they (can) only be enforced against a specific debtor, but if they (are/were) real rights, they (can) be enforced against any person. If the parents (leave) the land to only one child, there (will not be) such a problem.

Not all conditionals follow such a simple pattern. Study the following paragraph from *Introduction to the law of property* (Van der Walt and Pienaar 1997:61):

MINISTER OF COMMUNITY DEVELOPMENT v KOCH 1991 (A)

"An occupant of urban premises may be obliged at times to suffer some interference with his full enjoyment of such property in consequence of lawful private or public demolition or construction work in the vicinity...

... And in a case such as this, where the premises are situated in a redevelopment area where extensive demolition, road building and relocation of essential services have to be conducted, substantial and protracted interference may be lawful and will have to be endured. But in order to remain within the bounds of lawfulness the extent and duration of such interference would have to be reasonable."

Can you rewrite the three sentences in this decision by using the appropriate 'If...' construction? Decide what kind of conditional is used: general cause and effect, speculation about what might happen or speculation about what might have happened.

Sentences in which *unless* is used can also be rewritten as an 'if' sentence. By doing this you might also make the sentence easier to understand. Compare the following:

Sentence with *unless*

> 'It is inherent in the nature of ownership that possession of the *res* should normally be with the owner **unless** [somebody else] is vested with some right enforceable against the owner' (*Introduction to the law of property* Van der Walt and Pienaar 1997:60).

This sentence can be rewritten with *if*

> **If** [somebody else] is vested with some right enforceable against the owner, he will not have possession of the *res*.

The negative element in the word *unless* must be brought into the sentence with a simple *not*. It is a true test of your understanding of the work if you can 'transcribe' an *unless*-sentence in this way.

Try your hand at the following sentences and make them ordinary *if*-sentences.

a) The stipulations in the contract are applicable unless the owner and the lessee made separate arrangements.
b) Unless very specific steps are followed, there is nothing that the owner can do to stop people from occupying his land. (Careful!)
c) The short-term lease will be terminated in 30 days' time unless the parties can come to an agreement.
d) The sale would go through unless the bank did not approve the loan. (Careful!)
e) Unless the obligations of the owner to the community are maintained, the structure of ownership will not be accepted by that community.

C INTEGRATED SKILLS

1 SUMMARIZING MATERIAL FROM TEXTBOOKS

It is useful for purposes of note-making and summarizing to break up the text. By summarizing, in this instance, is meant summaries that you would use for study purposes, not elegant summaries with full sentences. Look at the following notes made on the concluding paragraph of the extract you read in A above (lines 99–103):

> Law of prop. =
> – real rts > corporeal things
> – prop rts = corporeal
> – customary prop rts

Try to summarize the paragraph preceding the conclusion (lines 83–98) in a similar way, using your own symbols.

Some textbook writers conclude each chapter with a brief summary. Such a summary might not be sufficient for study purposes but it usually gives a good overview of the chapter. If you need to study a chapter on your own and the textbook contains summaries at the end of each chapter, it is a good idea to start at the end! Read the summary at the end of the chapter so that you know beforehand what the important points are. By doing this you **focus** your own reading because you know what to expect and what is important.

Read the following summary and answer the questions that follow.

SUMMARY
Ownership is a real right that is often defined on the basis of entitlements. Although entitlements determine the extent of the owner's ownership and although ownership without entitlement is empty and impossible, ownership is more than the sum of entitlements. Ownership is a legal relationship between an owner and a thing or things, which implies that the owner can exercise certain entitlements in respect of the thing or things. It is, however, a legal relationship of an abstract nature, because it can differ from time to time in respect of the same relationship or from relationship to relationship.

(Introduction to property law, Van der Walt and Pienaar 1997:65)

1   Which word in the summary tells you what the text will be about?
2   Number each full sentence in the summary.

81

Now read the full text.

4.4 DEFINITION OF OWNERSHIP

DEFINITION

Ownership can be described as an abstract legal relationship, which implies that a legal relationship exists between the owner and a thing (object) in terms of which the owner acquires certain entitlements, and that a relationship exists between the owner and other legal subjects in terms of which the owner can require that others respect his entitlements regarding the object. Ownership is not the sum total of the entitlements of the owner, but the entitlements indicate the extent of the ownership. It is indeterminate in that it differs from time to time regarding the same relationship or regarding different relationships and is limited by statutory measures, limited real rights, creditor's rights of third parties and the interests of the community.

The indeterminate nature of ownership was confirmed in *Elektrisiteitsvoorsieningskommissie v Fourie*, where it was decided that the entitlement to enjoyment and use of the surface of the land was, in the case of immovables, an entitlement of ownership. This might, however, be amended from time to time by means of contract, which would create a different legal relationship between the owner and third parties.

Ownership without entitlements is impossible, since a real right cannot be without content. There is, however, no single entitlement that can be seen as the essence of ownership, since the entitlements only determine the extent of ownership as a real relationship.

The acquisition of limited real rights regarding the thing or of patrimonial rights against the owner is usually of a temporary nature, while the duration of ownership is indeterminate. As soon as the limitations fall away, the owner's ownership reverts to its original unlimited form. This characteristic is known as the elasticity of ownership and confirms that the extent of ownership is to be determined with reference to the owner's entitlements.

(*Introduction to property law*, Van der Walt and Pienaar 1997:64)

The repetition of the word **ownership** in the summary is an indication that the full text is about that concept. As you can see, the title is *Definition of ownership*, and the first sentence of the summary uses the word *defined*.

Look at the sentences that you numbered in the summary and try to find them in the full text. Are there aspects in the full text that you would like to add so that you have a summary that you could use for **study** purposes? Work with your fellow students and change the summary or add to it as you think necessary.

2 NOTE-MAKING SKILLS: USING THE TEXTBOOK

If you find that a lecturer sticks fairly closely to the textbook you can make notes in your textbook (use a pencil if you want to sell the book again) by using a system of signs and numbers. Successful note-making in a textbook depends to a large extent on how well you recognize words and phrases that advance or counter the author's argument.

Refer again to the text you read under A and the short summary you made of the paragraph (lines 83–98) above.

In this paragraph the word *However* (line 90) indicates an important counter argument. The paragraph that deals with the introduction of the *Constitution* (lines 56–70) starts with a *However*, in the middle of the paragraph there is a *Furthermore* and the last sentence of the paragraph starts with another *However*. You could circle these words to make them stand out in the text or you could use highlighters of different colours, although this could become too much to deal with if the lecturer moves quickly through the text.

We annotated (added notes and symbols to) this paragraph. Discuss with your lecturer and fellow students whether we indicated the most important points. Decide whether you could also use some of these signs or change them to suit your own style. You might need to revise unit 3 where the structure of arguments and connectors are discussed.

> The law of things, as it used to be defined traditionally in the narrower sense, deals with only some of these rights, namely those that relate to corporeal things. (You can refer back to chapter 2, where the characteristics of things are discussed.) In this narrower sense "things" do not include the rights mentioned under *(d)*, *(e)*,

(f), (l) or (m) above, since (d), (e), (f) and (m) are creditor's rights and (l) is an immaterial property right. Some of these rights are traditionally dealt with in the law of contract and immaterial property law respectively. In this narrower sense it was usually said that the law of things is restricted to real rights pertaining to corporeal things.

However, since the introduction of the *Constitution* of 1996 it has become impossible to restrict the scope of the law of property in this way. Even before the introduction of the *Constitution* in April 1994 some property lawyers argued that there were many exceptions to the traditional rule that the law of things related to corporeal things only, specifically with reference to a number of property rights in so-called incorporeal things. Furthermore, in 1994 it became necessary to extend the attention of lawyers to all kinds of property that might be protected in terms of section 28 of the *Constitution*. For practical reasons some property rights cannot *only* be dealt with extensively in the law of property course at university, since they are the object of specialized courses such as immaterial property law or company law. However, the law of property course NB has to at least recognize the fact that these rights are rights in property, and it has to deal with all other property rights, including those that do not relate to corporeal things.

(Introduction to property law, Van der Walt and Pienaar 1997:31)

Annotate the other two paragraphs provided in the full text above. Compare your version to those of your friends and try to find a system of signs and symbols that is both easy and manageable for you to deal with in a lecture.

3 MULTIPLE-CHOICE QUESTIONS

Many students are horrified at the prospect of multiple-choice questions in a test or examination while others regard them as 'monkey puzzles' that any fool can solve. Whatever your feelings, all students have to learn to cope with multiple-choice questions.

The instructions to these questions usually tell you how and where to answer. The first important point is to put your name and student number to your answer. Depending on whether you are doing the test on paper or directly on a computer, you should take great care that you type or write or punch out your student number correctly. Multiple-choice questions are usually marked by a machine that cannot guess whether your '2' is perhaps an '8'.

The second important point is that you should read instructions with great care so that you know whether to cross, circle, tick, type or punch out the correct answer.

Some multiple-choice items are of the type in which a question is asked (the **stem** of the item) and four or five different answers are given (the **alternatives**). Others have an incomplete sentence (the **stem**) and four different completions (the **alternatives**). If you struggle with an item, read the stem with each alternative, especially if you are dealing with the sentence-completion type.

Multiple-choice questions can be aimed at different levels of understanding: from basic knowledge of facts to highly complex reasoning skills. Your lecturers might examine both, so you should consider asking them to give you examples of the type of multiple-choice question they will ask.

Look at the difference between questions (a) and (b) (based on paragraph 4.4 *Definition of ownership* from *Introduction to property law*, Van der Walt and Pienaar 1997:64):

a) In the case of *Elektrisiteitsvoorsieningskommissie v Fourie* the court decided that ...

   A   ownership without entitlements was possible.

   B   enjoyment and use of the land was an entitlement of ownership.

   C   enjoyment and use of the land was, as was the case with movables, an entitlement of ownership.

   D   ownership reverts to its original unlimited form.

b) 'In the case of *Elektrisiteitsvoorsieningskommissie v Fourie* the court decided that the entitlement to enjoyment and use of the surface of the land was, in the case of immovables, an entitlement of ownership. This might, however, be amended from time to time by means of contract, which would create a different legal relationship between the owner and third parties' (Van der Walt and Pienaar 1997:64).

Which of the following deductions can be made from the above statements about the entitlements of ownership?

A   The entitlement of ownership includes the enjoyment and use of the surface of the land as is the case with other movables.

B   The enjoyment and use of the surface of the land are an entitlements of ownership that can be changed by contract which changes the legal relationship between the owner and third parties.

C   An entitlement of ownership is temporary and fluid and can be changed unilaterally by the owner.

D   When the entitlement of ownership is changed in a contract and the legal relationship between the owner and third parties changes, enjoyment and use of the land are forfeited.

As you can see from these examples, there is a great difference between these types of question:

Question (a)	Question (b)
knowledge of the facts of a case is required	understanding of case and theoretical implications are required
success depends on effective memorization	success depends on effective memorization and logical reasoning
there is less to read, therefore less time for answering is needed in the test	there is much to read and think about, therefore much more time must be allowed for answering in a test

If you prepared for the factual knowledge type of question (as in question a) and you received the other (question b), you will in all probability fail the test. It is crucial that you find out beforehand what type of multiple-choice questions your lecturer will ask.

The following hints on how to answer multiple-choice questions in tests and examinations may be helpful:

- Allow enough time for these questions. Don't think that you'll do them quickly in the last ten minutes. If they seem to be relatively short questions, you should allow **at least** 1 minute per question.
- If a test should consist of longer (paragraph-type) **and** multiple-choice questions, try to finish questions that require more writing first. If you then start on the multiple-choice questions and run out of time, you might lose 5 or 6 marks on the last few questions. If you do the

multiple-choice questions first and you leave out a longer question because you ran out of time, you might lose 20 marks or more.

- Some lecturers who might not be expert at setting multiple-choice questions give away the correct answer by making it the longest or shortest answer – maybe you will be lucky, but don't let them get hold of this book!

- If you have to answer on a card or answer sheet, make quite sure, **very, very sure**, that you circle or put your cross or punch a hole next to the correct number. It is very easy to skip a number and then put the answer for question 8 next to number 9 and so on. Use a ruler and check before you put pen to paper.

- Waters and Waters (1995:136) say that your chances of getting all the answers right by guessing, are 1 in 125, or 20% for the test. In law studies where you are getting specialist training, general knowledge will not help much either.

By the way, could you find the correct answers to questions (a) and (b)?

UNIT 5
READING
COMPLEX
TEXTS

A   READING
Extracts from *Law of succession: Students' handbook* by MJ De Waal,
MC Schoeman and NJ Wiechers (1996)

B   LANGUAGE FOCUS
1   THE SEQUENCE OF TENSES
2   THE APOSTROPHE

C   INTEGRATED SKILLS
1   MAIN IDEAS AND ARGUMENTS
2   NOTE-MAKING WHILE READING
3   MIND MAPS

The purpose of this unit is to build on what you learnt in unit 4. We use a
more complex text in one of your second year subjects, the law of
succession, to teach you how to use headings to predict the content of a
text. We look at how you go about finding main ideas in a text. We
continue our discussion on note-making, focusing this time on note-
making while reading. In the language section the sequence of tenses and
the correct use of the apostrophe are explored. In the study skills section we
show you how to use mind maps or spidergrams as an aid to your studies.

A READING

Refer back to the diagram that sets out the different components of South African law in unit 2. Where do you think the law of succession fits in and what do you think is it about?

WORDS AND THEIR MEANINGS

Before you read the extract below, work with a fellow student to find the meaning of the following words. Write down what you think each word means.

beneficiaries	legacy	intestate
heir	bequest	temporal
bequeath	propriety	dispose
residue	repudiates	nominate
voluntarily	liabilities	tacit
asset	revoke	incapacity
inheritance	vests	latter
legatees		

Now read **only** the headings printed in bold of the following extract from *Law of succession: Students' handbook* by de Waal, Schoeman and Wiechers (1996: 86–92):

4.2 BENEFICIARIES

The persons upon whom the testator's inheritance devolves are the beneficiaries. As far as the latter are concerned, a distinction must be drawn between heirs and legatees. The question as to whether a particular beneficiary is an heir or a legatee, is a matter of interpretation. An heir or a legatee obviously does not have to be a natural person; a testator may, for example, also institute a company, partnership, club or charitable institution as a legatee or heir.   5

4.2.1 Heirs

An heir inherits the entire inheritance, a proportional part of it, a particular part of it or the residue of the inheritance. A testator may nominate only one heir or he may nominate several heirs. The heir may qualify to benefit regardless of whether succession takes place in terms of a will, whether it is intestate or whether it takes place in terms of an antenuptial contract, as long as he inherits the   15   10

---

whole, the residue, a proportion or a particular part of the inheritance.

In Roman law the heir inherited as a so-called universal heir, which means that he took over the whole of the testator's estate and continued the *persona* of the testator. He inherited not only the testator's assets but also his liabilities. The heir was obliged to settle the testator's   20
debts as well as to pay legatees. The duties performed today by the executor of the estate were performed in terms of Roman law by the heir. This is why there always had to be an heir (*heres necessarius*).

The concepts of universal succession (*successio in universitatem*) and necessary heir (*heres necessarius*) no longer have any meaning in   25
modern South African law. An heir inherits only assets and not liabilities, and he is not personally obliged to settle the testator's debts or to pay legatees. The latter duties are nowadays fulfilled, as has been shown, by the executor from the assets of the estate.

4.2.2 Legatees   30

A legatee always inherits a specific asset or a specific amount of money. The legacy can be in any form, for example, the testator's farm, his shares in a company or an amount of R10 000. A legatee can be nominated only in a will or an antenuptial contract. There is no such thing as an intestate legatee.   35

A pre-legacy is a special bequest which has preference over all other bequests in terms of the testamentary instructions.[13] For example, a testator can stipulate that his wife must receive R30 000 before any other benefits are paid out.

A testator may bequeath his own or the assets of a third party by means of a legacy. The bequest of the asset of a third party will,   40
however, be valid only if the testator had known that the asset belonged to a third party. If the testator was under the misconception that the asset belonged to him personally, the legacy is null and void (unless it can be proved that he would in any case have made the bequest). In cases where the legacy is valid the executor must   45
attempt to obtain the third party's asset, or to pay the value of the legacy to the legatee.

If a testator bequeaths an asset which he holds in joint ownership with another, it is presumed that he intended merely to dispose of his own share.

An example would be a case where a testator, married in   50
community of property, bequeaths a joint asset.

4.2.2.1 Failure of a legacy

A legacy will fail under the following circumstances:
(a) If the testator voluntarily alienates the subject-matter of a legacy
    during his lifetime, it is said that the legacy fails through   55
    ademption. Ademption is thus a form of tacit revocation
    of the benefit. There has been no ademption if the testator had
    been forced to alienate the assets. An alienation which has taken
    place as a matter of convenience may well amount to ademption.
    Where the subject-matter of a legacy has been alienated but   60
    the testator had no intention to revoke the bequest, the legatee
    is entitled to the value of the legacy.
(b) If the legatee should die before the legacy passes to him.
(c) In the event that the legatee repudiates.
(d) In the event that the legatee is unfit to inherit.   65
(e) If the bequeathed asset is destroyed.
(f) If the legacy is made for a specific purpose and that purpose
    becomes impossible to execute.

4.2.3 Difference between heirs and legatees

Because of the administration of deceased estates by executors   70
in South Africa the distinction between heirs and legatees has
largely disappeared.

The following differences are, however, still important:

(a) After payment of the testator's debts, the executor of the
    deceased estate must first distribute or pay out the legacies   75
    to the legatees and only then hand over the inheritance to the
    heirs. If there is sufficient only to pay out the legatees, there
    will be nothing left over for the heirs. The heirs are thus in a
    weaker position than the legatees.
(b) Heirs are obliged to collate while at common law collation of   80
    benefits is not obligatory for legatees.
(c) There is a slight difference between heirs and legatees as far as
    accrual is concerned.

91

4.3 CONDITIONS AND *DIES*

4.3.1 Introduction   85
A bequest can be made unconditionally, conditionally or subject to a
time duration. A bequest is unconditional if the benefit vests in the beneficiary immediately upon the testator's death. In such a case there is no
possibility that the benefit he receives will ever be taken away from him
in the future if a particular uncertain event takes place. The bequest is   90
also not suspended subject to the occurrence of an uncertain future event.

Because testators often make bequests subject to conditions and *dies*,
it is important to give some attention to these. Conditions will be
dealt with first and then the *dies*.   95

4.3.2 Conditional provisions
Van der Merwe and Rowland describe a condition as follows:

> "A testamentary condition is a particular clause or provision in a
> will in terms of which the existence or condition of a beneficiary's
> right regarding the benefit allocated to him is made subject to the   100
> occurrence or otherwise of an uncertain future event. An 'uncertain
> future event' means that it is uncertain whether such an event will
> take place or not."

If it is clear that the event will take place at some or other time the
bequest is not conditional but subject to a time limit or a *dies*.   105

Conditions can be categorised in various ways:

4.3.2.1 Suspensive conditions
With a suspensive condition the operation of a clause and the vesting
of rights are suspended till the condition has been complied with
or fulfilled. Such a clause could read: 110

> "I leave my farm Mooifontein to my son X on condition that he
> obtains the LL.B. degree."

Such a provision means that the son has no claim to the farm until
he has met the condition.

4.3.2.2 Resolutive conditions   115
A bequest subject to a resolutive condition is a bequest which is
terminated if an uncertain future event occurs. An example of such a
condition is:

"I leave my farm to my wife. If she should marry again, my farm must pass to my son X."   120

It is uncertain whether the widow will get married again. If she does she will lose her proprietary right to the farm and it will become the property of X. If she does not marry again the farm will remain her property until she dies and after that it will pass to her heirs and not to X.   125

In the event that the testator fails to appoint a beneficiary who has to inherit the asset in case the condition is fulfilled, that condition is a *nudum praeceptum* and has no effect. In such a case, the appointed beneficiary inherits the asset unencumbered and the condition is ignored.   130

4.3.2.3 Potestative, casual and mixed conditions

A testamentary condition is potestative if the fulfilment of the condition lies within the power of the beneficiary. For example, the testator could stipulate that his son X will be his heir on condition that the son resign as chairman of the Potato Board. A condition is casual   135
if the fulfilment or non-fulfilment of it does not lie in the power of the beneficiary, for example, "if Metropolitan wins the Durban July". A condition is mixed if its fulfilment lies only partially in the power of the beneficiary.

4.3.2.4 Impossible conditions   140

If a testator lays down conditions which are impossible to fulfil, the condition is regarded as *pro non scripto* and the heir inherits unconditionally.

4.3.2.5 Conditions that are illegal or against public policy

If compliance with a condition will be illegal or if it is against public   145
policy, such condition is regarded as *pro non scripto*. The beneficiary then receives the benefit free of the condition provided that the bequest still makes sense if the condition is deleted. As far as assessing good morals is concerned, it has been said that "times change and conceptions of public policy change with them". Examples of   150
conditions regarded by the courts as against public policy and therefore as invalid are the following:
(a) Conditions calculated to destroy an existing marriage or
    conditions forbidding the beneficiary to get married. Therefore,
    if the condition leads to a marriage breaking up, but the testator 155
    did not envisage this, the condition is not invalid.

(b) A partial restraint of marriage is valid; therefore conditions prohibiting persons from marrying members of a particular religion, race or nationality are valid.

(c) A condition restraining the remarriage of the testator's surviving spouse is valid.   160

(d) A condition which terminates a benefit upon the insolvency of the beneficiary is valid.

(e) A condition excluding the jurisdiction of the court is against public policy.   165

A contentious question is to what extent section 8 (which prohibits discrimination) of the Constitution of the Republic of South Africa 200 of 1993 will affect the validity of testamentary provisions. If it is accepted that the Constitution does indeed have (at least limited) horizontal application, it may be expected that provisions of the   170 Constitution will indeed influence perceptions of public policy and good morals. Should that be the case, conditions and bequests which have been upheld up to date may be regarded in future as being in conflict with good morals and consequently as invalid.

4.3.2.6 Vague and uncertain conditions   175

A condition which is so vague and uncertain that it is impossible to determine what the testator intended is regarded as *pro non scripto*. Before the court declare a condition void they will first attempt to find a construction which will have the effect of giving it validity rather than nullifying it.

1 Judging only by the headings printed in bold, what do you think the text is about? Substantiate your answer.
2 Look at the very first heading, *4.2 Beneficiaries*. What do you think the section of the text under this heading will be about?
3 Look at the headings *4.2.1 Heirs* and *4.2.2 Legatees*. What do you think the sections of text under these headings are going to be about? Substantiate your answers.

Now read from the beginning of the text up to line 35 carefully. Decide whether you were right in your predictions about the content of the text.

After having done this exercise, you have very likely realized that you are able to predict the content of a section of text by looking at its headings. This is a skill that is very useful for a number of reasons:

- First of all, one is able to tell at a glance (by merely looking at the different headings) what a text is going to be about, and so decide where it fits in with what you already know and its relative importance. If you are looking for something on, for instance, resolutive conditions, you will see from the headings in which section you are most likely to find information on this particular topic.
- Secondly, one is able to get a general idea about how the writer's arguments in a text develop and is thus able to orientate oneself to understand better what the writer is saying. In this way one will come to a better understanding of the text in general.
- Thirdly, one is able to tell from the numbering in a textbook where a certain section of the text fits in, for example, it is clear that *4.2.1 Heirs* and *4.2.2 Legatees* are sub-sections of the larger class of *4.2 Beneficiaries*.

Another skill that is very useful in getting the gist of a text fairly quickly, is that of finding **main ideas** and **topic sentences** in passages.

4 Read the text under the heading *4.3.2.1 Suspensive conditions* up to *4.3.2.6 Vague and uncertain conditions* (lines 107-175) carefully. Try to find the main idea of each of these sub-sections.

As you no doubt can see from this exercise, it is not always easy to find the main idea of a text. Sometimes there are several ideas that are of equal importance. It is, however, important that you are able to isolate the main idea of a text as this is of help when you make summaries for study purposes or read a text for research purposes. Refer back to unit 2 where we discussed opening statements and clarifications. Do you agree that the following can be regarded as the main or most important idea in the first sub-section?

4.3.2.1 Suspensive conditions
With a suspensive condition the operation of a clause and the vesting of rights are suspended till the condition has been complied with or fulfilled.

Topic sentences are also of importance here. A topic sentence is a sentence that contains the meaning and purpose of a paragraph. The topic sentence of a paragraph is usually (but not always) the first sentence of the paragraph. When one reads to get a general idea of the content of a text, one looks for the topic sentence.

95

5   Reread the text that you had to read in question 4, and then draw lines
    to match the topic sentence for each paragraph with the heading of
    that paragraph in the table below.

4.3.2.1 Suspensive conditions	A bequest subject to a resolutive condition is a bequest which is terminated if an uncertain future event occurs.
4.3.2.2 Resolutive conditions	A condition that is so vague and uncertain that it is impossible to determine who the testator intended is regarded as *pro non scripto*.
4.3.2.3 Potestative, casual and mixed conditions	With a suspensive condition the operation of a clause and the vesting of rights are suspended till the condition has been complied with or fulfilled.
4.3.2.4 Impossible conditions	If compliance with a condition will be illegal or if it is against public policy, such condition is regarded as *pro non scripto*.
4.3.2.5 Conditions that are illegal or against public policy	A testamentary condition is potestative if the fulfilment of the condition lies within the power of the beneficiary.
4.3.2.6 Vague and uncertain conditions	If a testator lays down conditions that are impossible to fulfil, the condition is regarded as *pro non scripto* and the heir inherits unconditionally.

De Waal, Wiechers and Schoeman 1996:87–88.

B LANGUAGE FOCUS

1 THE SEQUENCE OF TENSES: SIMPLE PRESENT AND PRESENT PERFECT, PAST AND PAST PERFECT

Students often struggle to represent a sequence of events in their writing
because they are unsure of which tense to use to represent an event
occurring at a specific point in time.

Study the following sentences and say whether you are able to find
mistakes in the use of the different tenses (look at the underlined words):

- The letters of the respondent to the applicant <u>indicated</u> that they <u>were</u>
  to go to Kenya when they <u>are</u> married.

- The husband <u>started</u> extra-marital affairs after which he <u>leave</u> the marriage and <u>stay</u> with his new partner.

When you write in English you should try to stay within a specific 'family' of tenses: if you start off in the present, you can use the tenses that indicate the here and the now, for example:

> A legatee always <u>inherits</u> a specific asset or a specific amount of money. Once the inheritance <u>has been claimed</u>, other parties <u>can contest</u> the legatee's right to this asset or amount of money. While the different parties <u>are contesting</u> the legacy, nobody <u>enjoys</u> the benefits of the inheritance.

Certain words will tell you that the use of the 'family' of present tenses is applicable, for example words like *always*, *generally*, *as a rule*, and other words or phrases that tell you the author is explaining a general rule. When the authors of legal texts describe the facts of a case, they tend to describe what happened in the past tense, and one again, they will use the 'family' of past tenses:

> In *Ex Parte Brown* a husband and wife <u>left</u> in a mutual will a piece of land to their children in undivided shares. After the oldest child <u>had reached</u> maturity, she <u>wanted</u> to sell the farmhouse but the magistrate <u>refused</u> and <u>said</u> that while the younger children <u>were still growing</u> up, they <u>needed</u> the security of the family home.

Study the underlined sections in the following extract, paying particular attention to the tenses used. Say in each case whether the underlined verbs refer to a general rule, an action that is taking place in the present or an action that took place in the past.

4.2.2 Legatees   30

A legatee always <u>inherits</u> a specific asset or a specific amount of money. The legacy can be in any form, for example, the testator's farm, his shares in a company or an amount of R10 000. A legatee can be nominated only in a will or an antenuptial contract. There <u>is</u> no such thing as an intestate legatee.   35

A pre-legacy <u>is</u> a special bequest which has preference over all other bequests in terms of the testamentary instructions. For example, a testator can stipulate that his wife must receive R30 000 before any other benefits are paid out.

A testator may bequeath his own or the assets of a third party by
means of a legacy.   40

The bequest of the asset of a third party will, however, be valid only
if the testator had known that the asset belonged to a third party. If the
testator was under the misconception that the asset belonged to him
personally, the legacy is null and void (unless it can be proved that
he would in any case have made the bequest). In cases where   45
the legacy is valid the executor must attempt to obtain the third
party's asset, or to pay the value of the legacy to the legatee.

If a testator bequeaths an asset which he holds in joint ownership with
another, it is presumed that he intended merely to dispose of his own share.
An example would be a case where a testator, married in   50
community of property, bequeaths a joint asset.

4.2.2.1 Failure of a legacy

A legacy will fail under the following circumstances:
(a) If the testator voluntarily alienates the subject-matter of a legacy
    during his lifetime, it is said that the legacy fails through   55
    ademption. Ademption is thus a form of tacit revocation
    of the benefit. There has been no ademption if the testator had
    been forced to alienate the asset. An alienation which has taken
    place as a matter of convenience may well amount to ademption.
    Where the subject-matter of a legacy has been alienated but   60
    the testator had no intention to revoke the bequest, the legatee
    is entitled to the value of the legacy.
(b) If the legatee should die before the legacy passes to him.
(c) In the event that the legatee repudiates.
(d) In the event that the legatee is unfit to inherit.   65
(e) If the bequeathed asset is destroyed
(f) If the legacy is made for a specific purpose and that purpose
    becomes impossible to execute.

4.2.3 Difference between heirs and legatees

Because of the administration of deceased estates by executors in   70
South Africa the distinction between heirs and legatees has largely
disappeared.

The following distinctions are, however, still important:

(a) After payment of the testator's debts, the executor of the   75
deceased estate must first <u>distribute</u> or <u>pay out</u> the legacies to the
legatees and only then <u>hand over</u> the inheritance to the heirs. If there is
sufficient only to pay out the legatees, there <u>will be nothing left over</u> for
the heirs. The heirs <u>are</u> thus in a weaker position than the legatees.

(b) Heirs <u>are</u> obliged to collate while at common law collation of   80
benefits is not obligatory for legatees.

(c) There <u>is</u> a slight difference between heirs and legatees in the right of
accural.

a) The 'family' of present tenses

A sentence that is in the **simple present tense** tells one that something happens regularly, sometimes or from time to time. The event happens in the present but not at a specific point in the present. The first sentence of the extract is an example of a sentence in the present tense:

> A legatee always *inherits* a specific asset or a specific amount of money.

A sentence that is in the **present perfect tense** is used to describe an action which continues up to the present or which happened in the recent past. Look at the following example:

> The spouses *have massed* their estates.

One can also use the present and the present perfect together in a sentence in the following way:

> The same *applies* when the spouses *have massed* their estates.

Let us break this sentence down into the different tenses:

> The same *applies*   when the spouses *have massed* their estates.

When we use these two tenses together in a sentence, we usually want to indicate that one action (*have massed*: present perfect) has happened just before the other happens (*applies*: present tense).

b) The 'family' of past tense

The **simple past** is used to indicate that something happened at a definite past time, and is now no longer happening.

> The legatee *died* before the legacy could pass to him.

99

NOTE:

The difference between the use of the present perfect and the simple past is that although both tenses describe something which started in the past, we use the simple past when the action started and finished in the past, for example:

> He *has started* drawing up his will (present perfect). He *died* before the legacy could pass to him (simple past).

The **past perfect** tense is also known as the double past tense. It is used to indicate that two actions happened in the past but that one of the actions finished earlier than the other.

In past perfect formations we use the verb *had*:

> After his daughter *had decided* (past perfect) to marry a convicted felon, the testator *revoked* (simple past) his bequest.

The past and past perfect are used together in sentences in cases where we want to indicate what happened 'earlier' or 'later' than something else in the past. That which happened earlier is in the past perfect, that which happens later is in the simple past tense:

> She *had known* who stole the will before the police *told* her.

NOTE:

As a **general** rule we are able to say that the different tenses are used as follows in law texts:

- The present tense is used to describe rules and principles.
- The past tense is used to describe past actions, for example,
  - what the court *decided* in a specific case, what the judge *said* in a specific case,
  - the state of affairs before a specific ruling or legislation. The past perfect tense is used to describe events that happened **before** a case was brought to court.

Look at the following example:

In *S v S* the court *decided* that the appellant *had acted* illegally because it *is* generally accepted that when a person *knows* about a criminal act, she *is* also culpable.	past tense past perfect sense present tense present tense present tense

More is said about this in units 6 and 9. If you need more information on how to use these different tenses, ask your English lecturer for help or find a good grammar book in the library.

Now study the extract on pages 97–98 again (up to *4.2.2.1 Failure of a legacy*) and see if you can identify the different tenses and state why you think each has been used.

2 THE APOSTROPHE

Read the following passage, circling examples of the use of the apostrophe (').

> Sipho's father died rather unexpectedly. Although he survived the great war of '39, he was unable to survive the 'flu.
>
> Sipho and Sipho's brothers looked everywhere for their father's will, but they were unable to find it. They were especially worried over what was to become of their father's car. It's a pity that they're not able to find the will.

We use an apostrophe to

*   show that letter/s or number/s are missing:
    '39 = 1939
    I'm = I am
    does not = doesn't
    we are = we're
    he is = he's
    they are = they're
    it's = it is
*   to indicate possession:
    Sipho's = the father of Sipho
    father's car = the car of their father

In a few of the following sentences the apostrophe is used incorrectly. Correct these errors.

a) Theyr'e not going to find the will.
b) We've looked everywhere!
c) We can't drive the car, wer'e unable to find it's keys.
d) Did'nt father put the keys with his will?
e) I've no idea, he could've put them anywhere.
f) He's not always thinking, you know.
g) Go and look in Joss's room for the keys.

NOTE:

When something belongs to **one** person, but that person's name ends with an *s*, another *s* is added, for example

> Theuns's car; James's ring.

When something belongs to **more than one** person, the apostrophe comes after the *s*, for example

> the lawyers' books; the lecturers' offices.

C INTEGRATED SKILLS

In this section we look at what constitutes an argument and how it is structured, as well as at how one makes notes while reading.

1 MAIN IDEAS AND ARGUMENTS

Revise the section on how to identify main ideas in a text in unit 3 and also reread the *Tshabalala* case (also in unit 3). Reread Judge Howard's exposition of the legal principles relevant to the case carefully.

• Attempt to identify the main ideas in this part of the text.

It is very important to be able to find main ideas in a text as this enables you to determine how a writer's argument is constructed and how it develops. Because we will deal extensively with the tracing of an argument in unit 11, we will merely attempt to provide you with a short introduction in this unit.

A good writer of any expository or argumentative text normally has a clear argument that is easy to follow. An argument consists of the main ideas that are linked together so that they form a central train of thought which runs through a text. Once we have identified the main ideas of a text it is possible to use these to trace the writer's argument.

- Look at the main ideas that you have isolated in the exercise above. In the light of what we have just said about how a writer's argument is developed, try to pinpoint how the argument progresses, by, for example, rewriting it in the following way: First, the judge **states that** ... (thesis) then he **gives reasons** by saying that ... (justification).

2 NOTE-MAKING WHILE READING

One of the most important skills that you need to acquire in order to be successful students in any field is that of note-making while reading. Because you read to study it is very important to record what you read.

The first step in making notes is the selection of relevant points. It is a good idea to select the most important points in a passage by finding the topic sentences of paragraphs (see p 96 on how to find the topic sentence of a paragraph).

It is not necessary to write complete, grammatically correct sentences when making notes. Notes are there for you to refer to, and as long as you understand them they serve their purpose. Because of this, you should develop your own set of abbreviations that you can use for words that are used often and therefore are too much trouble to write in full.

Study the set of notes on the text printed below (the notes follow this extract).

- Decide whether you think this is a good set of notes. Give reasons for your answer.
- State what you think are the characteristics of good notes.

4.3.3 *Dies*

Unconditional benefits may be subject to a *dies* or time factor. Such 180
temporal provisions may be suspensive or resolutive. A benefit subject
to a *dies* must not be confused with a conditional benefit. In the case
of a condition the existence or lapsing of a right is dependent on an
uncertain future event. With a *dies* one is dealing with a moment
in time which will undoubtedly occur. For example, a testator could 185
stipulate:

"I leave my farm to my son X, but he shall not acquire it until
he is 21."

Here one has a suspensive *dies* that is certain. It is not a condition. The
beneficiary's rights vest at the time of the testator's death but they   190
become enforceable only after the occurrence of the event. Thus if
the son dies after the testator but before he turns 21, the son's
heirs will inherit the farm in his place. Like resolutive conditions, a
resolutive *dies* has the effect that already acquired rights will disappear
in the future. With resolutive conditions it is uncertain whether the   195
rights are actually going to disappear, while with a resolutive *dies* it
is certain that the rights are going to disappear. For example, a
testator could stipulate:

> "I bequeath my farm to my son X. He may keep the farm until
> he is 35 or until he dies after which it must pass to Y or his   200
> descendants. If Y has no descendants, the farm must go to Z."

In this case the son acquires the proprietary right to the farm subject
to a resolutive *dies*. Consequently, it is certain that the son's right in
respect of the farm will come to an end at the latest when he turns 35.
However, this may also happen sooner – in the case, namely,   205
where he dies before he reaches his 35th birthday.

4.4 THE MODUS

A testator who bequeaths an inheritance or legacy may burden
the bequest with a duty to perform (a *modus* or obligation) in
respect of the whole or part of the bequest. The *modus* should
not be confused with a wish or desire. In the case of the *modus* the   210
beneficiary is required to do something, or not to do something,
or to perform. Just as in the case of any other testamentary stipulation, the
modus will be regarded as *pro non scripto* if it is *contra bonos mores*,
impossible, or in conflict with the law. If, for example, the testator
should specify that "I leave my farm to my son (appointed   215
beneficiary) and he has to pay his sister (favoured beneficiary)
R100 000", the son is not allowed to accept the bequest without
the accompanying obligation. Upon the death of the testator, *dies
cedit* occurs in respect of the appointed beneficiary, but the rights are
vested subject to the execution of the obligation. The sister obtains   220
a personal right against her brother. It is precisely in this respect that
the important distinction between the *modus* and a conditional
bequest lies. The word "condition" is often used, while the intention
is to create a *modus* because the vesting of rights is not postponed.
In the case of a suspensive condition, the condition must first be   225
fulfilled before the rights of the beneficiary vest and the person in

whose favour the condition applies does not obtain any rights against the beneficiary. The *modus* differs from the resolutive condition in the sense that there is no question of a termination of rights (which have already taken effect) upon the occurrence or not of an   230
uncertain future event.

The beneficiaries maybe specified or ascertainable. The bequest may have a religious or educational objective, but the *modus* must be enforceable. A distinction must be made between cases where the appointed beneficiary is also the favoured beneficiary and cases   235
where the appointed beneficiary has to use the assets for an impersonal purpose. If the favoured beneficiary is not a person, the executor or the Master may be able to exact the execution of the stipulations. If only a moral obligation, which is not enforceable, has been placed on the beneficiary, it will not qualify as a *modus*. If there it is a   240
prohibitive stipulation which cannot be enforced, the bequest will be a *nudum praeceptum*.
When there is doubt as to whether a bequest is subject to a *modus* or a condition, the presumption is in favour of the *modus* since it is seen as a pure bequest.   245

The *modus* can manifest itself in different forms. Traditionally the modus is distinguished from other legal institutions. It is important to bear in mind that various other types of bequests could also in fact constitute *modus* bequests.

(De Waal, Wiechers and Schoeman 1996:93–96.)

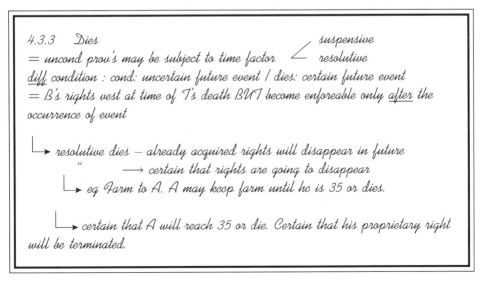

4.3.3   Dies   / suspensive
= uncond prov's may be subject to time factor   ∠   resolutive
diff condition : cond: uncertain future event / dies: certain future event
= B's rights vest at time of T's death BUT become enforeable only after the
occurrence of event

↳ resolutive dies – already acquired rights will disappear in future
     "   ⟶ certain that rights are going to disappear
       ↳ eg Farm to A. A may keep farm until he is 35 or dies.

       ↳ certain that A will reach 35 or die. Certain that his proprietary right
will be terminated.

> 4.4   The Modus
> = obligation on beneficiary to use the bequest, or returns, for a specific purpose
> ≠ conditional ≠ postpone vesting
>
>   MOD:
> diff susp cond: ben imm acquires rights to i/b subject to obligation
> to perform what MOD directs.
> = doubt: mod/cond? ⟶ modus – as it is unconditional
> = B becomes exclusive owner subj to personal duty to carry out obligation 3rd
> party has personal right against B
> = Compliance = c.b.m / illegal / impossible ⟶ MOD = pro non scripto

As you can see, these notes are much shorter than the printed text and, if they are good notes, can be learnt and studied for the examination.

- Reread the extract in A READING and make short notes on this extract.

3 MIND MAPS

Another way of making notes is in the form of a mind map or spidergram. As a mind map and a spidergram work on the same principle and look very much the same, our explanation on how to draw mind maps is also relevant for spidergrams. See unit 2 for an example of a spidergram.

A spidergram or mind map is a graphic, non-linear way of representing information on paper. The main topic of the information is put in a circle (or square) in the middle of a piece of paper. Lines are then drawn from the central circle (the legs of the spider) towards smaller circles which represent the main ideas of the text. Smaller, subsidiary circles may be added to indicate subsidiary ideas to the main ideas.

Many students find mind maps a more effective way of studying as they remember information represented in this way much more easily than information represented in a linear text. Mind maps enable one to set out the different arguments of a writer with greater ease. A mind map gives one the full picture of a topic, and thus helps one to see where a particular section of the information fits in with the rest.

Reread **all the reading material** in this unit (from *4.2 Beneficiaries* up to the end of *4.4 Modus*) and then complete the following mind map based on this material.

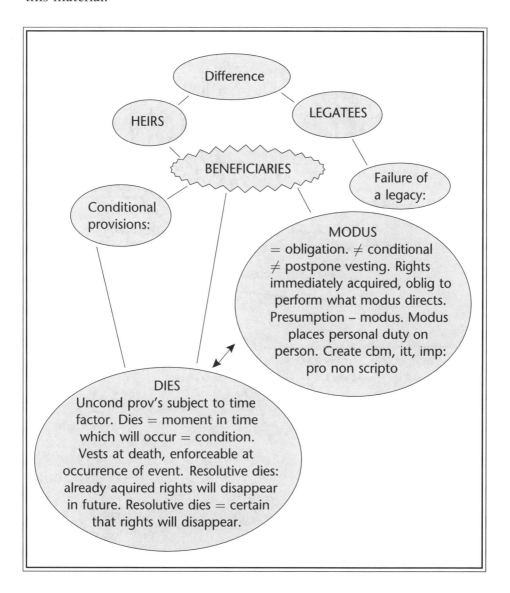

Remember that because everybody represents information in an individual fashion, not every mind map will look alike. There is no right or wrong way of making mind maps.

As you can see, not all the information in the text has been represented in the mind map. Mind maps usually represent only the most important points of a text.

"Then, after you tell them I've cut them out of my will,
I want you to give a sort of mean, nasty cackle"

UNIT 6
STRUCTURING ACADEMIC WRITING

A   READING

Extracts from *Law of persons: Students' textbook* by CJ Davel and RA Jordaan (2000)

B   LANGUAGE FOCUS
1   THE SEQUENCE OF TENSES

C   INTEGRATED SKILLS
1   PROBLEM-TYPE QUESTIONS
2   THE CORRECT USE OF TENSE IN ANSWERS TO PROBLEM-TYPE QUESTIONS
3   STUDY NOTES

As well as providing an introduction to some of the concepts in the law of persons, this unit deals with the way in which one writes longer academic texts, integrating material from different texts, and cross-referencing to these sources when commenting on a case or a specific problem. In the language section we look at the sequence of tenses as they appear in a text as a preparation for answering problem-type questions. In the study skills section we look at how one answers problem-type questions in an examination.

A READING

The extract that follows is taken from *Law of persons: Students' textbook* by Davel and Jordaan (2000:12). Go back to the diagram that you studied in unit 2. Where do you think the law of persons fits into the diagram? Look at the headings of the text below and think about the following:

- What aspect of the law do we study in the law of persons?
- How does the law of persons affect us in our everyday lives?
- The subheading of the extract below is *Nasciturus* fiction. What is the non-legal meaning of the word *fiction*?

WORDS AND THEIR MEANINGS

Before you read the extracts that follow you need to have an understanding of the different terms used in the law of persons. Look up the following words in your English and law dictionaries and discuss their meanings with your fellow students. Write down a brief explanation of each word. Remember to use your knowledge of the function of the word (noun or adjective) to help you.

natural person	legal subjects	juristic person
legal duties	adagium	status
foetus/fetus	potential	presumption
conception	interests	legal rule
postponed	subjective rights	objective law

Read the following extract from *Law of persons: Students' textbook* by Davel and Jordaan (2000:12).

2.3 PROTECTION OF THE UNBORN'S INTERESTS

2.3.1 Protection by means of the *nasciturus* fiction

2.3.1.1 Origin

In our introductory remarks about the moment at which legal subjectivity starts, we mentioned the fact that in legal literature there is more than one viewpoint in this regard[19]. An investigation into the origin of these two viewpoints takes us back to a Latin *adagium* which states: *nasciturus pro iam nato habetur quotiens de commodo eius agitur.* Freely translated, this means that the unborn (or *nasciturus*, as it is usually called in legal literature,) can be regarded as already having been born when it is to his (the unborn's) advantage. This *adagium*, according to the view that legal subjectivity starts with birth, embodies a fiction which is known as the *nasciturus* fiction. This fiction was already in existence in Roman law[20] and became part of Roman Dutch law[21]. In Roman Dutch law this fiction has been used specially in matters regarding status and in the law of succession.[22] Before the use of the *nasciturus* fiction in South African law is discussed,[23] attention must first be given to the various opinions regarding its content in current private law.

2.3.1.2 Fiction *versus* rule

For those who see the Latin phrase *nasciturus pro iam nato habetur quotiens de commodo eius agitur* as a fiction, the phrase means that, in certain circumstances, interests or potential interests are kept open, dependent on the live birth of the child involved.[24] This fiction thus takes cognizance of the fact that the *nasciturus* will be a legal subject after birth. By using the fiction, the interests of the potential legal subject are kept in abeyance. As soon as the *nasciturus* is born alive, the benefit concerned is then allocated to him or her. We want to emphasize that the use of the *nasciturus* fiction assumes that legal subjectivity *always* starts at birth.

On the other hand, there are those who are of the opinion that this *adagium* concerns circumstances in which legal subjectivity does not start at birth, but rather at an earlier stage, namely at conception.[25] As a result, they are willing to concede that legal subjectivity *usually* starts at birth, but they add that if it is to the advantage of the particular person, it would start at conception. Viewed like this, the *nasciturus* fiction[26] is no longer a *fiction*, but rather a legal *rule*. This legal rule makes provision for the advanced acquisition of legal subjectivity. Since the *nasciturus* already has legal subjectivity, rights can be allocated to it prior to birth.

Before the two viewpoints can be evaluated, it is necessary to clarify the conditions under which the fiction can actually be applied in our legal system.

[19] See para 2.1 above.

[20] D 1 5 7,1 5 26, 5 4 3, 50 16 231.

[21] Voet 1 5 5; De Groot 1 3 4; Van der Keessel *Praelections* 1 3 4, *Theses Selectae* 45 5. See also Spiro 1952 *SALJ* 77; Meyer 1963 *SALJ* 448; Van der Vyver 1981 *THRHR* 306.

[22] *Pincham v Santam Insurance Co Ltd* 1963 2 SA 254 (W) [3] 258; Van der Vyver 1981 *THRHR* 306.

[23] See para 2.3.4 below.

[24] Smit 212–13; Barnard, Cronjé & Olivier 13–14.

[25] Van der Vyver & Joubert 59.

[26] We use this terminology in the meantime, but see para 2.3.5 below where the different viewpoints are weighed up against each other.

Now attempt to answer the following questions:

1 Is the meaning of 'fiction' as used in the text at all similar to a lay person's understanding of what 'fiction' is? Explain.

2 How would you describe to a lay person the meaning of 'fiction' in the legal sense?

3 Reread the section under 2.3.1.1 *Origin*. How did the *nasciturus* fiction become part of South African law?

4 Reread the last sentence under the heading 2.3.1.1 *Origin*. What do you think will the next paragraph (the first paragraph under 2.3.1.2 *Fiction versus rule*) be about? Why is it necessary for the writer to include such 'statements of intent' in her writing?

5 Reread 2.3.1.2 *Fiction versus rule*. Two points of view are represented here. Summarize the different points of view.

6 Take a pencil (or different coloured pens) and mark instances in this section of the extract where

• the writer is outlining the historical context of the *nasciturus* fiction
• the writer presents the opinion of academics who see the *nasciturus* fiction as a **fiction**
• the writer presents the opinion of academics who view the *nasciturus* fiction as a **rule**

7 Quote words from this section which function to introduce the different points of view.

8 Reread the second paragraph under the heading 2.3.1.1 *Origin*. Which words indicate to you that the writer is representing someone else's viewpoint?

9 Study the following sentence taken from this section:

Viewed like this, the *nasciturus* fiction is no longer a fiction, but rather a legal rule.

Whose opinion do you think this is? Is it the writer's opinion? Or is it that of the academics whose point of view is represented in the preceding paragraphs? Give reasons for your answer.

10 Why do you think it is important to distinguish the writer's commentary on different academic opinions from the opinions themselves?

The next extract follows on the one printed above.

2.3.1.3 Requirements for application

Common law recognizes the following three requirements for the application of the *nasciturus* fiction and all these requirements form part of current private law.

(1) The application of the *nasciturus* fiction is subject to the condition that it must be to the advantage of the unborn.[27] This requirement will be met if both the child and a third person, for example, a parent, are jointly benefited. However, the benefit should not be *solely* in favour of the other person.[28]

(2) The benefit must accrue to the *nasciturus* after the date of conception.[29] It should be remembered that bequests (and specifically testatory bequests) vest in the heir on the day of the testator's death.[30]

(3) The *nasciturus* must be born in the legal-technical sense.[31]

2.3.4 Application possibilities

Subject to the requirements of our common law, the *nasciturus* fiction is used in several sections of private law to protect the interests of the unborn child. The most important juridical applications will now be discussed.

2.3.4.1 Law of succession

In accordance with the common law tradition in this regard,[32] the *nasciturus* fiction has often been used in the law of succession. This part of the law is divided into two distinct sections: on the one hand, intestate succession and, on the other, testate (or testatory) succession. Intestate succession involves those rules which are applied when the deceased did not leave a valid will to determine who would inherit his assets. The law of testate succession is concerned with those rules regulating succession according to the will of the testator as expressed in a valid will. The *nasciturus* fiction is used in both these divisions of the law of succession.

An heir will benefit from the law of intestate succession only if he is alive during the time which the estate 'falls open'. This stage is called *delatio* and

---

[27] *Inst* 1 4pr; D 1 5 7; Voet 1 5 5; De Groot 1 3 4; Van der Keessel *Theses Selectae* 45 4.

[28] Van der Vyver & Joubert 62.

[29] *Inst* 3 1 8; Van der Keessel *Theses Selectae* 45 4.

[30] Van der Vyver & Joubert 62.

[31] As defined in par 2.2 above. See also D 5 4 3, 50 16 231; C 6 29 3; Voet 1 5 5.

[32] See eg *Inst* 3 1 8, 2 14 2; D 1 5 26, 5 4 3; Voet 1 5 5; Van der Keessel *Theses Selectae* 45 5.

usually occurs at the death of the testator.[33] If this rule is strictly applied, it means that the unborn is ignored when an intestate inheritance occurs.[34] In these cases, however, the *nasciturus* fiction is used to keep the interests of the unborn in abeyance.[35] The division of the estate is then postponed until the birth of the *nasciturus* to determine whether it is a live birth.[36] If the child is born alive, it shares in the estate as if it had already been born at the time of the testator's death. If the foetus is stillborn, no rights can vest in it and the estate is divided without considering the foetus.

In the law of testate succession, the *nasciturus* fiction has often been used to negotiate a benefit for an heir in a case where the testator has died prior to the birth of the heir, but after the latter's conception.[37] This principle is so securely entrenched in our private law that in 1992 the legislator expressly included it in the Wills Act.[38] Section 2D(1)(c) now stipulates that (unless the opposite inference can be drawn from the will as a whole) a benefit which is due to a person's children, or to members of a class of persons (for example, grandchildren) mentioned in the will, vests in the children or other persons if they are alive, or have at least been conceived and are later born alive, when the benefit is transmitted. To put it differently, there exists a rebuttable presumption[39] that a testator wants not only those children or persons who are alive at the time of his death, but also those who have only been conceived by that time, to benefit. With this the *nasciturus* fiction has become a part of our statutory law.[40]

---

[33] Van der Merwe & Rowland 14–19

[34] Cronjé & Heaton 14.

[35] De Waal & Schoeman 5.

[36] Van der Merwe & Rowland 19; Cronjé & Heaton 14.

[37] *Estate Lewis v Estate Jackson* (1905) 22 SC 73 75; *Estate Delponte v De Fillipo* (1910) CTR 649 655 also reported in 1910 CPD 334 346; *Hopkins v Estate Smith* 1920 CPD 558 565–6; *Botha v Thompson* 1936 CPD 1 6–7 9–10; *Ex parte Administrators Estate Asmall* 1954 1 PH G4 (N) 13 15; *Ex parte Boedel Steenkamp* 1962 3 SA 954 (O) 958.

[38] 7 of 1953. Added by s 4 of the Law of Succession Amendment Act 43 of 1992.

[39] A presumption is an assumption made by the law on the basis of available facts. A rebuttable presumption is an acceptance which is made, but which can be rebutted by proving the contrary. In such a case the 'presumption' is actually a legal rule which states that a certain assumption must be made if certain facts are proved to exist.

[40] Jamneck 1994 *THRHR* 174.

If this presumption is not an accurate reflection of the testator's wishes, his contrary intention must be emphatically asserted in his will. Exactly *how* clearly this intention must be stated was highlighted by a judgment handed down long before this statutory amendment. In *Ex parte Boedel Steenkamp*[41] the court ruled that 'die baie sterk natuurlike vermoede' (referring to the *nasciturus* fiction) could not be rebutted when the testator emphatically declared in his will that the grandchildren 'wat by datum van dood in die lewe is', had to inherit the estate. In this case the remainder of the estate had been bequeathed to a daughter and her children of the first generation in equal shares. The testator added the condition that they (the grandchildren) had to be alive at the time of his (the testator's) death. The court was so convinced that the *nasciturus* fiction had to apply, that it resolved not to take the word 'in lewe' literally.[42] The court ruled that these words show that the testator could not have foreseen that his daughter would be pregnant at the time of his death and therefore that the *nasciturus* fiction had to apply.[43]

---

[41] 1962 3 SA 954 (O) 958.

[42] See Cronjé & Heaton 15 who offer a few objections, but conclude that this case illustrates that a testator who does not want to benefit a *nasciturus* will have to make this quite clear. After recent amendments to the law this viewpoint must be even more strictly subscribed to.

[43] Textbook writers sometimes aver that the *nasciturus* fiction is also applied when claiming maintenance for an unborn child in divorce proceedings: Van der Vyver & Joubert 63; Cronjé & Heaton 17. It must immediately be emphasized that the authority on which these authors rely, namely *Shields v Shields* 1946 CPD 242 and *Pretorius v Pretorius* 1967 2 PH B17 (O), do not contain a single reference to the *nasciturus* fiction. In our view it is absolutely unnecessary to apply the *nasciturus* fiction in these circumstances, because the presumption *pater est quem nuptiae demonstrant* will, in any case, mean that the former husband of the particular woman will be regarded as the father of that child until the contrary is proved. This will result in the fact that either in the settlement between the parties or in the divorce order itself an amount will be determined which the particular man will have to pay as maintenance from the date of birth of the child.

2.3.4.1.2 Law of delict

In *Chisholm v East Rand Proprietary Mines Ltd*[44] the *nasciturus* fiction is extended to the law of delict and applied in an action by dependants. This action hinges on the fact that members of a family, who are dependent on a breadwinner for their maintenance, have a claim for damages against a third party who has negligently caused the death of the breadwinner. The third person has thus infringed their personal right[45] to maintenance.[46]

In the *Chisholm* case the plaintiff's husband had died in a mine accident. It was found, however, that the accident had been negligently caused by another employee of the defendant. At the time of the breadwinner's death, the claimant was pregnant with their first child. She then claimed damages from the defendant due to the infringement of her and her child's right to maintenance. The court ruled that the first question to be answered was whether provision must be made for the maintenance the father would have provided for the child.[47] According to the court, this issue depends on the second question, namely, whether the child has a separate base for a claim, distinct from the mother's.[48] With reference to *Jameson's Minors v CSAR*,[49] the court answered this question in the affirmative. The court ruled that the application of the *nasciturus* fiction results in the fact that the unborn child in an action for damages is in the same position as other children.[50] Consequently the plaintiff's claim succeeded.[51]

A

[44] 1909 TH 297 301.
[45] See par 1.2 above in connection with this type of subjective right.
[46] For an extensive discussion of the dependant's action see Davel.
[47] 301.
[48] Ibid.
[49] 1908 TS 575.
[50] 301.
[51] In *Stevenson v Transvaal Provincial Administration* 1934 TPD 80, the court unfortunately did not come to this conclusion as easily. In this case the dependant's action was instituted on behalf of a child that had been born one month after the death of the breadwinner. The court was confronted with the fact that claims against the TPA must be instituted within six months after the ground on which the action is based, arose, because of a statutory provision to this effect. The court found that, if the *nasciturus* fiction were to be applied, the six months had to be calculated from the moment the breadwinner died. If that were done in this case, the action would fail due to the fact that the claimant *himself* had suffered loss by the death of the breadwinner. He insisted on the claimant's being a legal subject the moment the delict occurred. Viewed in this way, he reached the conclusion that the action should fail due to the fact that the claimant (applicant) was not a legal subject when the

In the fields of the law of delict another meaningful development has taken place. In *Pinchin v Santam Insurance Co Ltd*[52] the *nasciturus* fiction has even been extended to cover not only patrimonial loss but also to cover cases of reparation.[53] The court ruled that the *nasciturus* fiction can be used to claim compensation for the infringement of a person's physical integrity if the loss arose out of pre-natal injuries. A pregnant woman was injured in a car accident due to the negligence of the other driver. The defendant was the statutory insurer of the other vehicle, as provided for in the Compulsory Motor Vehicle Insurance Act.[54] After the child's birth it was found that it suffered from cerebral paralysis and brain damage. The child's father claimed reparation on behalf of the child on the assumption that the injuries were sustained in the car accident. (In his own capacity he also claimed compensation for medical expenses which arose from the accident.) With reference to the *nasciturus* fiction, the court ruled that a child would be entitled to compensation due to injuries it has sustained as a fetus.[55] The plaintiff, however, did not succeed in proving a balance of probabilities that the brain damage was sustained during the accident and he was therefore not successful in this case.

B

C

breadwinner died (88). We disagree with the court's view that the dependants can claim only if they are in fact legal subjects when the breadwinner dies, or if they are legal subjects through the application of the fiction when the breadwinner dies. (See our viewpoint in par 2.3.1.5 below: application of the fiction does not suppose in any case that legal subjectivity commences before birth.) We suggest that the court in the Stevenson case actually wanted to emphasize that the dependants had an independent action, ie an action not deferred to them via the deceased breadwinner (see in this regard, Davel 48–51). As will be shown later, the elements of a delict can exist at different times and places. In this case, that will mean that, although the act was performed negligently at a particular point in time, the delict will be completed only when the legal subject suffers the resultant damage. Due to this fact, the six months must be calculated from the date of the birth of the child.

[52] 1963 2 SA 254 (W).

[53] The term reparation is used to indicate that damage in these instances is not due to patrimonial loss, ie it concerns non-patrimonial damages.

[54] 56 of 1972. Now the Road Accident Fund Act 56 of 1996.

[55] 1963 2 SA 254 (W) 259 260. See also how the court acknowledges the claimant's success regarding the question of law when making an order as to costs (263).

However, the court undoubtedly, through this judgment of Judge Hiemstra, answered in the affirmative the question whether a person's right to physical integrity is protected in cases where the unlawful conduct took place prior to the birth of that person. Judge Hiemstra even mentioned by way of *obiter dicta* further possible applications. He predicted that our law would allow an action if a mother was administered with a substance (for example, thalidomide) with the intention of deforming her unborn child.[56] According to the court, a child could also institute an action if it could be proved that the mother's unsuccessful attempts to abort the fetus, injured it to such extent that it was handicapped after birth.[57]

[56] 259. Hiemstra J submits that intent is not necessarily the only form of fault that should be recognized in these instances. Negligence should also be taken into account.

[57] 260. See in this regard Bedil 1981 *SALJ* 463.

(Davel and Jordaan 2000: 13-16)

11 Revise the notes on predicting content by looking at the headings (unit 5). Do you think the different headings in this extract are an accurate reflection of the content that follows?

12 Most texts that you will study as a student of the law include footnotes indicated by the small numbers in subscript in the main text. What do you think is the function of these footnotes?

13 Find footnote 31 in the extract. This footnote provides a cross-reference to another section in the textbook. Why does the writer include such cross-references in the text?

14 To what other types of texts does the writer refer us in the footnotes? What is the purpose of footnote 32? And footnotes 33 to 36? What is the purpose of footnote 38?

Study the three bracketed sections of the extract. In each of these sections the writer has integrated a discussion of a court decision into her discussion of the legal position.

15 Why do you think writers of textbooks often include discussions of specific court cases?

16 What does the writer attempt to illustrate with each of the discussions of court cases?

Do you think all writers incorporate court decisions and other opinions in the same way? (Also refer to unit 7 for a discussion on how statutes are integrated into a text).

118

B LANGUAGE FOCUS

Reread the writer's discussion of the *Chisholm* case (marked 'A' in the extract), underlining all the instances where the writer has used a verb in a sentence.

1 Read the first paragraph of this discussion carefully. Why do you think the writer uses the present tense in the second sentence of the extract?
2 Reread the second paragraph up to '*maintenance*'. Why do you think it is written in the past tense?
3 Study the following sentence:

> The court ruled that the application of the *nasciturus* fiction results in the fact that the unborn child in an action for damages is in the same position as other children. Consequently the plaintiff's claim succeeded.

How would you account for the use of the different tenses in this paragraph?
4 What tense should one use to
   a) state the legal question decided in a case?
   b) relate the facts of a case?
   c) relate the court's decision?
   d) state the general rule that can be deduced from a case?
   e) indicate the court's reasons for reaching a specific decision?

Reread the writer's discussion of the *Pinchin* case (marked 'B' in the extract), marking all the instances where a verb has been used.

5 Why is the sentence starting 'The court ruled ...' written in the past tense?
6 Explain the use of the past tense in the following sentence:

> A pregnant woman was injured in a car accident due to the negligence of the other driver.

(Revise the use of tenses in unit 5 if you had trouble with these exercises.)

C INTEGRATED SKILLS

1 PROBLEM-TYPE QUESTIONS

One of the most basic skills that you will have to master in the course of your study is the answering of problem-type questions. By now you will have realized that you are not examined merely on your theoretical knowledge, but also on your ability to apply theoretical knowledge to concrete problems.

Work with a fellow student and study the following problem-type question, and discuss how you would answer it (you do not have to answer the question, you merely have to indicate **how** you would answer it).

> You are approached by Mrs M, a young mother whose husband was killed in a motor vehicle accident. The accident happened exclusively due to the negligence of a certain Mr X, a rich businessman. At the time of her husband's death, the woman had three young children, and was pregnant with the fourth.
>
> Mrs M would like to know from you whether she has an action against Mr X for the maintenance of her unborn child, or whether only her three children who have already been born have a claim.

Problem-type questions are usually asked in the form of the presentation of a long (and often complicated) set of facts and you have to decide on a course of action. Remember that the lecturer wants to test your knowledge of the legal rules and cases that were referred to in class/your textbook. You should attempt to find the most **relevant** rules, principles and cases to support your advice or opinion.

You should approach problem-type questions in the following way:

a) First of all you select the **essential facts** from those given in the question. Remember with which subject you are dealing: the lecturer might include non-essential facts from other areas of the law, might add irrelevant detail, for example the fact that Mr X is a rich businessman.

    Do you agree that the sections underlined below are the essential facts of the question in the light of the extracts you read earlier?

> You are approached by Mrs M, a young mother <u>whose husband was killed in a motor vehicle accident</u>. The accident happened exclusively due to the <u>negligence of a certain Mr X</u>, a rich businessman. At the time of her husband's death, the woman had three young children, and <u>was pregnant with the fourth</u>.
>
> Mrs M would like to know from you whether she has <u>an action against Mr X</u> for the maintenance of her <u>unborn child</u>, or whether only her three children who have already been born have a claim.

b) Once you have selected the essential facts, it will be possible to identify the **key issue** or **legal question**.

In our example, the question whether Mrs M has an action against Mr X for the maintenance of her unborn child, seems to be the key issue.

c) At this point it is possible to **plan** your answer. Make a rough plan of
   i) the legal question raised by these facts.
   ii) the legal position on this question, consisting of the general principles and specific legal rules, exceptions to the general legal rule, and any **authority** in the form of cases on the issue. Mention any other considerations that need to be taken into account.
   iii) the application of the legal position to the facts.
   iv) the conclusion.

d) At this stage you are ready to answer the question.

Keeping these guidelines in mind, now attempt to answer the question above. Compare your answer with those of fellow students to see where you went wrong, or ask a law lecturer to 'grade' your answer.

Using the approach outlined in a) – d) answer the following problem-type question. Afterwards, compare your answers with those of fellow students.

> Mrs M is pregnant with her first child. She is taking 'flu medicine which should not be prescribed to pregnant women as it may cause serious defects in the unborn child. She warns her doctor that she is pregnant, but he answers: 'Anyone can take these tables. It's not a problem.' Her child is born seriously deformed. Outline the legal position, and say whether Mrs M and/or the baby have a claim.

2 THE CORRECT USE OF TENSES IN PROBLEM-TYPE QUESTIONS

NOTE:

Revise the sections on **tense** in unit 5 before you read further.

Students often struggle to answer problem-type questions because they are not sure of the **tense** that they should use.

What you have learnt about the different tenses used to relate the facts and decision of a court case in B LANGUAGE FOCUS, (this unit) is relevant here. The following notes serve as an additional guideline on what tense to use when answering problem-type questions.

- When giving a short answer to a problem-type question, modal auxiliaries and the future tense are used as you are making a prediction about what may happen. For example,
    Mrs M *should succeed* with her action for maintenance, or
    Mrs M *will probably succeed* with her action for maintenance.

- When identifying the issues raised in the question the present tense is used. For example,
    Our concern here *is* whether Mrs M's unborn child . . .

- When discussing the legal position applicable to the facts, the present tense is once again used. For example,
    Mrs M *must show* that . . .
    Mrs M *must convince* the court that . . .

- However, when relating the facts of an authoritative case, the past or past perfect tense is used. For example,
    In the *Chisholm* case the plaintiff's husband *had died* in a mine accident and she was *left* pregnant with her first child.
    At the time of the breadwinner's death, the claimant *was* pregnant with their first child.

- The court's ruling in the case is also placed in the past tense. For example,
    The court *ruled* that the application of the . . .

- When applying the legal position to the facts, the present and future tenses are used. For example,
    These facts *are* analogous to those of the *Chisholm* case . . .

In this instance, the court *will have to* / *must* / *has to* rule on whether . . .

Obviously, these guidelines are an over-simplification. Students will, however, be able to use these guidelines as a starting point when deciding which tense to choose.

Study the following extract, taking special note of the sequence of tenses:

122

2.3.5 Critical evaluation of the viewpoints regarding the beginning of legal subjectivity

In *Christian League of Southern Africa v Rall*[74] the different viewpoints   1
regarding the beginning of legal subjectivity came under review. The
applicant, an organization promoting Christian ethics and morals,
applied to the Supreme Court to be appointed as curator *ad litem*[75] of
the defendant's unborn child. Within the framework of the Abortion   5
and Sterilization Act,[76] Rall had applied for a legal abortion because
she had been raped. The applicant wanted to serve the interests of
the unborn child in the action before the magistrate (under section
6 of the abovementioned Act). The question before the court was
whether there were legal grounds for the appointment of a curator   10
ad litem to represent a fetus in matters regarding the termination
of the pregnancy. In answer to the question the court first clearly
stated that legal subjectivity begins at birth.[77] The court then took
note of the *nasciturus* fiction and its application in our case law.[78]
The court also considered the viewpoints of the different authors   15
after the *Pinchin* case and expressed the opinion that the following
view is to be preferred. Preference should be given to the view which
recognizes that the Aquilian action would grant damages to a person
against whom a delict had been committed even prior to his birth.[79]
Judge Steyn continued by stating emphatically that the *nasciturus*   20
fiction does not confer legal subjectivity on the unborn, but that it
only ensures that any benefits due to it should be held *in suspenso*
until its birth.[80] In so doing, Judge Steyn confirmed the view that
the Latin *adagium* establishes a *fiction* and that it is not an exception
which provides for the putting forward of legal subjectivity.[81] In   25
this case, the court concluded that the *nasciturus* fiction should not be

---

[74] 1981 2 SA 821 (O).

[75] The title for a curator who is appointed to assist somebody in legal proceedings.
See also par 6.7.3 below.

[76] 2 of 1975, see s 3(1)(*d*) and s 6.

[77] 827.

[78] 827–8.

[79] 829, ie the viewpoint of Joubert. The court concedes that the wording of s 11 of
the Motor Vehicle Insurance Act 29 of 1942, namely 'bodily injury to *any person*'
(our emphasis), may perhaps justify the application of the *nasciturus* fiction in
Pinchin's case.

[80] 829 and see par 2.3.1.2 above.

[81] See par 2.3.1.2 above.

123

extended any further and pointed out that the Abortion and
Sterilization Act[82] expressly protects the fetus by means of several
prescriptions and administrative procedures, linked to penal sanction.[83]

From this case it seems that the standpoint determining that,   30
in certain circumstances, the *nasciturus* fiction is actually a legal rule
permitting the bringing forward of legal subjectivity, is rejected. In
addition, Van der Vyver[84] concedes that to regard conception as the
moment at which legal subjectivity begins, would cause problems,
because the exact moment of conception can never be determined   35
with certainty. In addition to this there is the further objection that this
view cannot accommodate cases in which the unlawful conduct has
occurred prior to conception. Assume that a woman uses certain
medicines containing thalidomide for the purpose of contraception.
She does, however, fall pregnant and the child is born without arms.   40
Assume that it can be proved that this physical defect was caused by
the thalidomide found in the medicine: could the child claim damages?
Assume that it is not the pharmaceutical company, but the child's
mother, who caused his defects, for example, by failed attempts to
abort the foetus; is she accountable to her child for damages if her   45
guilt can be proved on a balance of probabilities? These questions
were raised in *Pinchin v Santam Insurance Co Ltd*.[85]

[82] 2 of 1975. In *G v Superintendent, Groote Schuur Hospital* 1993 2 SA 255 (C) 259D–
   E the court was uncertain about the correctness of the *Rall* case in this regard. The
   court was of the opinion that protection should be provided for a fetus if its very
   existence is threatened. However, see par 2.4 below.
[83] This position has since been changed drastically, see par 2.4 below.
[84] Van der Vyver & Joubert 66.
[85] 1963 2 SA 254 (W) 259.

(Davel and Jordaan *2000: 17–18*)

a) Underline all the verbs in this extract.
b) In lines 1–5 the past tense is used because it describes a court case that
    happened in the past. Why is the past perfect tense used in the next
    sentence? ('Rall *had applied ... had been raped.*')
c) Why is there a switch back to the simple past after this sentence? (Line
    6 and further on.)
d) In line 20 there is a switch to the present tense: 'Judge Steyn continued
    emphatically that the *nasciturus* fiction *does not* ..., but that it only
    ensures ...'. Why is the present tense used here?

124

e) Why is the past tense used in lines 25–27, while the present tense is used in line 28 ('the Abortion and Sterilization Act expressly *protects* ...')?

f) Why does the writer of this text say: 'Judge Steyn *confirmed* the view ...' (in line 23), but 'Van der Vyver *concedes* that ...' (in line 33)?

On the basis of your answers to the above questions, decide what the tense of the verbs in brackets should be in the following discussions of court decisions:

g) "In *Barens en 'n ander v Lottering* 2000 (3) SA 305 the court had to decide what constitutes proper service. The court (consider) Magistrates' Court Rules 9(3)(b) and 9(5) respectively. Rule 9(3)(b) (provide) that a process may be served by delivering it "at his residence" to someone "apparently not less than 16 years of age and apparently residing there". The court (find) that a person may have more than one residence ... Therefore, this case (is/was) authority for the preposition that processes must be served according to the Rules".
(Cassim in 'From the law reports', *Codicillus* 42(1): 63, 64).

h) *Godbeer v Godbeer* 2000 3 SA 976: "The facts were largely undisputed. The applicant (is/was) born in Scotland and (meet) the respondent while in South Africa ... The applicant (submit) that the move to the United Kingdom would be in the best interests of the children, because they (will) be close to their mother's family ... The court (state) that it was the respondent's access to the children which was the only material consideration that (weigh) against the applicant's decision ... and, while the Court (is/was) the upper guardian of all minors, it should not override the custodian parent's decision as to what (is/was) in the best interest of the children." (Ferreira in 'From the law reports', *Codicillus* 42(1): 65, 66).

3 STUDY NOTES

a) Refer to the general rules for the use of different tenses in unit 5.

b) Always read through your answers carefully so that you can eliminate careless errors! Using the correct tense ensures that you express yourself clearly.

UNIT 7
READING
AN ACT (1)

A READING
1 Extracts from *Doctor, patient and the law* by S A Strauss (1991)
2 Sec 78 of the Criminal Procedure Act, 51 of 1977

B LANGUAGE FOCUS
1 PASSIVES
2 MODAL VERBS

C INTEGRATED SKILLS
1 PARAPHRASING
2 REFERRING TO ACTS AND STATUTES

This unit is concerned with the skills you will need to read an act. We look at the type of language used in statutes, and try to anticipate some of the problems this language use causes students. In this regard we deal with complex sentences, passives and the use of 'shall' in sentences. We also briefly look at how one refers to an act or statute when writing an essay or answering a question in an examination.

You should regard this unit as a preparation for unit 8 in which we look at how an act is organized and structured.

126

A READING

Before you read, briefly consider the following:

- Why does a country need to write its law down in acts and statutes?
- Do you think acts and statutes should be freely available for everyone to read or should only lawyers, judges and politicians know what is written in them? Why/why not?
- Write down the names of acts or statutes that you have come across in your law studies.
- What do you think is the difference between an act and a statute?
- What do you think is the difference between a bill and an act?

Now study the following provision from the Criminal Procedure Act, 51 of 1977:

> 78 A person who commits an act which constitutes an offence, and who at the time of such commission suffers from a mental illness or mental defect which makes him incapable –
> (a) of appreciating the wrongfulness of his act; or
> (b) of acting in accordance with an appreciation of the wrongfulness of his act, shall not be criminally responsible for such an act.

Are you able to summarize the content of this section of the act by reading through it once? If you are not able to do this, do not despair. Most people experience difficulty in reading the most simple acts and statutes!

We experience difficulty in understanding the language of statutes because of the very nature of this language. The writers of these texts use long, complex sentences, they tend to write in the passive, and use words rarely employed in everyday language. What is needed is a strategy to decode or decipher the language that is used in these texts.

To begin with, it is important to remember what you learnt about breaking up long, complex sentences in unit 3. We are going to use the same skills here.

Look again carefully at the extract from the text printed above.

- Can you identify keywords?
- Can you identify breaks in the sentence?
- What does the dash (—) tell us?

- Why would subsections and numbering such as (a) and (b) be used? Do they perhaps aid in the understanding of what is in the text?
- Are you able to identify the gist of what this section of the act is about?
- Why do you think 'shall' is used instead of 'will'?

In the following example the provision has been broken up into more understandable sub-sections. Try to see if ~~you are able to understand~~ what the provision is about:

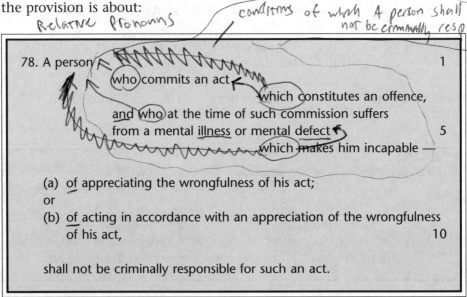

Relative Pronouns

conditions of which A person shall not be criminally responsible

78. A person
   who commits an act
         which constitutes an offence,
      and who at the time of such commission suffers
      from a mental illness or mental defect
                        which makes him incapable —

   (a) of appreciating the wrongfulness of his act;
   or
   (b) of acting in accordance with an appreciation of the wrongfulness
       of his act,

   shall not be criminally responsible for such an act.

1

5

10

When one is confronted with a long and complex sentence (such as the one we see here) it is always better to break it up into more understandable parts and make sure that we know what each part means before we attempt to understand the meaning of the whole. If at first this method seems cumbersome, don't despair, you will be able to use this technique much more quickly as you become used to it.

It is always a good idea to use certain words as markers — if we know that specific words introduce specific types of information it will be much easier to analyze a sentence.

a) Look at the word 'which' in line 3. When do we usually use 'which'? To which word does 'which' refer in this case?
b) To which word does 'who' (second line) refer?
c) Do you think the 'which' in line 3 refers to the same person or thing as the 'who' in line 2? Explain your answer.
d) The dash in line 6 is used very effectively to break the flow of the sentence. We also know that normally a dash is followed by a qualifi-

cation of what has been said before, or a description, or an explanation. What do you think is the function of the phrase that follows the dash in line 6?

e) Why does 'of' in lines 7 and 9 not start with a capital letter? What does 'of' in this case refer to?

f) Now look at the word 'shall' in line 11. Who is the subject of this verb? If we remove those parts of the sentence that come between the subject of the sentence and its main verb, the sentence reads as follows:

> 'A person who commits an act .... shall not be held responsible for such an act.'

What occurs in the middle of these two sections of the act are the conditions under which a person shall not be held responsible for an act.

It seems much easier now, doesn't it? At this stage you should be able to write down the gist of this provision in your own words.

g) Examine the provision again and briefly state the circumstances under which one cannot be held responsible for one's actions (clue: look carefully at (a) and (b)).

THE INTEGRATION OF DIFFERENT SOURCES

In unit 6 we looked at the way in which one integrates references to court cases in a textbook or into another section of writing. Writers of textbooks often discuss sections of acts or statutes in their books. In this unit we are going to look at how this is done.

Read only the headings in the following extract from *Doctor, patient and the law* by S A Strauss (1991:126–128):

Criminal incapacity or non-responsibility

Legal criterion for non-responsibility

Criminal responsibility is a legal concept and not a medical or psychiatric concept.[50] In South Africa the criterion for criminal responsibility is contained in section 78 of the Criminal Procedure Act, which provides as follows:

"A person who commits an act which constitutes an offence, and who at the time of such commission suffers from a mental illness or mental defect which makes him incapable —
(a) of appreciating the wrongfulness of his act; or
(b) of acting in accordance with an appreciation of the wrongfulness of his act, shall not be criminally responsible for such act."

Responsibility a prerequisite for criminal liability

Criminal responsibility is an indispensable prerequisite for criminal liability in regard to any offence,[51] whether *mens rea* be required in the form of intent or negligence, or whether no *mens rea* be required for the crime in question.[52] Before the question can be asked whether the accused had a specific form of fault – where fault is, in fact required — it must be established that he was responsible at the time of the act.[53] The criterion of non-responsibility embodied in section 78(1), in particular the use of the word "incapable" in the context of the subsection, confirms this view. It would be juridically untenable to assess the responsibility of the wrongdoer by asking whether he had the intent to commit the deed with which he is charged.[54]

Mental illness or defect

In order not to be found criminally responsible for his conduct, it must first be established that the accused was suffering from a mental illness or defect at the time of the act.

As I have mentioned, "mental illness" and "mental defect" are not defined in the Act. Whether mental illness or defect was present or not is therefore a question of psychiatric evidence, as indicated expressly in

---

[50] J C de Wet & H L Swanepoel *Strafreg* (4th ed; 1985) 113.

[51] *S v Mahlinza, supra*, at 414–5.

[52] By virtue of express statutory exclusion, so that liability will be "strict" or "absolute".

[53] De Wet & Swanepoel *op cit* 117; *S v Mahlinzo, supra*; *Rumpff Report* par 12.26.

[54] *S v Adams* 1986 (4) SA 482 (A) 901 C–E.

section 78.[55] It is impossible and dangerous too, for a court to try and seek a general symptom by which a mental disorder can be recognised.[56] As we have seen, "mental illness" has been defined in the Mental Health Act, but certifiability under that Act does not per se lead to the conclusion that an accused is not criminally responsible or that his responsibility will be diminished.

"Mental illness" or "mental defect" refers to a pathological disturbance of the mental faculties of the accused[57] and not simply to a temporary mental aberration in a normal individual, which is not attributable to mental abnormality or is due exclusively to external stimuli such as brain, concussion, the use of alcohol,[58] drugs or medicines, or is the result of provocation.

It must therefore be shown that the condition of the accused constitutes a recognised pathological deviation.[59]

The fact that the mental condition of the accused could have deviated to a certain degree from what is normal is not proof of a state of illness.[60] "Intelligent people also sometimes think and do stupid things, more particularly when emotions are abused."[61] It would

---

[55] If the issue of non-responsibility on account of mental illness is raised at criminal proceedings, the court must in terms of section 78(2) direct an inquiry in accordance with section 79 – as to which, see above.

[56] *S v Mahlinza, supra,* 417.

[57] *Ibid* 418; *Rumpff Report* par 9.4.

[58] See e g *S v Stellmacher* 1-983 (2) SA 181 (SWA): A farmer who was on a strict diet, after a day of hard work in the sun, went to a bar and drank brandy on an empty stomach. He had a pistol with him. He fired several wild shots in the bar, killing another customer without any apparent motive. He claimed in court that he had gone "blank". According to medical evidence, excessive consumption of alcohol could cause temporary brain dysfunction in a healthy individual, as a result of hypoglycaemia. The court held that this does not constitute mental illness. However, it caused the accused to act automatically, in a state of amnesia, and he was accordingly found not guilty. Note that if the Criminal Law Amendment Act I of 1988 had been in force at the time (and of application to South West Africa/ Namibia) the accused could have been convicted in terms of section 1 of that Act (see text and see below 353).

[59] The formal report of the psychiatric examination of the accused in terms of section 79 of the Criminal Procedure Act must contain, *inter alia*, a diagnosis of his mental condition (section 79(40(b)).

[60] *S v Harris* 1965 (2) SA 340 (A) 360.

[61] Chief Justice Steyn, in the *Harris* case at 358.

likewise be wrong to interpret an inclination to violence in the accused as being in itself an indication of mental illness.[62]

It is not necessary, however, to prove that the origin of the accused's mental illness or defect lies in his mind. It could just as well be organic in origin, e g arteriosclerosis (hardening of the arteries).[63] So too, functional (as distinguished from mere temporary, alcohol-induced) hypoglycaemia (shortage of blood-sugar) can occasion mental illness[64] as can a traumatic head-injury.

On the other hand, however, mere concussion, which causes a temporary interruption in the flow of blood to the brain and loss of consciousness, does not constitute mental illness;[65] such a contrition could in fact cause automatism, which means that legally the accused is regarded as not having acted at all.[66]

Moreover, it need not be proved that the mental illness was of a permanent nature[67] or that it is incurable.[68] The doctrine of partial or limited mental illness — according to which one part of a person's mind is normal and the remaining part abnormal[69] — no longer has any support. [70]

The illness of the accused must have existed at the time of the conduct. A person who suffers from mental illness and commits an unlawful act during a *lucidum intervallum*, can in fact be found to have been responsible at the time of the act. This would be so even where a court had previously held that the person was mentally deranged.[71]

Although, as we have seen, mere occasional mental aberration as the result of the use of alcohol does not constitute mental illness, the consumption of alcohol, especially if it is chronic, can result in a condition which can be clearly diagnosed as mental illness,

[62] Cf C J R Dugard 1967 *SALJ* 134.
[63] Cf the English case of *R v Kemp* [1957] 1 QBD 399; [1956] 3 All ER 249, cited with approval in *Mahlinza, supra,* 417.
[64] Cf S v Bezuidenhout 1964 (2) SA 651 (A).
[65] Cf the submission in *Kemp, supra,* 253F.
[66] See below 129.
[67] *Mahlinza, supra,* 417.
[68] *Kemp, supra,* 253.
[69] Cf R v Kruger 1958 (2) SA 320 (T).
[70] Cf Rumpff Report par 5.15; E M Burchell & P M A Hunt *South African Criminal Law and Procedure* (2nd ed, 1983) 265.
[71] *S v Steyn* 1963 (1) SA 797 (W).

e g *delirium tremens.*[72] The same would apply to the long-term use of drugs or medicines which results in serious brain dysfunction.

[72] Cf *R v Bourke* 1916 TPD 303, 307; *R v Holliday* 1924 AD 250.

In this extract the writer discusses the interpretation of section 78 of the Criminal Procedure Act, 51 of 1977. The sub-headings are used to tell the reader what a paragraph is about.

In the light of our discussion of section 78, are you able to predict the topic of each paragraph by looking at the three sub-sections? Write down what you expect to be discussed under each heading.

Were you right in your predictions about the content of each sub-heading?

Now read the whole text carefully.

Note how the writer discusses different aspects of section 78. He takes key-concepts from the section and then looks at how these have been interpreted by law writers and the courts.

Look carefully at the first sentence under the sub-heading 'Mental illness or defect'. The writer starts his discussion by summarizing the content of section 78. He goes on to look at the content of the section in detail.

Reread the rest of what has been written under this heading and try to find answers to the following questions:

h) What are the key words or key concepts that the writer thinks need to be defined?
i) How does the writer suggest one determines whether mental illness is present or not?
j) Does the fact that 'mental illness' has been defined in the Mental Health Act of 1973, help us in our search for an accurate definition of what it is? Quote from the text to substantiate your answer.
k) What then are the properties or qualities of a 'mental illness' or 'mental defect'?
l) What does the writer want to tell us when he stresses the fact that a deviation from what is normal cannot be considered proof of mental illness?

133

Use your answers and your brief notes about what is discussed under each sub-heading to write a summary of this section of the text.

This serves as one example of how a writer may integrate a discussion of an act into a textbook. Often the text of the actual act or statute will not be reprinted as it has been done here, and you will have to find your own copy of the act in the library (see unit 2). It is also important to realize that you will in most cases be expected to know the contents of an entire act, instead of just one sub-section of that act. You will be expected to interpret a sub-section of an act in the light of what was written in the act as a whole.

B LANGUAGE FOCUS

You may have noticed that the language used in acts and statutes differs from everyday 'informal' language, and also from the language that we find in textbooks. We can say that this language is more 'formal' than that which we use when we are talking to our friends. (Refer to unit 13 for a further discussion of 'formality' in language use.)

Writers of statutes make extensive use of language structures such as passives and modal verbs, especially those expressing obligation, such as *shall*. It is therefore necessary to examine these language structures. (For more on the language used in legal writing, see unit 9).

1 PASSIVES

English sentences containing a subject, verb and object are either **active** or **passive** sentences.

The passive is not very common in informal speech or writing but is a regular feature of formal impersonal texts, such as legal or scientific texts. It is very important that you recognise and understand the passive form as it is commonly used in legal English.

Passives are often used in the following places:

Notices	No smoking is allowed in the courtroom.
Newspapers	The Attorney-General was given no choice by the Minister but to resign.
Textbooks	The South African legal system has been influenced profoundly by Roman Dutch Law.
Legal documents	One month's notice has to be given by the lessee before this contract can be terminated.
Statutes	No person shall be held responsible for such an act.

134

You should take care not to overuse the passive voice, mainly because it can make your writing stilted and longer than it needs to be. Stewart (1995:536) points out that passives 'make complicated demands on comprehension' and 'make it possible to supply or withhold information about the agent of the process', which may be to the disadvantage of ordinary people who also need to understand the law. She gives an example from the Human Rights Commission Bill [B 8F-94] 10 (2):

> The entry and search of any premises under this section shall be conducted with strict regard to decency and order.

It is not clear who will do the searching in this case, although such information is clearly important. One could argue that lawyers and lawmakers will know who the agent is but Stewart argues (1995:532) that, '[a]ll the users of law have the right to be informed in language which they can understand'.

The purpose and context of legal writing will also determine the use of the passive voice. If a textbook writer states that, as a general rule, *the supreme court or maintenance court can be approached at any time to claim maintenance for one's children*, the passive seems more justified than when a lawyer writes the same sentence in an advice column for a women's magazine. In such a case the active voice is more appropriate, for example, *You can approach the supreme court or maintenance court at any time to claim maintenance for your children.*

The next example illustrates how misunderstanding can arise in a sentence where the passive dominates. Campbell et al (1988: 272) advise lawyers who are collecting information from clients as follows:

> Analysis of the facts will be facilitated if the information obtained through interviews and correspondence is brought together in a well-ordered statement of facts.

The over-abundance of passives and the repetition of 'facts' create comprehension problems at a first reading. Can you improve on this sentence? This is our effort:

> A lawyer can facilitate his analysis of the facts by bringing together information obtained through interviews and correspondence in a well-ordered statement of facts.

Transform the following sentences into the passive and decide whether it is necessary to identify who did the action (the agent). Remember to first find the object of the passive sentence and then work from there.

a) The man paid maintenance to his ex-wife.

b) The Constitutional Court has decided to strike down the act.

c) Parliament voted on the proposed bill amending the Abortion Act.

d) Professional privilege protects interviews between patients and doctors.

e) The lawyer is challenging the new act in the High Court.

f) The President will pardon the prisoner next week.

Transform the following passive sentences into the active:

g) It is submitted that, as a matter of law, the decision is correct.

h) That fact was attested to by all the witnesses for the state.

i) It was decided that serial killers will no longer be granted parole.

j) The reciprocal duty of support is ended by divorce.

If you struggled with these sentences you should ask your English lecturer to provide you with additional exercises and explanations.

C INTEGRATED SKILLS

1 PARAPHRASING

To paraphrase is to rewrite a section of a text in your own words. During the course of your studies you will often be required to paraphrase the content of a statute, a court case or an article written by a legal academic. Because it is impossible or unnecessary to repeat exactly what someone else has said or written, we paraphrase by repeating only the essence of what they have said in our own words. Look carefully at the following extract from the Criminal Law Amendment Act, No 1 of 1988:

1(1)   Any person who consumes or uses any substance which impairs his faculties to appreciate the wrongfulness of his acts or to act in accordance with that appreciation, while knowing that such substance has that effect, and who, while such faculties are thus impaired, commits any act prohibited by law under any penalty, but is not criminally liable because his faculties were impaired as aforesaid, shall be guilty of an offence and shall be liable on conviction to the penalty, except the death penalty, which may be imposed in respect of the commission of that act.

(2)   If in any prosecution for any offence it is found that the accused is not criminally liable for the offence charged on account that his faculties referred to in subsection (1) were impaired by the consumption or use of any substance, such accused may be found guilty of a contravention of subsection (1), if the evidence proves the commission of such contravention.

136

a) Using all the skills you have learnt in this unit, (for example breaking up the sentence in more manageable sections), attempt to paraphrase (rewrite in your own words) the main idea of this section.

b) Can you suggest circumstances in which this section will find application?

2 REFERRING TO ACTS AND STATUTES

You will often have to refer to acts and statutes when writing a test, examination or term paper.

- Remember that the name of an act is a proper noun and that you therefore need to use capital letters, for example:
  Mental Health Act 18 of 1973, Child Care Act 74 of 1983 or Internal Security Act 74 of 1982.

- Note that the 'A' of Act is also a capital letter when it is part of the name of the act.

- When using the name of an act in a sentence, remember that only the name of the act needs to be in capitals, a preceding word such as 'the' does not, e.g. the Mental Health Act or the Child Care Act.

- Students often ask whether it is necessary to provide the number of the act when referring to it. This seems a waste of time when your reader knows which act it is you are referring to. We would suggest that you use the full title of the act (including its number) when you refer to it for the first time. Always give the full reference (number, year and full title) in a formal document, for example in a term paper. Abbreviate the title of the act in an examination. Abbreviate the title of the act (or use the words 'the act') when you make subsequent references to it. Even when abbreviating and in examinations, always provide the year in which the act was promulgated — this is more important than the number of the act.

- In term papers, dissertations or essays in which you make use of footnotes, the number of the act could be given in a footnote, for example:

...... Section 39(I) of the Child Care Act[1] makes provision for a ....
....

1. Act 74 of 1983.

UNIT 8
READING
AN ACT
(II)

This unit should be seen as a continuation of unit 7 where you were introduced to some of the language structures used in acts. In this unit you are shown how an act is organized and structured. In the language section we examine the use of modal verbs to express degrees of certainty or uncertainty. Finally we look at how one should draft and plan argumentative writing.

A READING

Before you read the newspaper articles and the extract from the constitution on the right to freedom of religion (printed below), think about the following:

- Much has been written in the media about the possible decriminalization of the use of dagga. What is your point of the view on this?
- Do you think that some drugs are more harmful than other drugs? Are the effects of dagga and those of heroin the same?
- Why do you think it is a criminal offence to be in the possession of, or to use, drugs? Whose interests does the state want to protect by making it a criminal offence?
- Many people use cannabis or dagga for religious reasons. Do you think they should be allowed to use dagga without fear of possible prosecution? Why/why not?

Now carefully read the articles that appeared in the *Beeld* of 28 January 2002 and the *Natal Witness* of 21 March 2002, and also the extracts from the Constitution of the Republic of South Africa Act 108 of 1996:

Rastas take high road on dagga

Johannesburg - Rasta priest and member of the Rasta National Council Solomon Ngema says Rastafarians will continue to smoke their dope, regardless of what the Constitutional Court has ruled.

He was speaking after an appeal by Rastafarian candidate lawyer Gareth Prince to be allowed to smoke dagga as part of his religion was dismissed in the Constitutional Court.

Judge-President Arthur Chaskalson, who read out the judgment, said five of the nine judges who heard the case were not in favour of allowing Prince to use the drug.

The challenge against the laws that criminalise the use of dagga was brought last year by Prince. The laws are the Drugs and Drug Trafficking Act and the Medicines and Related Substances Control Act.

Prince was refused admission to the Law Society of the Cape of Good Hope because he had two previous convictions for dagga possession and had declared he would continue using the drug as part of his religion.

Prince's advocate John Abel said he was disappointed at the decision, which he said went against trends in Europe and Canada where dagga was used for medicinal and religious purposes.

Rastas vow to continue smoking

Prince himself said: "I am not prepared to make a comment on the ruling until I have seen the Constitutional Court's judgment."

Prince, who lives in Cape Town, was not able to attend court.

Department of Health attorney Neville Gawala said the government was pleased with the decision.

However, Rasta priest Ngema said Rastafari would continue to smoke dagga, despite the ruling.

"As Rasta we have no problem with ganja, we use it as a herb. The main point is that Rastas should not take ganja as a drug, but as a herb for service of the mind ... so we have the right to use ganja."

Chaskalson said the five judges not in favour felt that if the use of dagga was legalised under certain restrictions to Rastafari, it would make law enforcement difficult.

139

Rastafarian attorney to challenge concourt ruling on dagga

JOHANNESBURG - Rastafarian candidate attorney Garreth Prince said on Wednesday he will challenge the Constitutional Court's judgment on the use of cannabis at the African Commission on Human and Peoples' Rights in May.

"I am taking up the matter with the African Commission, even though they don't have jurisdiction to tell the government what to do, but they can add persuasive value," Prince told a packed lecture hall at the University of the Witwatersrand in Johannesburg.

The African Commission is an organ of the Organisation of African Unity (OAU). Established in 1987, it is an enforcement mechanism created under the African Charter on Human and Peoples' Rights. It promotes and protects rights in the African Charter, engages in conflict resolution and investigates violations of rights.

Prince lost a Constitutional Court battle earlier this year in which he wanted cannabis or dagga to be legalised for Rastafarian religious purposes.

The court ruled against him, saying if an exemption is permitted in general terms for the use of harmful drugs by people for religious purposes, the state's ability to enforce its drugs legislation will be substantially impaired.

Prince, a candidate attorney who was refused admission to the Law Society of the Cape of Good Hope because of two convictions for possession of dagga, said the organisation has treated him unfairly.

"But they will not stop me. I still want to be a lawyer. I believe that justice will prevail even though it might take time.

When a student asked him how he makes his living, he responded: "I sell fruit and vegetables."

Freedom of religion, belief and opinion

15. (1) Everyone has the right to freedom of conscience, religion, thought, belief and opinion.
    (2) Religious observances may be conducted at state or state-aided institutions, provided that —
       (a) those observances follow rules made by the appropriate public authorities;
       (b) they are conducted on an equitable basis; and
       (c) attendance at them is free and voluntary.
    (3) (a) This section does not prevent legislation recognising
          (i) marriages concluded under any tradition, or a system of religious, personal or family law; or
          (ii) systems of personal and family law under any tradition, or adhered to by persons professing a particular religion.
       (b) Recognition in terms of paragraph (a) must be consistent with this section and the other provisions of the Constitution.

a) Briefly summarize the factual background to each of the articles using the information given in them.
b) Read the section taken from the constitution (Freedom of religion, belief and opinion). How is this section relevant to the newspaper articles?

140

c) Comment on the use of 'high road' in the title of first article.

d) Summarize the content of the first article in your own words.

e) Comment on the use of 'dope' instead of 'dagga' or 'drugs' in the first paragraph of the first article. What effect does this create?

f) Why did the Constitutional Court refuse Prince's claim? Do you agree with this judgement? Substantiate.

g) Explain the phrase "challenge against the laws" (par 4 of the first article).

h) The following statement is not a true reflection of the Constitutional courts judgement:

"We're not in favour of *allowing Prince to use the drug*".

Do you agree? Substantiate.

i) Comment on the use of 'concourt' in the heading of the second article. Why do you think the writer used 'concourt' instead of 'Constitutional Court'?

j) Reread the third paragraph of the second article. What is the purpose of this paragraph?

k) Why do you think the writer ends the article with Prince's statement that he sells fruit and vegetables? What effect does the writer intend?

l) Why does Prince want to challenge the Constitutional Court's judgment at the African Commission?

m) Rewrite paragraph 5 of the second article in your own words.

n) Study the extracts from the Drug and Drug Trafficking Act 140 of 1992 (reprinted on pp 145–150 below). Which section of the Act do you think is relevant to Prince's situation?

As you can see from the newspaper extracts, discussions on the different rights guaranteed in the South African Constitution are very topical. The Constitution is an example of an act and in the next few pages we are going to look at exactly how such an act is structured.

READING AN ACT

As you will spend a substantial amount of time during your legal training reading acts and statutes, it is important that you know how an act is structured.

Study the following extract from the Constitution of the Republic of South Africa Act 108 of 1996:

GOVERNMENT GAZETTE, 18 DECEMBER 1996   No. 17678   1

Publicat Governm Gazette 17678 + date o gazette

CONSTITUTION OF THE REPUBLIC OF SOUTH AFRICA, 1996   Act No. 108, 1996

To introduce a new constitution for the Republic of South Africa and to provide for matters incidental thereto

long title

CONTENTS

Conten of act

. . . *(Sections left out)*

GOVERNMENT GAZETTE, 28 JANUARY 1994   No. 15466   2

CONSTITUTION OF THE REPUBLIC OF SOUTH AFRICA, 1993   Act No. 200, 1993

PREAMBLE

We, the people of South Africa,

Recognise the injustices of our past;

Honour those who suffered for justice and freedom in our land;

Respect those who have worked to build and develop our country; and

Believe that South Africa belongs to all who live in it, united in our diversity.

We therefore, through our freely elected representatives, adopt this Constitution as the supreme law of the Republic so as to —

> *Heal the divisions of the past and establish a society based on democratic values, social justice and fundamental human rights;*

> *Lay the foundations for a democratic and open society in which government is based on the will of the people and every citizen is equally protected by law;*

> *Improve the quality of life of all citizens and free the potential of each person; and*

> *Build a united and democratic South Africa able to take its rightful place as a sovereign state in the family of nations.*

May God protect our people.

Nkosi Sikelel' iAfrika. Morena boloka setjhaba sa heso.
God seën Suid-Afrika. God bless South Africa.
Mudzimu fhatutshedza Afurika. Hosi katekisa Afrika.

Preamble (note: not contained in all acts)

143

No. 17678   5

CONSTITUTION OF THE REPUBLIC OF SOUTH AFRICA, 1996   **Act No. 108, 1996**

Chapter 1

Founding Provisions

Chapter Heading

Republic of South Africa

1. The Republic of South Africa is one, sovereign, democratic state founded on the following values:
   (a) Human dignity, the achievement of equality and the advancement of human rights and freedoms.
   (b) Non-racialism and non-sexism.
   (c) Supremacy of the constitution and the rule of law.
   (d) Universal adult suffrage, a national common voters' roll, regular elections and a multi-party system of democratic government, to ensure accountability, responsiveness and openness.

Section

Supremacy of Constitution

2. This Constitution is the supreme law of the Republic; law or conduct inconsistent with it is invalid, and the obligations imposed by it must be fulfilled.

Citizenship

3. (1) There is a common South African citizenship.
   (2) All citizens are –
       (a) equally entitled to the rights, privileges and benefits of citizenship; and
       (b) equally subject to the duties and responsibilities of citizenship.
   (3) National legislation must provide for the acquisition, loss and restoration of citizenship.

Section

Sub

See whether you are able to identify the different components (marked above) of the following act:

DRUGS AND DRUG TRAFFICKING ACT 140 OF 1992

[ASSENTED TO 2 JULY 1992]   [DATE OF COMMENCEMENT: 30 APRIL 1993]
(English text signed by the State President)

as amended by

Justice Laws Rationalisation Act 18 of 1996
International Co-operation in Criminal Matters Act 75 of 1996
Proceeds of Crime Act of 1996
Prevention of Organised Crime Act 121 of 1998

ACT

To provide for the prohibition of the use or possession of, or the dealing in, drugs and of certain acts relating to the manufacture or supply of certain substances or the acquisition or conversion of the proceeds of certain crimes; for the obligation to report certain information to the police; for the exercise of powers of entry, search, seizure and detention in specified circumstances; for the recovery of the proceeds of drug trafficking; and for matters connected therewith.

ARRANGEMENT OF SECTIONS

. . . *(sections of text left out)*

145

CHAPTER I
APPLICATION OF ACT (ss 1-2)

1 **Definitions**

(1) In this Act, unless the context indicates otherwise–

'convert' ...
[Definition of 'convert' deleted by s. 79 (*b*) of Act 121 of 1998.] A

'dangerous dependence-producing substance' means any substance or any plant from which a substance can be manufactured included in Part 11 of Schedule 2;

'deal in', in relation to a drug, includes performing any act in connection with the transshipment, importation, cultivation, collection, manufacture, supply, prescription, administration, sale, transmission or exportation of the drug;

'declaration of forfeiture' means a declaration of forfeiture made in terms of section 25 (1);

'defined crime' ...
[Definition of 'defined crime' deleted by s. 79 (*b*) of Act 121 of 1998.] A

'dependence-producing substance' means any substance or any plant from which a substance can be manufactured included in Part I of Schedule 2;

'designated officer' means any officer referred to in section 8;

'drug' means any dependence-producing substance, any dangerous dependence-producing substance or any undesirable dependence-producing substance;

'drug offence'
(*a*) in relation to a drug offence committed in the Republic, means an offence referred to in section 13 (*f*);
(*b*) in relation to a drug offence committed outside the Republic, means any act or omission which, if it had occurred within the Republic, would have constituted an offence referred to in that section;

'economic offence' ...
[Definition of 'economic offence' deleted by s. 79 (*b*) of Act 121 of 1998.] A

'financial institution' ...
[Definition of 'financial institution' deleted by s. 79 (*b*) of Act 121 of 1998.] A

'interest' includes any right;

'manufacture', in relation to a substance, includes the preparing, extraction or producing of the substance;

... *(sections left out)*

CHAPTER 11
ILLEGAL ACTS (ss 3-7)

Acts relating to scheduled substances and drugs

3   Manufacture and supply of scheduled substances

No person shall manufacture any scheduled substance or supply it to any other person, knowing or suspecting that any such scheduled substance is to be used in or for the unlawful manufacture of any drug.

4   Use and possession of drugs

No person shall use or have in his possession-

(*a*) any dependence-producing substance; or
(*b*) any dangerous dependence-producing substance or any undesirable dependence-producing substance,
unless—
(i)   he is a patient who has acquired or bought any such substance–

    (*aa*) from a medical practitioner, dentist or practitioner acting in his professional capacity and in accordance with the requirements of the Medicines Act or any regulation made thereunder; or

    (*bb*) from a pharmacist in terms of an oral instruction or a prescription in writing of such medical practitioner, dentist or practitioner,
and uses that substance for medicinal purposes under the care or treatment of the said medical practitioner, dentist or practitioner;

    ... *(sections left out)*

66 Repeal of laws

The laws mentioned in Schedule 3 are hereby repealed to the extent indicated in the third column thereof.

67 Saving in respect of pending prosecutions

Nothing in this Act shall affect any prosecution instituted before the commencement of this Act, and any such prosecution shall be continued and concluded as if this Act had not been passed.

68 Short title and commencement

This Act shall be called the Drugs and Drug Trafficking Act, 1992, and shall come into operation on a date fixed by the State President by proclamation in the *Gazette*.

A

147

- Why do you think is it important for us to know the different components of an act?
- Why is it important to know the promulgation date of an act?
- What is the purpose of the long title of an act?
- Look at the sections marked with an 'A' in the Drugs and Drug Trafficking Act 140 of 1992. What do these sections indicate?
- What is the purpose of the defining section of an act?
- Find an example of a section and a sub-section in the act quoted above.

B LANGUAGE FOCUS

1 MODAL VERBS: DEGREES OF CERTAINTY AND UNCERTAINTY

Modal verbs are different from other verbs because they do not usually stand alone in a sentence. They are almost always used in front of a main verb.

> I *must* go to court now.
> He *might* be found guilty.
> The judge *ought* to know that the defendant is lying.

Modal verbs change the meaning of the main verb slightly:

I must speak about these crimes.	strong obligation
I might speak about these crimes.	slight possibility
I ought to speak about these crimes.	moral obligation

All these words express different degrees (modalities) of obligation.

Examples of modal verbs are *can, could, may, might, will, would, shall, should, need, must, ought to,* etc.

- Modal verbs are used to express obligation, possibility, willingness to do something, ability, permission, necessity, for example:
  > this law must be obeyed,
  > he shall not be held criminally responsible for such acts
  > before you can claim, you might have to prove your case
  > you need to establish fault on the part of the defendant.

- Words such as *must, have to* or *has to* are used to indicate that there is an obligation upon a person to do something. The past tense form of *must* and *have/has to* is *had to*, for example:
  > He must settle for a lower sum of money.
  > He had to settle for a lower sum of money.

- One uses *need* to in a sentence if one wants to indicate that it is necessary to perform a certain action to be able to achieve something, for example:

148

> The attorney needs to file all the necessary documents before he can institute his claim.

or in the past tense,

> The advocate needed to read the attorney's brief before he could start preparing his defence.

- One can also use the negative forms of *have to* and *need to*, for example:
  The defendant needn't have lied about his alibi as the murder was committed only later in the evening.
  or
  He doesn't have to make a statement, we are not charging him with anything.

- The use of *shall* often presents problems and is used in formal written laws, such as statutes, and in other government publications. *Shall* has more or less the same meaning as *must* but is much stronger. This word is used to indicate command, obligation or duty, for example:
  'You shall marry me!' 'You shall go to that class!', 'You shall not go there!'.

Shall is also often used in statutes to indicate that upon the completion of a certain condition, something is brought about, as in section 78 (above):

> A person who commits an act which constitutes an offence,
> . . . shall not be criminally responsible for such act.

- It is possible to make passive sentences with modal verbs:
  They will send you to jail. (active)
  You will be sent to jail. (passive)

  They ought to pay advocates more money. (active)
  Advocates ought to be paid more money. (passive)

If a modal verb is used in the passive, the construction is:

MODAL VERB	+ BE (infinitive)	+ MAIN VERB
must	be	sent
need to	be	claimed
ought to	be	examined

Transform the following sentences into the passive:

a) The judge needs to impose a more severe sentence.
b) The attorney will question the suspect.
c) You need to claim compensation for loss of income.
d) The witness ought to tell the truth.
e) The court must decide the issue.

149

Sometimes we use modal verbs to express the certainty or uncertainty (likelihood) of an event happening.

Study the following examples that were taken from the statutes in section A READING.

- ... all South Africans *will be* entitled to a common South African citizenship in a sovereign and democratic state ...
- ... all the people of South Africa *should be* mandated to adopt a new Constitution ...
- A member of Parliament *may* address Parliament in the official South African language of his or her choice.
- Any application pursuant to the provisions of this act *shall be* made in the manner prescribed in the rules.

Do you think the likelihood of the event happening is equally great in all these examples? Explain your answer.

Now study the following sentences:

a) The advocate *might* win the case.
b) The advocate *will* win the case.
c) The advocate *should* win the case.
d) The advocate *may* win the case.
e) The advocate *shall* win the case.

In each case, the word in italics expresses the certainty/uncertainty of the advocate winning the case. Which example would you say expresses the greatest certainty?

Certainty/uncertainty may also be expressed by adverbs (or adverbial phrases/adjectival phrases). In each of the following pairs of sentences state which event is *most likely* to happen:

- You are *bound* to succeed with the appeal.
  It is *virtually certain* that you will succeed with the appeal.

- There is *every chance* that the advocate will ask for another postponement.
  There is *a chance* that the advocate will ask for another postponement.

- There is *no way* that judgement will be given in her favour.
  It is *most improbable* that judgement will be given in her favour.

- *It may well be* that she has been admitted as an advocate.
  It is *very probable* that she has been admitted as an advocate.

150

Refer back to the sentences we used as examples and make sure that you know which modal verbs to use to express the different degrees of certainty/uncertainty.

C INTEGRATED SKILLS

1 ARGUMENTATIVE WRITING: PLANNING AND DRAFTING

In this section we concentrate on advanced organisation of an argument, the use of *connectors* and writing a conclusion. In the discussion that follows we focus on longer pieces of writing because we believe that the writing of an assignment, that is, a longer piece of writing, is both excellent mental training and preparation for the type of writing you will be required to do in advanced legal courses.

Reread the newspaper article entitled 'Rastafarian attorney to challenge concourt ruling', taking special note of how the writer presents his argument. Attempt to divide the article into the following sections:

  i) the problem
 ii) the thesis (writer's point of view)
iii) the justification.

From this exercise you will see how a simple argument is structured.

Step 1: Getting Started

You should read the instructions of every assignment carefully. An assignment is usually set on the work that you have recently completed and you will therefore have to refer back to the sections in the textbook and/or articles given as recommended or additional reading.

The instructions will probably refer you to specific cases, legislation and/or sections in your textbook. This is your starting point.

Planning an assignment and getting hold of the relevant material is often regarded as the 'easy' part of writing; getting started by writing the first sentence on an empty piece of paper is usually a problem. Rest assured that you share this problem with many famous writers. You could solve the problem in two ways:

- Think up an introductory sentence or copy it from a good writer and begin all assignments in this way. This may seem ridiculous, but you can hardly go wrong if you start all assignments in the following way:
    'In this assignment/ essay I [will] argue that ... / discuss the following .../ describe the problem of ...'

151

You tell your reader what you are going to do and at the same time you gain clarity in your mind about what you intend doing.

OR

- You start writing anywhere and on any part of the assignment. Get the one important point that you want to make out of your system and carry on from there. You can always move paragraphs around, split them up, and write an introduction and conclusion right at the end. This option does not, however, mean that you don't need any planning. You still have to have a global idea of the points that must be mentioned in your assignment.

Whatever option you choose, your first paragraph must say what you are going to do in the assignment. You might find that you have to rewrite the introductory paragraph once you have a complete draft. The following are phrases that you could use in an introductory paragraph:

In this assignment I [will] . . .

. . . argue for/ against

. . . defend the point of view that . . .

. . . look at . . . (Very vague: clarify!)

. . . discuss/ talk about . . .

. . . examine/ analyze/ investigate/ explore . . .

Step 2: Organizing Facts, Opinions and Sources

After reading the material, ideas on the topic can be listed in random order, but always with reference to the article or book that supports or provides them. If your lecturer has provided you with a scheme of work, you may try to fit in your ideas under the various sub-headings. Alternatively, you will have to devise your own scheme of work. You will probably use at least some of the following sub-headings:

- the problem
- state of affairs in legislation
- state of affairs in the latest court decisions
- arguments by academic writers
- justification for a specific point of view
- conclusion

When they mark your assignment, your lecturers will probably asses your assignment in terms of the following criteria:

- Understanding the problem: do you demonstrate a grasp of the problem **in the context of the specific subject**?

152

- **Correct** identification of issues and relevant law
- **Appropriate** application of law
- **Appropriate** conclusion
- Correct use of **relevant** references, cases, statutes
- Correct use of legal concepts and principles

However, it is not enough to have the appropriate information, you also need to present it in a coherent and academic fashion. As you saw in the texts that you have read, writers use specific words called *connectors* to indicate the logical links in their arguments. (Refer to unit 3 for a list of such words.) Some of these words indicate the **beginning** of an argument, some a **continuation** or an **opposing** point and some indicate the **final** conclusion of an argument.

- Determine the function of each connector in the list below — to introduce, continue, oppose or conclude an argument:

but	and	although	secondly
firstly	however	moreover	thus
therefore	in fact	consequently	despite
nevertheless	accordingly	indeed	finally

You need to use these words as **markers** that will help your lecturer to follow your reasoning. The words will also help you to present your argument well. Remember that it is possible to have a series of conclusions in your assignment as you move from one argument to the next.

Step 3: Drawing the Threads Together

In the **conclusion** of your assignment you should take care to refer back to your topic and the introductory paragraph. It is not customary to introduce new ideas in a concluding paragraph. This is also the time to check that you actually did what was asked and what you promised to do in your introduction. This is the **revision** phase, when you edit your work to eliminate errors and to check that your text 'flows', that is, that your text runs smoothly from one idea to the next by means of connectors.

Use the following checklist when next you have finished an assignment:

GLOBAL REVISION Did you ... • write on the topic? • introduce your arguments? • use paragraphs? • link ideas? • conclude your arguments?	
LANGUAGE REVISION • Check punctuation: capitals and full stops. • Check connectors: can the text be made easier to understand by adding 'however' or 'although'? • Check spelling. • Check agreement between nouns and verbs. • Check tense: argumentative writing is done mostly in the present tense, except where you refer to the facts of a case or things that happened in the past. • Check conditionals: did you use 'If...' sentences? Are they correct? (See unit 4.) (For language revision you should use the spell and grammar check that your word-processing programme provides.)	
STYLE REVIEW • Check numbering: do all the numbers follow? • Check headings: do you distinguish clearly and consistently between main headings and subheadings? • Check references: Do you acknowledge your sources? Are the sources that you mention in the text also in the list of references at the end of the assignment? Did you list separately all the statutes and cases that you used in the text?	

Now plan and draft your own argument:

> Your client, the editor of *Hassle Magazine,* asks you to defend his magazine in a defamation case. In a recent article in his magazine he referred to a Cabinet Minister as the 'backside of a donkey'. She is now suing him for damages.

Write an argument in defence of your client's freedom of speech/press freedom.

a) Start your plan by filling in the following table:
   i)   the problem
   ii) the thesis (your point of view)
   iii) the justification

b) Now prepare a paragraph containing a topic sentence and supporting ideas (see unit 3) for each point of your thesis. Provide a heading for each point.
c) Draft your argument. Include references to cases and legislation.
d) Revise the draft argument by checking with friends or fellow students whether it makes sense.
e) Write your argument down in the form of an essay.
f) Make sure that you edit your essay by using the checklists on the previous page.
g) Make a list of references (articles, books, cases, legislation) that you used in this assignment.

For more on argumentative writing, see units 11 & 12.

2 STUDY NOTE

When having to write a paper or assignment on a particular topic, students often feel at a loss about where to find books containing information on that topic.

A good way of overcoming this problem is to look at the footnotes, endnotes and bibliography of a book or article written on the topic in question. Here the names of the books and articles the author consulted when researching the topic are listed. You can use these titles as a starting point for your own study and research. (See unit 14 for more about finding sources).

UNIT 9
EXPRESSING AND EVALUATING OPINIONS

A READING
'Plain words' by Dick Usher *Fair Lady* (17 May 1995)

B LANGUAGE FOCUS
1 WORD FORMATION
2 EXPRESSING OPINIONS
3 QUOTING AND REPORTING SPEECH

C INTEGRATED SKILLS
1 VOICING OPINIONS AND SUPPORTING THEM
2 STUDY NOTE

In this unit we move away from strictly 'legal' texts and introduce the issue of plain English. The focus in this unit is on the style writers of popular articles use to communicate their ideas. We discuss the expression of opinions in argumentative writing, including the structure of such writing. In the section on language we explain direct and indirect speech.

A READING

Before you read the text below, think about the complex language that lawyers use:

- Is 'legal language' accessible to the general public?
- Do you think people who object to the language used in legal contracts and legislation have a valid point?
- Why are contracts, legislation and (sometimes) law textbooks written in 'difficult' language?

Go back to unit 2, B(2) *Complete and incomplete sentences*, and read the sentence provided in (j). Do you think this sentence from an antenuptial agreement can be formulated in language that is plainer and yet still be a valid reflection of what the contract has to say?

READING: 'PLAIN WORDS' (Dick Usher, *Fair Lady*, 1995)

Study the title and the two sentences printed directly below it. What do you think is the function of these sentences?

Now read the first five paragraphs below in 3 minutes and answer the first six questions that follow.

Plain words

For too long South Africans have struggled to decipher documents riddled with convoluted legalese, contract jargon and fine print obfuscation, but our new government has plans to end all that. Viva the Plain Language Campaign! By DICK USHER

If you're one of the world's millions who have nearly lost their minds trying to make sense of a contract, take heart: the Plain Language Campaign is about to fight a battle for the public's right not to be faced with gobbledygook such as, 'A reference to eggs or to egg products or to eggs and egg products shall be construed as a reference to citrus fruit'.
    I tested this piece of gibberish on my duck, who at the time was pecking an orange which had fallen off the tree.

1

He appeared taken aback by the thought that he might be trying to lunch off a possible future relative. He wasn't reassured when I told him it was Australian, culled from the state of Victoria's Marketing of Primary Products Act, or that this particular gem has passed into history, thanks to the efforts of the Victoria Law Reform Commission which undertook the translation of the state's statute into plain English. 2

The practice of bamboozling the public with balderdash is far from being an Australian phenomenon – or problem. Almost anyone in South Africa who is not a lawyer has had difficulty making sense of contracts and official documents. Sometimes the lawyers themselves aren't too certain what's going on, which is why so much of our civil courts' time is given to settling disputes about what, precisely, was meant when a contract or law was originally drafted. 3

It's not surprising then that ordinary folk confronted with a hire purchase agreement, a lease or an insurance policy feel that the document has been written to obscure the issue rather than to promote clarity and understanding. 4

And, thinking about an annual problem we all have to contend with, I'm certain that a large cause of my dilatoriness in completing my income tax return is that the damn thing is so intimidating. It's not a user-friendly document at all. 5

IN MANY OTHER countries, organisations have for years been campaigning with considerable success to have plain, intelligible language used in all official documents and contracts and almost any other printed matter intended to convey information to the public at large. 6

Most such campaigns have been driven from the ground up by groups of people who had simply had enough of dealing with forms and notices of which they couldn't make the slightest sense. 7

In Britain, for example, the Plain English Campaign was called in by the government to review all the documents it produced. Director George Maher, who was in South Africa recently to liaise with an emergent local campaign for plain language, said that the organisation undertook the mammoth task of checking 171 000 documents. This 8

took several years and in the end about 36 000 documents
were scrapped and another 58 000 revised.

'It's estimated that this brought about an immediate   9
saving of roughly £15 million and nearly £250 million over
the next 10 years,' said Maher.

'Eventually, it's impossible to calculate the cost of
producing the material: if nobody reads it because   10
nobody can <u>understand</u> it, then you have wasted your
money and time. You haven't fulfilled your main purpose
of informing people.

'Beyond that, there are work hours wasted in trying to
make sense out of laws and government regulations, of
contracts and agreements; and there's the time spent in   11
court by highly paid professionals in search of rulings
about what these things intended to say in the first place.'
For Europeans, thanks to strong pressure from consumer
and other lobbies, relief is at hand. The European Union   12
recently put out a directive requiring all contracts that
affect the public to be written in plain language. If they're
not, and the matter comes to a dispute, the drafters of
such agreements will probably find courts ruling against
them on the grounds that the agreement could not be
understood by one of the parties.

In South Africa, irritation about government and
corporate obscurantism has not reached levels sufficient   13
to kick up a groundswell of protest, but it definitely exists.
So do the problems.

Geoff van Zyl, Cape regional manager of the Consumer
Council, says that the organisation receives many
complaints from which it is evident that consumers   14
neither read nor understand the full <u>implications</u> of
agreements they enter into.

The Ombudsman for Life Assurance's annual report
complaints that 'linguistic complications are frequently
encountered . . .' and that on a number of
occasions there have been complaints that 'stem from the   15
fact that the complainant has not fully understood the
policy: Frequently one feels . . ., the complainant deserves
sympathy . . .

'To write to a farm labourer in the Hex River Valley and
assume that he has the benefit of a classical educa-   16
tion by introducing phrases like uberrima fides ('in the

utmost good faith) is somewhat absurd and should be avoided,' he comments.

However, although we're a bit behind Europe, Canada and Australia in such matters, moves are being made to get a plain language campaign off the ground. As a start, the Department of Justice hosted and sponsored a seminar in Cape Town on the subject in March. Several leading lights in similar campaigns from other countries shared their experience, successes and failures. 17

Among them were Maher and Australian lawyer Christopher Balmford, who worked on rewriting legislation for the Victoria Law Reform Commission and who now heads a plain language department in Melbourne at the Phillips Fox law firm. 18

Balmford says that the problem is partly the conservatism of lawmakers and many legal professionals who argue that legal documents must be correct, unambiguous and precise and that this is not compatible with plain language. 19

'In the meantime, the general public remains convinced that the profession has a vested interest in obscurity: that by couching documents in unintelligible jargon, lawyers are making sure that they have a steady flow of business. But it's simply not true that plain language and precision are incompatible. Neither is incomprehensibility good for business. It's been our experience that producing documents ordinary people can understand makes them want to come back to you.' 20

Unlike the public-driven campaigns of other countries, the move towards plain language in South Africa comes from the top. ANC MP Willie Hofmeyr got the ball rolling with a letter to a newspaper. The response from lawyers, educators, translators and journalists was enthusiastic, and a number of organisations dealing with advice and legal aid at grass-roots level have pledged their support. 21

Even before the Department of Justice moved – with Minister Dullah Omar committing himself to eradicating the complex language used in forms, White Papers, legislation and pamphlets – insurance company Norwich Life rewrote all its policies in plain language. 22

'We did it because it was plain to us that an intelligent layman could no longer understand them,' says John Beak,

Norwich's chief executive officer. 'People often submitted
claims without really knowing whether they were valid or not.'   23
    The rewritten policies have only been in use since
October last year, so he can't say if they've been responsi-   24
ble for improved business, 'but being able to understand
what the company is saying must add to customer
satisfaction.'
    In everyday life, the advantages of plain language are
many and identifiable, but it goes a lot further than easing
the path of hire purchase. Eventually, it gets down to   25
questions of democracy and making government
accessible and accountable.
    After all, if you can't understand what the government is
doing because much of what it's up to is hidden   26
behind a barrier of bureaucratese, how do you keep
control of it?
    Fortunately, the burgeoning Plain Language Campaign
has support in Parliament, and there is also pressure   27
for the new constitution to be written in plain language.
Wouldn't it be nice to know what our rights are without
having to take legal opinion?

Answer the following questions without looking at the text again.

1   Write down at least two documents which the writer regards as
    complicated and obscure.
2   What do you think are the meanings of the words *gobbledygook*,
    gibberish, bamboozling and *balderdash* in the context of this article?
3   Would you expect these words in a formal document?
4   What do you think are the meanings of the words *culled, phenomenon,
    dilatoriness* and *intimidating* in the context of this article?
5   Would you expect these words in a formal document?
6   Do you think the writer uses these two sets of words (in questions 2
    and 4) to make a specific point? If so, what do you think is the point?

Now read the rest of the text.

7   How does the second part of this text differ from paragraphs 1–5?
8   What is different in the second part?
9   What does the absence of words such as *gobbledygook* and *balderdash* in
    the second part of the text say about the author's intention in this part
    of the text?

· 161

Study the following jumbled summary of the text. Try to arrange the sentences so that they reflect the original line of argument. Pay particular attention to words such as *similarly* and *eventually* because they indicate the progression of the argument.

- The public believes that lawyers deliberately obscure the meaning of their documents so that they can make money from subsequent confusions.
- Eventually, the use of plain language will be to the advantage of everybody; one must know one's rights to be able to control the actions of government.
- In Britain all government documents have been reviewed and this led to savings of millions of pounds.
- Since then the Minister of Justice and one insurance company undertook to make documents more readable.
- In South Africa agencies such as the Consumer Council and The Ombudsman for Life Assurance receive complaints about the complexity of legal and insurance documents.
- Similarly, the European Council requires contracts that affect the public to be written in plain language.
- A plain language campaign has recently been launched in Cape Town and a seminar on the matter was held with speakers from Britain and Australia.

This article contains factual information as well as the opinions of people who are regarded as experts because of their position, training, experience or all of these. Study, for example, the quotations from The Ombudsman for Life Assurance's annual report (these quotations can be found in paragraphs 15 and 16 of *Plain Words*). How does the Ombudsman refer to himself? What **support** does the Ombudsman offer for his opinion that complicated language in itself disadvantages customers? In paragraph 16 the Ombudsman writes that the use of Latin terms in correspondence with people who did not receive a classical education 'is somewhat absurd and should be avoided'. Would you agree that the Ombudsman is careful when formulating his opinion? Which one of his words may give such an impression? Note too, that the writer of this article ends paragraph 16 by saying that the Ombudsman **comments**: he is not stating facts but commenting on certain facts, which means that the Ombudsman draws his own conclusions from a set of facts. You should be aware of the difference among the following:

- a person *states* something
- a person *comments* on

- a person *argues* that
- a person *claims* that
- a person *alleges* that

and so on.

Opinions or comments on the public's problems with life insurance documents are generally taken seriously when they are voiced by a person such as the Ombudsman or Ombudsperson. We usually say that she has **authority** and this makes her opinions and arguments more valid than those of somebody who knows nothing of such matters. In this case the Ombudsman expresses his opinions carefully, by using the impersonal form 'one feels...' (instead of *I think*) and by saying that the use of Latin terms is 'somewhat absurd...' (instead of *plain ridiculous*). He quotes cases which he has handled (in paragraph 15) and the specific case of the farm labourer in the Hex River Valley (paragraph 16) **in support** of his opinions, in other words he offers **factual evidence** for his opinion. Note too that the quotations in paragraphs 15 and 16 come from an annual report: generally people are more formal in the way they express opinions **in writing**. The way in which we argue is usually by presenting facts, expressing opinions and supporting our facts and opinions. These are the basic elements of an **argument**.

Now examine the opinions expressed by the Australian lawyer Christopher Balmford in paragraphs 19 and 20 of *Plain Words*. How do they differ from the Ombudsman's opinions in paragraphs 15 and 16 as regards the following:

- Do the position and experience of the lawyer lend **authority** to his opinions?
- Does the lawyer offer **support** for his opinions?
- Is the lawyer more discreet or more direct than the Ombudsman in the way he expresses his opinions?
- Does the lawyer express his opinions in writing or in speech?

Do you agree wholeheartedly with the lawyer's points of view in paragraphs 19 and 20?

Perhaps you could discuss this with your fellow students. Do you think the lawyer's opinions will sound fair to the average layperson who does not know the law very well? If you think the public would probably like these points of view, what does this state of affairs imply for the reputation and acceptability of the law in general and lawyers in particular?

163

Say whether you agree with the following statements and discuss your views with fellow students.

- Opinions voiced in interviews with the media need not always be supported because people recognize them as opinions and not statements of fact.
- Some opinions are of such a general nature that they need not be supported. (If you support this statement, be prepared to give examples to test the nature of their generality!)
- Unsupported opinions that seem general are mostly popular stereotypes which are not always harmless. (If you support this statement, be prepared to give examples of stereotypes and their possible danger.)

SOMETHING TO DO

Get hold of several newspapers and identify opinions voiced by prominent politicians, the police, community leaders, entertainers and so on. Compare them to the list of opinions below (which also come from newspapers) and say which are fairly harmless opinions and which you would regard as dangerously general (in the sense that they reinforce negative stereotypes). Indicate those opinions that you think need closer clarification and/or factual support.

- Lawyers are conservative.
- People like a champion for what they perceive to be a cause for the common people.
- The Chief of Police regards any criticism of the police system as support for the increasing audacity of criminals.
- People like a juicy piece of gossip and the divorce of a former beauty queen and her rich businessman-husband offers abundant satisfaction for this voyeuristic need. (How many opinions are expressed in this sentence?)
- The threat by COSATU to strike on 15 May is a heavy blow for an economy that is already staggering under repeated setbacks on world markets.
- The trainer of the South African team remained calm during the match and ascribed the success of his team to regular and focused training.
- The new minister said that the role of women in Parliament is to soften the harsh rationality of their male counterparts with more sympathy and compassion.

WORDS AND THEIR MEANINGS

In the text *Plain Words* the writer is concerned with 'plain' as opposed to 'complicated' language. To this end he makes frequent use of synonyms and antonyms for the word *understand*. He also uses a variety of adjectives to describe texts that are difficult or easy to understand.

Go through the text and see how many words you can find that relate to the concept of *understanding* and *misunderstanding* and write them down in the table below:

SYNONYMS	ANTONYMS
understand	misunderstand
clarity	obscure

B LANGUAGE FOCUS

1 WORD FORMATION

One of the features of the English language is the ease with which it transforms existing words to fulfil new functions. There are two notable examples in the text *Plain Words: legalese and obscurantism.*

It is clear where these words come from and what they mean, but do they imply something positive or negative? We can say that words have a dictionary meaning and an emotional meaning; that means, words have an effect on readers or listeners that can be positive or negative. This characteristic is called the *connotation* of words and it can change in time and from person to person. Some words have a relatively fixed connotation, for example, *love, peace, home.* However, *home* can also have a negative connotation when a person says, 'I don't have any parents. I grew up in a home, you know'. In this case *home* refers to an orphanage, with which people generally have negative associations.

In their context, do you think the words *legalese* and *obscurantism* have a positive or negative connotation?

Words ending on *-ism* and *-ist* are often used to describe a school of thought, a belief or practice (as in *feminism*) or support for such a belief (as

165

in *feminist*). In the case of *feminist* the word can act either as a noun, for example, *The feminists applauded the new act* or an adjective, for example, *Her feminist attitude gave her the courage to stand her ground*. As adjectives such words sometimes add *-istic*, as in sad*ism* (a practice) — sad*ist* (the person who practises sadism) and sad*istic* (describing the practices). It is often said that words ending in *-ism* or *-ist* have a negative connotation because they indicate an extreme point of view or an exaggerated belief. As indicated above, positive or negative connotations depend on the way in which individual persons experience such words.

Words ending on *-ese* follow the example of proper nouns for languages, for example, *Japanese* and *Chinese*. When the word ending is attached to other words, it usually describes the use of language in a specific domain, therefore *legalese* refers to the use of legal language. Do you think this word has a negative or positive connotation in the text *Plain Words*? Another example of such a word is *bureaucratese*; a term used to describe the language of bureaucracy (paragraph 27).

Study the following words and decide whether they have positive and/ or negative connotations. Use your dictionaries if you do not know the meaning of the words. Discuss your answers with your fellow students.

defeatist	obscurantism	legalistic
constitutionalism	professionalism	escapist
atheist	revisionistic	alarmist
favouritism		

2 EXPRESSING OPINIONS

We talked about the way in which opinions are expressed in writing and in speech. Generally the type of document that you write and the circumstances in which you speak will determine how formal and how careful you are about the way in which you express your opinions. (Refer to and revise the section in unit 8 dealing with expressing degrees of certainty and uncertainty.) It is one thing to write a letter to a friend saying, 'The English course is a useless waste of time', it's quite another to write at the bottom of your English assignment, 'And by the way, sir, I think this course is a waste of time'. Of course the conventions of formality, politeness and the written word change over time and from one group to another but, as law students know, it is not acceptable to say almost anything about anybody.

In the text *Plain Words* the Ombudsman expresses his opinion by using an impersonal form (*one*), words that mitigate (soften) harsh words (*somewhat absurd*) and the auxiliary *should*, which sounds less authoritarian than *must.* The expression of opinions, requests and apologies can all be made more formal and less direct by using these techniques. A direct opinion such as

'I'd be careful if I were you!'

can be made more formal and less direct by saying

'One	should	perhaps	take more care.'
↓	↓	↓	
impersonal form	auxiliary	mitigator (softener)	

Compare, for example, the following two opinions:

A professor asks two lecturers in her department for their views on an article that she has written. Lecturer A says, 'Perhaps you should clarify a few of the issues that seem fairly contentious to me.' Lecturer B says, 'You'd better get rid of the sweeping statements.' Depending on the relationship between the professor and each lecturer, each of these responses is appropriate.

We do not prescribe polite behaviour in this book. The point that we want to make is that you can make opinions and requests more formal and more indirect by following various strategies:

- Use impersonal forms such as *one* instead of *you* or *we*.
- Use auxiliaries such as *would, could, might* and *should*.
- Use mitigators (softeners) such as *perhaps, somewhat, possibly, please*, and so on.
- Use the question form, for example, *Don't you think you might be over-reacting?*

Look at the following situations and the responses and say whether you think the speaker/writer should be more formal or informal. Try to change those responses you think are inappropriate. Remember, it might be just as inappropriate to be too direct and informal as it is to be too formal and distant.

a) A student objects verbally, in class, to the amount of work the class has to do for the next period: 'Sir, this is just too much. Couldn't we spread the work over the next two weeks?'
b) A student writes to the registrar of a university to complain about the time it takes to process his application: 'This kind of inefficiency is pure racism and I demand an apology.'

c) At the beginning of a meeting of your local Law Students' Society the chairperson says to the secretary, 'Sir, I think it might be a better idea if you wrote down the minutes instead of relying on your memory.'

d) A member of the local Bar Association speaks to law students about job opportunities. Afterwards, as she drinks coffee with students and their lecturers, she discusses the salary of candidate attorneys and says to the students around her, 'Yes, and I suppose you just want to make money once you finish your studies!'

e) You apply for a post as a candidate attorney and in your covering letter you write: 'I am sure that such a prestigious firm would probably not have an opening for an inexperienced student. Yet I would appreciate it if you could take the time to read my application.'

Check your answers with your fellow students and your lecturer. Do you agree in all the cases? Remember that appropriate language is dependent upon the circumstances of and participants in a conversation.

3   GENDER NEUTRAL LANGUAGE

In unit 4 we referred briefly to the convention that writers use gender neutral language. This is also a practice that you should follow in your writing. Language is very powerful and the way in which we write influences our thinking: if a judge is always referred to as *he*, we tend to close our minds to the possibility of *female* judges and similarly to *female* presidents or *female* class representatives. The following general guidelines will help you to write in gender neutral terms:

- Avoid the use of the so-called generic *he*: use *s/he, her/him*, etc.
  Another possibility is to use the plural, for example:
    Each student must pay *her/his* fees in full at the end of March.
    As opposed to:
    Students must pay *their* fees in full at the end of March.

- Use alternatives for words like:
    Man (as in 'Man does not live by bread alone'): Use *one* or *people* or *humans*
    Mankind: humankind/humanity
    Manpower: personpower, human resources
    Manning: staffing
    Man in the street: the average person/ average voter/ a broad power base
    The working man: the average worker/ average wage earner
    The reasonable man: the reasonable person

168

> *To man* (*a ship/ an exhibition*): To *staff* a ship or an emergency room/ to *run* an exhibition
> *Spokesman*: Representative
> *Chairman*: Chair/ presiding officer/ convenor

- There is a tendency to move away altogether from gendered terms, as indicated by relatively new job titles such as *flight attendant* (instead of steward/ stewardess), *camera operator* (instead of cameraman), *sales agent* (instead of salesman) and *waitron* or *server* (instead of waiter/ waitress) and so on.

- In the end a list of suitable words is a poor substitute for gender sensitivity. All students of law need to be aware of the power of the language that they use and the ability of that language to affect people's lives and their perception of justice and equality.

4 QUOTING AND REPORTING SPEECH

Something that you probably remember from your secondary-school days is *reported speech*, or *direct* and *indirect* speech as it is often called by language teachers. We assume that you remember the rules for reported speech: ask your lecturer to refresh your memory or refer to a grammar book.

As you read textbooks and cases you will see that the words of academics, judges, appellants, respondents, defendants and others are reported in different ways. Two very important rules are generally followed. A distinction is made between reporting words that were actually **said** and reporting words that appear in **print**.

- If you write an assignment in which you discuss varying points of view expressed by academics in textbooks or journals, you generally **quote** a writer in the **present tense**:

    Van der Merwe state**s** that '........'.

    This is done because the words and the point of view or theory they represent are there on the page: they exist in the present. Therefore you talk about them in the present. Despite the fact that the words may have been written many years ago, they exist in the present.
- If you report words that were actually spoken, then you follow the rules of reported speech.

    The defendant's real words are:

    'I **was** unaware of the existence of a contract.'

    You report the words according to the rules of reported speech:

    The defendant contended that he **had been** unaware of the existence of a contract.

    Was changes to *had been* according to the rules of reported speech.

169

References to court decisions, therefore, are in the past tense because they are a report of the verbal proceedings in the courtroom.

NOTE:

It is important to note that discussions of what was said in court are very seldom introduced by the neutral verb *say* and that the different introductory verbs (like *ask*, *allege*, *state*) have different meanings.

Study the following list and state in each case how the underlined verbs differ in meaning from a neutral verb such as *say*.

f) In the *Beginner's guide for law students* Kleyn and Viljoen (1995) state ...
g) In *Steyn v LSA Motors Ltd* 1994 1 SA 49 (A) the appellant, an amateur golfer, contended that ... The respondent, however, claimed that ... but later conceded that ... The court acknowledged that ... The court found that ... and concluded that ...
h) The attorney for the defence suggested that ...
i) Spiller (1986:216) in *Roman-Dutch Law* asserts that ...

Discussions and reviews of cases such as you find in your law textbooks and in law journals often include sentences like those in the exercise above. It is important to note that these sentences are not necessarily a report of the court's or the defendant's exact words, but are often a report of the **gist** of what was said. That is why words such as *conclude* and *allege* are used, because they indicate both the **stage** of the court proceedings (as in *conclude*) and the **function** of a specific speech (as in *allege*). The writer interprets the function of what various people in court say and paraphrases their speech.

Two problems arise when speech is reported in this way:

*   The person who reports must be very sure that the words are, in fact, an allegation, or a claim, or a concession. Go back to the underlined words in sentences f-i (above) and make quite sure that you know what these words mean. Check the meaning with your lecturer and/ or in a dictionary.
*   It is difficult to decide when speech or utterances are **reported** and when they are **described**. For example, what do you think is the difference between the following two phrases in one sentence?
    [The court] **considered** it an unprofitable exercise to deal with these two aspects separately ...

and **held** that the decisive question was whether a reasonable man in the position of the appellant would have considered ...

It is in the second phrase that speech is being reported. The distinction is important when you have to, for example, discuss the relevance of a case to a specific rule, because as soon as you **report** speech, you have to watch your grammar! The one thing that should alert you to watch out for reported speech is the word *that*: the minute you write it down you should take special care with the formulation of your sentence.

You probably remember from your secondary school days that 'universal truths' or 'general rules' do not change when they are reported, for example

>The man *said* that the sun *rises* every day.

and **not**

>The man *said* that the sun *rose* every day. (Unless you are writing a science fiction story!)

The same rule applies in discussions of cases. Study the following example:

>'In delivering judgement, Grosskopf JA initially stated that it is a clear principle in our law that if an accused effectively dissociates himself from the common purpose ...' (Jordaan 1994:75 see STUDY NOTE).

Because a principle of law is being referred to, the present tense is maintained in the verbs following *stated*: 'it **is** a clear principle ... **dissociates** himself ...'. You will find that discussions of cases often move from the past tense to the present tense and back, as the writer indicates what happen*ed* in real life (the facts of the case) and the rules that *are applied* (and which are always valid).

Study the following extracts from discussions of law reports and underline the correct verb.

j) 'The court rejected the decision in *Zillie v Johnson and Another* 1984 2 SA 186 (W) that public interest on its own, without having to prove that the defamatory statements (are/were) true, (can/could) be a defence against a defamation action. The court held that *Zillie* (give/gave) the press a licence recognized neither by SA law nor (with the exception of the USA) by the legal systems of most other countries in the English-speaking world.

'The court held that although the traditional defence (did/does) not constitute a closed list of categories of justification, it (did/does) not mean that a court (is/was) free to consider the issue of liability for the publication of a defamatory statement by a newspaper independently of the substantive requirements of the traditional defence ...'

(From a discussion of Neethling v Du Preez and Others; Neethling v *The Weekly Mail and Others 1994 1 SA 708 (A)*, Roos 1994:103.)

k) 'The court examined the meaning of the word 'required' and decided that it (has/had) to be given a generous and purposive interpretation. In each case the enquiry should be a factual one and the question should be asked whether the information required (is/was) for the protection or exercise of a person's rights'.

(From a discussion of *Khala v Minister of Safety and Security* 1994 4 SA 218 WLD, Ehrenbeck 1995:72.)

1) 'The court also considered whether an accused (has/had) a right under section 23 to information in a police docket. It was stated:
'... it (must/ had to) indubitably be so that an accused in a criminal trial (is/was) entitled to access to information ...'

(From a discussion of *Khala v Minister of Safety and Security* 1994 4 SA 278 WLD, Ehrenbeck 1995:73.)

m) 'Relying on a recent decision of the appeal court ... the court stated that liability in such situations (requires/required), in essence, that the accused (must/ had to) have the intent in common with the other participants to commit the substantive crime charged ...'

(From a discussion of *S v Singo 1993 1 SACR 226 (A)*, Jordaan 1993:76.)

You will probably agree that this is not an easy exercise at all. Check your answers with your lecturer and fellow students and if you made many mistakes, find out where and why you went wrong.

C INTEGRATED SKILLS

In A READING we discussed opinions and when it is necessary to support them. We also referred to the difference between presenting an opinion verbally and in written form. You will find that you need the skill of arguing both verbally (when in class, seminars and study groups) and in written form (when writing assignments and tests). In unit 8 we discussed argumentative writing. We will discuss oral argumentation next.

1 VOICING OPINIONS AND SUPPORTING THEM

Look at the following characteristics of a group discussion and rank them from most to least important, with 1 as most and 10 as least important or irrelevant.

☐ Controversial points are raised to liven up the discussion.

☐ The chairman's role is to say the most.

☐ All participants must be prepared to listen to each other.

☐ Opinions must be substantiated.

☐ One should try to get one's own view accepted by everybody.

☐ Intelligent, well-spoken participants should speak the most.

☐ Each speaker should have an opportunity to voice his or her opinion within a specific time limit.

☐ In the end the whole group has to agree.

☐ Somebody should take notes of arguments and try to keep a clear mind as to their relevance and the way in which they interlock.

☐ A speaker's argument has to link up with what was said previously.

Discuss your ranking with fellow students and your lecturer; depending on your ranking you might decide to reach consensus or to allow each student his or her own ranking! Perhaps you could agree on the five most important characteristics.

The following are ways in which you could formulate an opinion and support it. Read through the list and decide which are informal (and could be used in group discussions with your fellow students) and which examples are formal (and could be used in class or even in court!).

- I have to disagree when you say ... because ...
- No, I simply cannot go along with that because ... With all due respect I have to disagree ...
- Oh nonsense! How can you say that when you know that ...
- In my opinion such an argument will lead to ... and therefore I think we have to realize that ...
- Such a position is untenable because ...
- If what you say is true, then ... and therefore ...
- Okay I agree, but what about ...

Note in particular that all these phrases refer to the other person's point of view and even repeat it to some extent. You must prove that you actually

173

listened to the other person and that you understand what they say. There is nothing more irritating than a person who just waits for you to draw a breath before they jump in with their point of view that has nothing to do with what went before. Take care that you do not become one of the following types of discussion disruptors:

Mr Knowitall, who thinks that you will agree with him as soon as you have all the relevant information, which he will keep on explaining to you

Ms Brokenrecord, who keeps on repeating the same point, usually at increasing volume.

Ms Label, who calls you names (like socialist or fascist) instead of thinking up valid points against your arguments.

Mr Noidea, whose only contribution is, 'If you're so critical, then what **is** the right answer?'

Ms Thinedgeofthewedge, who immediately takes an argument to its absurd conclusions along the lines of, 'If women wear mini-skirts today, they will surely walk around naked tomorrow'.

AN ARGUMENT:

... consists of opposing views, therefore you must make
quite clear which points you are arguing **for** and which **against**.

... consists of logical links expressed by words
such as *because, therefore, however, but,* and so on.

... makes use of statements, questions and conditionals to move
forward and not in circles or from one irrelevant point to the next.

Before you continue, revise briefly the work you did in unit 2 (A READING, questions 17–19), unit 3 (B LANGUAGE FOCUS, CONNECTORS), unit 4 (B LANGUAGE FOCUS, CONDITIONALS) and unit 8 (C INTEGRATED SKILLS).

Use the text *Plain Words* and the reading material in unit 10 to write a two-page paper on *Plain English and the law*. You must argue for or against the Plain English Movement and you may use other sources as well.

2 STUDY NOTE

The extracts from discussions of cases in 2 QUOTING AND REPORTING SPEECH (under B LANGUAGE FOCUS), as they appear in both examples and exercises j–m, were taken from the journal *Codicillus*. As explained in unit 1, we use the referencing style appropriate to texts written in faculties of arts and education.

UNIT 10
PLAIN LEGAL LANGUAGE

This unit continues the discussion of unit 9 on the nature of the language in which legal documents, acts and statutes are written. We compare different versions of the South African and Liberian constitutions and consider the effect the language in which these constitutions are written has on their comprehensibility. We look at different ways to make 'difficult' legal language understandable, such as breaking up long complicated sentences into shorter ones (a revision of unit 7), substituting difficult words with simple ones and eliminating wordiness. Finally, we study the correct use of prepositions in sentences.

A READING

Before you read the text below, consider the following:

- What do you think is the purpose of a constitution?
- What does one usually find in a Bill of Rights?
- Whose rights are protected in a Bill of Rights?
- Does South Africa have a Bill of Rights? Where would we find such a document?
- Do you think lay-people (people who have no training in the law) know the contents of our constitution?
- Have you ever seen a copy of South Africa's constitution? Have you ever experienced difficulty in reading a legal document such as a lease or hire-purchase agreement? Why do you think these documents are considered difficult to understand?

Read the following extracts from two different South African constitutions carefully:

1 THE CONSTITUTION OF THE REPUBLIC OF SOUTH AFRICA ACT 200 OF 1993

Equality

8. Every person shall have the right to equality before the law and to equal protection of the law.

(2) No person shall be unfairly discriminated against, directly or indirectly, and, without derogating from the generality of this provision, on one or more of the following grounds in particular: race, sex, ethnic or social origin, colour, sexual orientation, age, disability, religion, conscience, belief, culture or language.

(3) (*a*) This section shall not preclude measures designed to achieve the adequate protection and advancement of persons or groups or

177

categories of persons disadvantaged by unfair discrimination, in order to enable their full and equal enjoyment of all rights and freedoms.

(*b*) Every person or community dispossessed of rights in land before the commencement of this Constitution under any law which would have been inconsistent with subsection (2) had that subsection been in operation at the time of the dispossession, shall be entitled to claim restitution of such rights subject to and in accordance with sections 121, 122 and 123.

(4) *Prima facie* proof of discrimination on any of the grounds specified in subsection (2) shall be presumed to be sufficient proof of unfair discrimination as contemplated in that subsection, until the contrary is established.

2 THE CONSTITUTION OF THE REPUBLIC OF SOUTH AFRICA, ACT 108 OF 1996

Equality

9.(1) Everyone is equal before the law and has the right to equal protection and benefit of the law.

(2) Equality includes the full and equal enjoyment of all rights and freedoms. To promote the achievement of equality, legislative and other measures designed to protect or advance persons, or categories of persons, disadvantaged by unfair discrimination may be taken.

(3) The state may not unfairly discriminate directly or indirectly against anyone on one or more grounds, including race, gender, sex, pregnancy, marital status, ethnic or social origin, colour, sexual orientation, age, disability, religion, conscience, belief, culture, language, and birth.

(4) No persons may unfairly discriminate directly or indirectly against anyone on one or more grounds in terms of subsection (3). National legislation must be enacted to prevent or prohibit unfair discrimination.

(5) Discrimination on one or more of the grounds listed in subsection (3) is unfair unless it is established that the discrimination is fair.

Now try to answer the following questions about the two texts.

a) Compare text (1) Sec 8(1) to text (2) Sec 9(1).

8(1) Every person shall have the right to equality before the law and to equal protection of the law.

9(1) Everyone is equal before the law and has the right to equal protection and benefit of the law.

How does the phrasing of the two sections differ?

b) Revise the notes on the use of 'shall' in unit 7. What effect does the fact that 'shall' is left out in the 1996 constitution (text (2)) create?

c) Compare the following phrases:

'... shall have the right to equality ...'
'... is equal before the law ...'

Do these two phrases differ at all in their meaning? Or in any way at all? Which of the two sounds most formal?

d) Is there any difference between '[e]very person' (1) and 'everyone' (2)? Explain.
e) Formulate the gist (main points) of text (1) in your own words.
f) Formulate the gist of text (2) in your own words.

Do you agree that the Constitution of the Republic of South Africa Act 108 of 1996 (text (2)) has been written in language that is slightly less formal and less difficult to understand than the language of the Constitution of the Republic of South Africa Act 200 of 1993 (text (1))? The writers of text (2) tried to use less formal language because of a growing concern about the lack of accessibility of the law to the lay-person.

Attempts to make legal language more accessible to people who are not involved in the legal profession enjoy a lot of attention in the media. It is argued that a Bill of Rights is of very little use if the citizens of a country do not know what their rights are because they are unable to understand the language in which these rights are presented.

• Do you agree with this point of view? You can perhaps debate this issue with your fellow students.

g) Reread texts (1) and (2). Although it is clear that text (2) is an improvement on text (1) as far as the level of difficulty of the language is concerned, do you think that someone without any legal training will be able to understand the text? Substantiate your answer.
h) Try to rewrite text (2) in language that would be even easier to understand.

179

- Lawyers are often accused of consciously making the law and legal texts more difficult than necessary, and intentionally 'mystifying' the law, so that they can make a living out of interpreting texts for the lay-person. Do you think this allegation is justified? Substantiate your answer.

Carefully study the following two versions of the Liberian constitution:

3 CONSTITUTION OF THE REPUBLIC OF LIBERIA

FUNDAMENTAL RIGHTS

Article 11

a) All persons are born equally free and independent and have certain natural, inherent and inalienable rights, among which are the right of enjoying and defending life and liberty, and pursuing and maintaining the security of the person and of acquiring, possessing and protecting property, as provided for in this Constitution.

b) All persons, irrespective of ethnic background, race, sex, creed, place of origin or political opinion, are entitled to the fundamental rights and freedoms of the individual, subject to such qualifications as provided for in this Constitution.

c) All persons are equal before the law and are therefore entitled to the equal protection of the law.

4 SIMPLIFIED VERSION OF THE APPROVED REVISED DRAFT CONSTITUTION OF THE REPUBLIC OF LIBERIA from CONSTITUTIONS OF THE COUNTRIES OF THE WORLD (G H Flanz, Ed. 1996)

CHAPTER III
FUNDAMENTAL RIGHTS
(RIGHTS FOR EVERYBODY)

Article 11   Sections a), b) & c)

God made all people equal before the law, to live and be free, to own, and defend their property as written in this Book and these rights shall not be taken away from any person except this Book says so.

Compare the two texts.

i) Is the content of these two texts more or less the same? Discuss.
j) What is the most important difference between texts (3) and (4)?
k) Article 11 of the simplified version (text (4)) lacks the clear distinction between the three sub-sections of the section that occurs in the original (text (3)). Do you agree that it is so? What effect do you think it creates?
l) Comment on the lay-out (what the text looks like on the page) of the two versions.
m) Is it possible to rewrite art 11 of text (4) in even simpler language? Which words would you change and why? Work with a fellow student and write down your version of this section.
n) Rewrite the following words, phrases and sentences in simple legal language:

> ... the plaintiff shall hereinafter be deemed a ...
> ... it was established that the defendant was not present at the scene of the crime ...
> ... for such and any other relief as to the court may seem meet and just. This clause in his last will and testament is null and void. After consideration of the facts, the court shall reach a decision. Please note that you are hereby requested to quit, surrender, deliver up possession to me of the premises hereinafter described ...
> This contract is deemed void *ab initio*.

Are you able to begin recognising principles of clear writing? Look carefully at the sentences above. They are wordy, written in the passive voice, they contain difficult words and make use of latin phrases. Refer to the strategies under C) INTEGRATED SKILLS to see how one corrects these sentences.

o) Rewrite section 2 of Act 4 of 2000 in plain legal language:

Prohibition of dissemination and publication of information that unfairly discriminates:

> 12 No person may —
>   (a) disseminate or broadcast any information;
>   (b) publish or display any advertisement or notice,
>   that could reasonably be construed or reasonably be understood to demonstrate a clear intention to unfairly discriminate against any person: Provided that *bona fide* engagement in artistic creativity, academic and scientific enquiry, fair and accurate reporting in the public interest or publication of any information, advertisement or notice in accordance with section 16 of the Constitution, is not precluded by this section.

181

B LANGUAGE FOCUS

1 ARTICLES

There are two kinds of *articles* in English: *a/an* and *the*. Nouns, or words that function as nouns must be preceded by an article. Nouns which do not take **an** article are **the** exception rather than **the** rule!

2 PREPOSITIONS

Prepositions are words which indicate the relation of objects, ideas, people, animals and so on to each other, for example:

the relation *between* different organs of state

you want to claim damages *from* someone

the state enters *into* a contract

the state encroaches *upon* the area of private law

Examples of prepositions are:

after; at, before; on; since; to; until; etc   (time)
across; along; at; below; behind; by; on; etc   (place)

Read the following extract from the Constitution of the Republic of South Africa Act 108 of 1996 and see whether you can spot the prepositions. Try to determine whether the prepositions indicate time, place or manner.

Application

7.(1) This Chapter shall bind all legislative and executive organs of state at all levels of government.

(2) This Chapter shall apply to all law in force and all administrative decisions taken and acts performed during the period of operation of this Constitution.

(3) Juristic persons shall be entitled to the rights contained in this Chapter where, and to the extent that, the nature of the rights permits.

(4) (*a*) When an infringement of or threat to any right entrenched in this Chapter is alleged, any person referred to in paragraph (*b*) shall be entitled to apply to a competent court of law for appropriate relief, which may include a declaration of rights.

> (*b*) The relief referred to in paragraph (*a*) may be sought by—
>   (i)   a person acting in his or her own interest;
>   (ii) an association acting in the interest of its members;
>   (iii) a person acting on behalf of another person who is not in a position to seek such relief in his or her own name;
>   (iv) a person acting as a member of or in the interest of a group or class of persons; or
>   (v)   a person acting in the public interest.

Prepositions in legal texts often cause students difficulty. Test your knowledge of prepositions by choosing the correct preposition to complete the following sentences. Work with a fellow student and see how many you get right.

a) He will take you ____ court for breach ____ contract.
b) You will get involved ____ a court case.
c) The lawyer was engaged in negotiation ____ their return to the country.
d) The prisoner was remanded ____ custody.
e) The union entered ____ wage negotiations.
f) The court gave judgement ____ the matter.
g) The buyer's signature was added ____ the contract.
h) This contract should have been signed ____ the presence of the judge.
i) The courthouse is ____ the corner *from* the police station.
j) A fight took place ____ the witness and the accused.
k) The woman was raped while she was standing ____ the bus-stop.
l) He was walking away ____ his attacker when he was killed.
m) The forensic pathologist looked ____ the blood sample ____ a microscope.
n) I found the murder weapon ____ the bed ____ which the victim was lying.
o) He said the court will be adjourned ____ three o'clock.
p) The clerk was late for work ____ Tuesday.
q) You must have your summary ____ the case ready ____ Wednesday.
r) The witness testified that he finished the work ____ a very short period of time.
s) They are both parties ____ the contract.
t) He was arrested ____ a charge of murder.
u) She is suspected ____ helping a convicted felon to escape.

C INTEGRATED SKILLS

1 SIMPLIFICATION OF COMPLEX LANGUAGE

Study the following extract from the original (unsimplified version) of the Liberian Constitution:

CITIZENSHIP

Article 27

a) All persons who, on the coming into force of this Constitution were lawfully citizens of Liberia shall continue to be Liberian citizens.

b) In order to preserve, foster and maintain the positive Liberian culture, values and character, only persons who are Negroes or of Negro descent shall qualify by birth or by naturalization to be citizens of Liberia.

c) The Legislature shall, adhering to the above standard, prescribe such other qualification criteria for and the procedures by which naturalization may be obtained.

Article 28

Any person, at least one of whose parents was a citizen of Liberia at the time of the person's birth, shall be a citizen of Liberia; provided that any such person shall upon reaching maturity renounce any other citizenship acquired by virtue of one parent being a citizen of another country. No citizen of the Republic shall be deprived of citizenship or nationality except as provided by law, and no person shall be denied the right to change citizenship or nationality.

Constitutions of the countries of the world G H Flanz (Ed) 1996

- Imagine that you have been given the task of drafting a plain English version of this chapter of Liberia's constitution. Can you think of a few ways in which you would go about making this text simpler or more understandable?

You could make use of the following strategies:

a) Breaking up long, complicated sentences into shorter, simpler ones

In unit 7 we saw that it is possible to come to a better understanding of long and complicated legal sentences by breaking them up into shorter units. Using the skills you have learnt, rewrite article 28 so that it consists of shorter and simpler sentences.

184

b) Substitution of difficult words with words that are easier to understand

Another method of simplifying a text is to substitute difficult words or complicated phrasing with easier, more understandable language. Try to find synonyms (words/phrases with the same meaning) for the following words and phrases. Remember that you are to select language that would be easier to understand!

'adhering' in art 27(c)
'other qualification criteria' in art 27(c)
'naturalization' in art 27(c)
'procedures' in art 27(c)
'obtained' in art 27(c)
'Any person, at least one of whose parents' in art 28
'time of the person's birth' in art 28
'provided that' in art 28
'renounce' in art 28
'acquired by virtue of one parent' in art 28
'deprived' in art 28
'as provided by law' in art 28

('art'= 'article')

c) Redundancy

The term 'redundancy' means the use of too many words to convey something, or an excess of words to convey something that could have been said much better in fewer words, eg 'At this point in time today...' Redundant words can be omitted without loss of significance or meaning. In legal language we often find instances of redundancy. The importance of eliminating redundancy when simplifying legal English is obvious.

Study the following sentence and attempt to identify and correct an instance of redundancy:

'... looking back in retrospect we were not allowed to enjoy, utilize and exercise our right of freedom of expression ...'

Are you able to detect instances of redundancy in texts (1), (2), (3) and (4)?

• Now attempt to rewrite the entire Chapter IV (articles 27 and 28) of the Liberian Constitution in simple English.

Compare your attempt with the official plain language version:

CITIZENSHIP
(TO BE LIBERIAN MAN)

Article 27

All persons who were proper Liberian citizens long time ago will still be citizens according to this big Law Book. For us to live together as true Liberians, only black man, or person whose mother or father is black can be Liberian citizen. The Legislature will pass law to show how any black foreigner can become Liberian citizen.

Article 28

If any foreigner has a child by a Liberian citizen, that child will be a Liberian citizen too, but when that child becomes man or woman he or she must tell the government whether he will not be a citizen of different country where his mother or father comes from. Only the law can say that a person is a citizen again and any Liberian can change his or her citizenship.

Constitutions of the countries of the world G H Flanz (Ed) 1996

i)   Do you think this is a successful attempt at simplifying the original text of the constitution? Why/why not?
ii) Are you perhaps able to detect any errors in the text in which words are left out? Do these omissions hamper comprehension?
iii) Quote an example of **sexist language** from this extract. (Sexist language is language which assumes the inferiority of one gender.)
iv) Rephrase:
> 'Only the law can say that a person is a citizen again and any Liberian can change his or her citizenship.'

Simplify the following clauses so that they are understandable to the parties to the contract:

---

13 Alterations, additions and improvements[9]
9 See Preliminary Note pars 5.2 and 10.

13.1 The Lessee shall not make any alterations or additions to the Premises without the Lessor's prior consent, but the Lessor shall not withhold its consent unreasonably to an alteration or addition which is not structural.

186

13.2 If the Lessee does alter, add to, or improve the Premises in any way, whether in breach of clause 13.1 or not, the Lessee shall, if so required in writing by the Lessor, restore the Premises on the termination of this lease to their condition as it was prior to such alteration, addition or improvement having been made. The Lessor's requirements in this regard may be communicated to the Lessee at any time, but not later than the (*specify*) day after the Lessee has delivered up the Premises pursuant to the termination of this lease; and this clause 13.2 shall not be construed as excluding any other or further remedy which the Lessor may have in consequence of a breach by the Lessee of clause 13.1.

13.3 Save for any improvement which is removed from the Premises as required by the Lessor in terms of clause 13.2, all improvements made to the Premises shall belong to the Lessor and may not be removed from the Premises at any time. The Lessee shall not, whatever the circumstances, have any claim against the Lessor for compensation for any improvement to the Premises.

14 Exclusion of lessor from certain liability and indemnity

14.1 The Lessee shall have no claim for damages against the Lessor and may not withhold or delay any payment due to the Lessor by reason directly or indirectly of

14.1.1 a breach by the Lessor of any of its obligations under this lease;

14.1.2 any act or omission of the Lessor or any agent or servant of or contractor to the Lessor, whether or not negligent, willfully wrongful, or otherwise actionable at law, and including (without limiting the generality of the aforegoing) any act or omission of any cleaner, maintenance person, handyman, artisan, labourer, workman, watchman, guard, or commissionaire;

14.1.3 the condition or state of repair at any time of the Property, the Building, or any part of the Property or the Building,

14.1.4 any failure or suspension of, or any interruption in, the supply of water, electricity, gas, air conditioning, heating, or any other amenity or service to the Premises, the Building, or the Property (including, without generality being limited, any cleaning service), whatever the cause;

14.1.5 any breakdown of, or interruption in the operation of, any machinery, plant, equipment, installation or system situated in or on, or serving the Property, the Building, or the Premises, and including (but without limiting the generality of the aforegoing) any lift, escalator, geyser, boiler, burglar alarm, or security installation or system, again regardless of cause.

Butterworths forms and precedents (1994) Vol 6 Part 1: 36–37

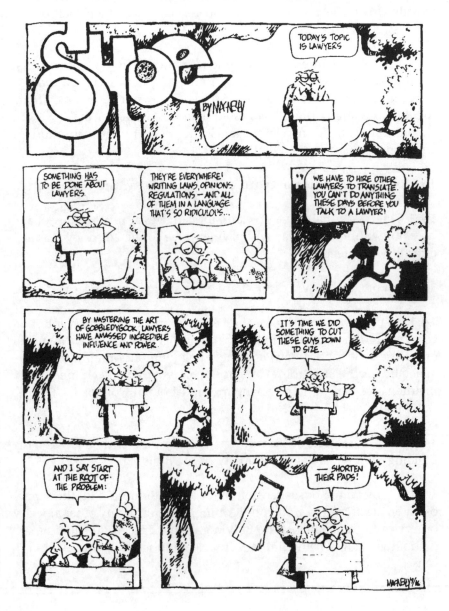

Please do **not** take the following advice:

PRINCIPLES OF LEGAL WRITING

1. Never use one word where ten will do.
2. Never use a small word where a big one will ~~de~~ suffice.
3. Never use a simple statement where it appears that one of substantially greater complexity will achieve comparable goals.
4. Never use English, where Latin, *mutatis mutandis,* will do.
5. Qualify virtually everything.
6. Do not be embarrassed about repeating yourself. Do not be embarrassed about repeating yourself.
7. Worry about the difference between "which" and "that".
8. In pleadings and briefs, that which is defensible should be stated. That which is indefensible, but which you wish were true, should merely be suggested.
9. Never refer to your opponent's "arguments;" he only makes "assertions," and his assertions are always "bald."
10. If a layperson can read a document from beginning to end without falling asleep, it needs work.

IMIS NON CURAT LEX

UNIT 11
CRITICAL READING SKILLS: 'Filthy Lucre'

In this unit we use a satirical essay about how the Lotto millions may be misappropriated as a starting point for an examination of purpose, tone, attitude, emotive language and point of view. We continue our examination of argumentative writing, and concentrate on tracing an argument and listing and consolidating counter arguments. In the language section we study the structures of contrast, reason and purpose.

A READING

Before you read the essay printed below, briefly consider the following:

- What is the purpose of the Lotto lottery?
- Do you think politicians are generally honest and honourable? Why/ why not?
- What are the connotations of the words 'filthy lucre'?
- Would you consider money raised by the Lotto to be 'filthy lucre'?

Now read only the **first three** paragraphs of the following essay by B Ronge (*Sunday Times Magazine* of 2000, p8):

FILTHY LUCRE

Just who will benefit from the Lotto millions?
Not those who need it most, suggests BARRY RONGE

Forget about *Cluedo*. The next big mystery game is going to be called *Lotto*: *Where did the Money Go*?

If I had the time and skill I should design this boardgame myself, patent it, and be ready to make a killing when the big Lotto scandal hits, because it is going to hit.

That's as certain as another petrol price increase. There's just too much money lying around and too many unanswered questions dangling in the air for a scandal of some kind not to erupt.

We are, in general, living in a society in which the only clear sign of concentrated intellectual activity has been the variety and complexity of the scams it has produced.

False academic qualifications, bogus passports, auctions of Matric exam papers, fake licences for driving cars, buses and planes, pension rip-offs. Struggle accounting and pyramid schemes have been the most visible but you could go on and on.

For a culture so uniquely skilled, a vast sum of money set aside for the deliciously vague and inconclusive purpose of nation-building and community upliftment must offer attractive possibilities.

The public are unclear on exactly how much cash is actually involved here. Every week we are told how much is being given away, but you need only three brain cells to know that the payout is a mere fraction of what is actually paid in. But what is that fraction? Is it half, one-quarter or two-thirds that is paid back to the public each week?

Let's be laughably generous and assume that it is half. I wrote this column a day after a R10-million payout was made, which means that if they pay out half, there is another R10-million sitting in a kitty somewhere, going nowhere.

Work out the interest on R10-million. It's quite enough to pay for that crappy little TV show on which the winning numbers are revealed, although I think that show pays for itself with product placement and TV advertising.

The interest on the money for that single week would certainly cover all the other advertising costs involved in persuading people to buy a Lotto card. But these hoards of cash are collected on a weekly basis. By now the collective sum must be vast, but where is it and what's going to happen to it?

In a country as needy as ours, in crucial areas like housing, education, HIV-Aids issues and poverty relief, it can't be too difficult to identify a set of organisations that could benefit from these amassed funds. Yet our government is stymied. They just don't know where to start, which is, in itself, a mystery.

How hard can it be to distribute a hoard of cash that grows larger each week to a country that grows poorer every week? Yet nothing is being done, and I firmly believe that the devil makes work for idle hands. The law of averages tells me that someone is going to start skimming and that the skimming will rapidly turn into looting.

So who are the likeliest suspects in the great Lotto cash mystery? My prime suspect is sport. To start with, it is surrounded with an aura of emotional and racial manipulation that makes negative criticism seem like an act of treason.

Although it is sponsored on almost every level it is always short of money, standing there with its begging bowl held at such an angle that it does not obscure the sponsor's trademark on the sportsman's tracksuit.

Our sportsman carry more trade advertising on their clothing than travelling salesmen out on a job. The amount of sponsorship money involved in the total sports package, including TV rights and endorsements, would make your head spin — yet they are always broke. As we have seen, some of them have to go to extraordinary lengths to get by on what they earn. That makes them my prime suspects.

Next on my list is the military and munitions conglomerate who, at a time when we are normally at peace, are spending more money on weapons and military matters than we ever did when we were facing the 'total onslaught'. It can't all come of the national fiscus and while it would take a high degree of ingenuity to make this look like some community need, it's not impossible. There are still some people who think that the spending of millions on *Sarafina 2* was a justifiable initiative in the war on HIV-Aids.

Then comes that amorphous government agency, headed by no one in particular, which, nonetheless, conjures up millions to spend on public celebrations for Freedom Day, Women's Day, May Day and any other public holiday, which seems to have some vague community connection. The source of that money is mysterious, which makes it a good fit with the equally mysterious Lotto cache.

> And what about the aged, the arts, the disabled, our national parks and heritage conservation issues? They have been assigned their role in this scenario. They have been cast as the victims, the acceptable losses that exist in any war of survival and liberation.
>
> Some of them are pretty close to death and when they die they will be the victims of whoever has hands on the Lotto loot. Identifying that owner is going to be one of the deadliest and most mystifying games of the year. Think of it as a combination of *Monopoly* and *Trivial Pursuit*, words that precisely define its key elements.

Now answer the following questions:

a) Look carefully at the heading of the article. From the heading are you able to predict what the article will be about?

b) Judging by the title of the article, what do you think is the writer's intention in this article?

c) Consider the sub-heading of the article:

   Just who will benefit from the Lotto millions?

   In it we are given a clue as to the contents of the article. What, in your view, is the gist of the article?

d) Look carefully at the second paragraph of the article.

   i) Do you think the writer really intends designing a boardgame? Substantiate.

   ii) Judging from the first three paragraphs, are you able to predict the writer's aim in writing this article?

Now read the rest of the article.

e) Outline the stages in the writer's argument. (Refer to unit 8 on how to trace an argument. A clue: look at the first sentence of each paragraph.)

f) What effect does the writer achieve by using contractions such as *That's* and *It's*?

g) Comment on the writer's choice of words in paragraph nine. What do you think is his attitude to 'that crappy little TV show'?

h) What effect is achieved by the use of short statements, such as *'That's as certain as another petrol price increase'* (par 3)?

Now that we have a general understanding of the structure of the writer's argument, we look at the article in more detail.

Many students see language exclusively as a means of transferring information. Because of this belief they tend to view what they read as objective and unbiased.

However, language conveys more than information — it also expresses the emotions and attitudes of the writer or speaker, and it is often used to influence the attitudes of the reader. Many students fail to perceive that the writer of any piece of writing such as a newspaper or magazine article, essay, paper, textbook, novel, etc has a purpose — he or she has a reason why they are writing. The writer will have a certain attitude towards that which he or she is writing.

In the next few pages we will look at different features of argumentative writing which express the emotions or attitudes of the writer such as tone, attitude, emotive language, point of view, fact and opinion, and purpose.

1 THE WRITER IN RELATION TO THE TEXT

A writer has a certain **attitude** to the topic which he or she is writing about. A writer may for example not agree with a certain point of view that is being put forward, he or she may disapprove of a government policy on which he or she is reporting, or the writer may feel sadness at a death he or she is writing about. It is important that we determine a writer's attitude, as such knowledge will enable us to decide how to regard that which we are reading.

Look carefully at the following extracts from the essay printed above and from a law textbook. Try to see if you are able to determine the writer's attitude in both cases.

> We are in general, living in a society in which the only clear sign of concentrated intellectual activity has been the variety and complexity of the scams it has produced.

- What attitude towards South African society does the writer express in this extract?

> 'As far as the ethical side is concerned, I can see nothing wrong with this type of scheme and that seems to be the generally accepted view in the medical profession'. (*Doctor, patient and the law*, S A Strauss 1991:58.)

- What would you say is the writer's attitude towards the 'scheme' that he is writing about?

Remember that although academic texts are generally regarded as 'objective', this does not mean that the writers do not express their attitudes to problems, theories or court decisions.

Point of view signifies the perspective from which a writer or speaker presents his or her material. Point of view depends on where the writer situates himself or herself in relation to the material. It is very important that you determine the point of view of a writer of a text as this will determine the way in which you view that which he or she writes, for instance, whether he or she presents only his or her personal point of view or whether he or she attempts to remain 'neutral' towards that which he or she is writing about (it is to be doubted whether anybody can really remain neutral). Study the following examples:

> My prime suspect is sport. To start with, it is surrounded with an aura of emotional and racial manipulation that makes negative criticism seem like an act of treason.
>
> Although it is sponsored on almost every level it is always short of money, standing there with its begging bowl held at such an angle that it does not obscure the sponsor's trademark on the sportsman's tracksuit.

- Judging solely by this extract, how does the writer view sport?
- Which words in this extract indicate the writer's point of view?
- Quote the words from the following extract which indicate the writer's point of view.

    > 'Whatever the ethical considerations may be, there is no doubt in my mind, legally speaking, that a doctor would be entitled to administer medical treatment — including intravenous treatment — at that stage.' (S A Strauss 1991:413.)

- From what point of view are most academic texts written? Discuss this question with your fellow students.

A writer's **purpose** is the reason why he or she is writing something. A writer or speaker may aim to amuse, inform, criticise, or even to provoke action. It is sometimes difficult to determine a writer's purpose as it is not always explicit. An author may also say that his or her purpose is one thing while it is in fact quite another.

- What do you think is Barry Ronge's purpose in the essay you have read? What does the first sentence of the second last paragraph tell us about his purpose? Can you think of any other possible purpose that he may have for writing this essay?
- What do you think is the writer's purpose in the following extract?

    > 'The next question to be considered in regard to the criminal responsibility of the epileptic, is whether he may be dealt with under Chapter 13 of the Criminal Procedure Act.' (S A Strauss 1991:139)

195

2 MANIPULATING LANGUAGE

Tone is closely linked to attitude. When one speaks of someone's tone of voice, one is referring to the way in which that person's voice is modulated so that it expresses emotion or sentiment, such as anger or joy. When we talk about a writer's tone, we are referring to the corresponding style in writing. Just like spoken language, written language can be impatient, lively, imploring, despondent, bantering, suspicious, angry, disappointed or grim.

- What do you think is the tone of the article 'Filthy Lucre'?
- How do you think does the writer achieve this?
- What would you say is the relationship between tone and attitude?

Emotion is exploited in language in an attempt to convince the reader to make a decision based on emotion rather than reason. Lawyers sometimes make use of emotive language when arguing cases in court. **Emotive language** is used in almost every aspect of our daily lives, such as in advertising and in political speeches. Words with a strong emotional connotation reinforce the emotional appeal of a text. Think for instance of words such as *love, Apartheid, bastard* and *poverty*. (Revise B(1) *Word Formation* in unit 10.)

- Study the following extracts from the essay and identify words which have emotive connotations:

    In a country as needy as ours, in crucial areas like housing, education, HIV-Aids issues and poverty relief, it can't be too difficult to identify a set of organisations that could benefit from these amassed funds. Yet our government is stymied. They just don't know where to start, which is, in itself, a mystery.

    ... Yet nothing is being done, and I firmly believe that the devil makes work for idle hands. The law of averages tells me that someone is going to start skimming and that the skimming will rapidly turn into looting.

- Can you think of any examples of emotive language in your legal textbooks? Do academic writers commonly make use of emotive language? Discuss.

As you will be able to see from your answers to these questions, the different aspects of language that we discussed above cannot be seen as separate features of a text but overlap with one another. Not all of these are always present in equal degrees in all texts.

196

• Work with a friend and discuss the following questions:

> Do you think emotive language is appropriate in academic writing?

> How would you define the tone that is appropriate for academic texts?

Read the following extract from Bram Fischer's speech during his trial and then answer the questions which follow.

STATE CASE

MR. KENTRIDGE: My lord, I have no witnesses for the defence. The accused, who is, of course, well aware of his legal rights, wishes to make a statement from the dock.

THE ACCUSED:

I am on trial, my lord, for my political beliefs and for the conduct which those beliefs drove me to. My lord, whatever labels may have been attached to the fifteen charges brought against me, they all arise from my having been a member of the Communist Party and from my activities as a member. I engaged upon those activities because I believed that, in the dangerous circumstances which have been created in South Africa, it was my duty to do so.

My lord, when a man is on trial for his political beliefs and actions, two courses are open to him. He can either confess to his transgressions and plead for mercy, or he can justify his beliefs and explain why he has acted as he did. Were I to ask for forgiveness today, I would betray my cause. That course, my lord, is not open to me. I believe that what I did was right, and I must therefore explain to your lordship what my motives were; why I hold the beliefs that I do, and why I was compelled to act in accordance with them.

My belief, moreover, my lord, is one reason why I have pleaded not guilty to all the charges brought against me. Though I shall deny a number of important allegations, this Court is aware of the fact that there is much in the State case which has not been contested. Yet, if I am to explain my motives and my actions as clearly as I am able, then this Court was entitled to have had before it the witnesses who testified in chief and in cross-examination against me. Some of these, my lord, I believe were fine and loyal persons who have now turned traitors to their cause, and to their country, because of the methods used against them by the State. Their evidence, my lord, therefore may in important respects be very unreliable.

My lord, there is another reason, and a more compelling reason for my plea and why even now I persist in it. I accept, my lord, the general rule that for the protection of a society laws should be obeyed. But when the laws

> themselves become immoral, and require the citizen to take part in an organised system of oppression — if only by his silence and apathy — then I believe that a higher duty arises. This compels one to refuse to recognise such laws.

Unpublished court record of *The State v Abram Fischer*,
Transvaal Provincial Division, 28 March 1966

a) Try to establish the accused's tone, attitude, point of view and purpose.
b) Comment on the use of emotive language and the effect this achieves.
c) Illustrate that you are able to distinguish between fact and opinion.

You should include relevant quotations from the text to substantiate your answers.

B LANGUAGE FOCUS

When constructing spoken and written arguments, it is very important to use the structures of contrast, reason and purpose correctly as they will enable you to understand exactly how the writer's argument fits together. In this section we will briefly examine these structures. Revise the section on *Connectors* in unit 3 before you continue.

1 STRUCTURES OF CONTRAST

Structures of contrast connect two ideas that are in opposition. If two events or circumstances are in contrast, it means that one of them is surprising or unexpected in view of the other. Study the following example from the Fisher speech quoted in section A:

> I accept, my lord, the general rule that for the protection of a society laws should be obeyed. But when the laws themselves become immoral, and require the citizen to take part in an organised system of oppression — if only by his silence and apathy — then I believe that a higher duty arises.

• Which two ideas are in contrast here?

Words such as *but, despite, in spite of, yet, however, even so* and *nevertheless* may be used to compose structures of contrast.

The following sentences contain structures of contrast, some of which are used incorrectly. Rewrite these sentences and correct those structures of contrast that have been used incorrectly.

198

a) In spite the fact that lawyers do not like working over weekends, they sometimes have to be available during weekends.
b) Despite that the fact that partners earn more money, they do less work.
c) Even though he spends most of his time lecturing, he is still able to represent a few clients in court.
d) Instead of he pays his assistants to do his marking, he does all the marking himself.
e) He worked until late that night, but he could not finish his preparation before the hearing.
f) For all his skill, he has accomplished very little.
g) Although that the prisoner hadn't eaten for days, yet he still looked strong and healthy.

NOTE:

- *Despite* is written as one word and never followed by *of, in spite* is written as two words and should always be used with *of*.

2 STRUCTURES OF REASON

One uses structures of reason to connect two ideas of which one is the cause (the reason why something occurs or exists) and the other is the result (the consequence of something occurring or existing). In other words, one idea is **the reason for** another idea. Study the following examples:

a) It is difficult to understand what the witness is saying.
b) She speaks with a heavy accent.

If we want to connect these two sentences and indicate that sentence (a) occurred because of sentence (b) we will combine the two sentences with a structure of reason:

It is difficult to understand what the witness is saying *as* she speaks with a heavy accent.

It is difficult to understand the witness *because* she speaks with a heavy accent.

It is clear that this sentence consists of three important sections:

MAIN CLAUSE	LINKING WORD	REASON CLAUSE
it is difficult to understand what the witness is saying	as (*because* and *since* can also be used)	she speaks with a heavy accent.

Look at the following example from Bram Fisher's speech, and attempt to break it up in three sections (as was done with the sentence above):

> Some of these, my lord, I believe were fine and loyal persons who have now turned traitors to their cause, and to their country, because of the methods used against them by the state.

Words and phrases such as *since, on account of* and *for* can be used in the same way.

The following sentences contain structures of reason, some of which are used incorrectly. Rewrite these sentences and correct where necessary.

a) The lawyer found it difficult to make sense of what actually happened on the night of the murder because of his client told so many lies.
b) He told his client that it would be difficult to represent him on account his lies.
c) The client countered that he was lying for no one would believe the truth.
d) He said that he could not possibly have committed the murder that he was accused of since he had an alibi for that time.
e) Because the hospital is very far from the murder scene, he could not have committed the murder.
f) For account of the heavy traffic, he could not have reached the murder scene in time.
g) The lawyer was very angry with his client for lying.

NOTE:
- Use a comma in the sentence only when you use *for*, and not when you use *as* and *because*.
- It is possible to swing the sentence around and introduce it with *as, since* or *because*, for example:

As the witness is speaking with a heavy accent, we are unable to understand what she is saying.

- However, one cannot use *for* in the same way at the start of a sentence. You should take careful note of this as it is a mistake often made by students:

  For the witness was speaking with a heavy accent, we were unable to understand what she was saying. **This is incorrect!**

- *For* is often used with a verb ending in an -ing, for example

  He was angry with the witness *for lying*.

3 STRUCTURES OF PURPOSE

We use structures of purpose to introduce the reason for/intention behind an action or event. Study the following example:

a) The judge asked the witness a question.
b) He wanted to get the facts straight.

If we want to indicate that sentence b) is the reason for/intention behind the judge's action in sentence a), we will combine the two sentences with a structure of purpose:

  The judge asked the witness a question in order to get the facts straight.
  The judge asked the witness a question so as to get the facts straight.

Because may be used to indicate both reason and / or purpose, for example:

  I broke the law *because* I believed it to be unfair. (reason)
  I broke the law *because* I wanted to show my solidarity with the detainees. (purpose)

Once again we are able to distinguish three parts of the sentence:

MAIN CLAUSE	LINKING WORD(S)	CLAUSE OF PURPOSE
The judge asked the witness a question	in order to	get the facts straight.

Look at the following example from Bram Fisher's speech, and attempt to break it up in three sections (as was done with the sentence above):

  I engaged upon those activities because I believed that, in the dangerous circumstances which have been created in South Africa, it was my duty to do so.

Words and phrases such as *to, in order that, in case, so that* and *because* can be used in a similar way.

201

The following sentences contain structures of purpose, some of which are used incorrectly. Rewrite these sentences and correct those structures of purpose that have been used incorrectly.

a) Peter caught the early bus to the university so as to be there on time.
b) Peter has to study hard so that to be a lawyer.
c) Peter has to pay attention in class in order to understand the work.
d) Peter listens carefully in order so that he understands the *ratio decidendi* of the case.
e) Peter's friend takes notes to study from them.
f) Peter leaned over as to examine his friend's notes.
g) Peter borrowed his friend's notes in case of his own notes were not adequate.

NOTE:

- One uses *so as to* and *in order* to in situations where more formal language usage is required.
- It is possible to swing the sentence around and start it with the linking word:

In order to get the facts straight, the judge asked the witness a question.

C INTEGRATED SKILLS

1 CONSTRUCTING COUNTER ARGUMENTS

In many of the academic writing tasks that you will be given at university you will need to present an opposing view or argument. Much of your professional career will also depend on your ability to argue against an opponent and present counter arguments.

In unit 5 we pointed out that writers often present a **thesis** or **statement** on which they then elaborate or provide justification and evidence for the thesis. When you counter somebody's arguments you need to attack both the thesis and the evidence, using structures of reason, contrast and purpose. For example:

202

In paragraphs 4 and 5 of *Filthy Lucre*, Ronge makes the following **statement**:	You can counter the **statement** by simply making your own statement:
We are, in general, living in a society in which the only clear sign of concentrated intellectual activity has been the variety and complexity of the scams it has produced.	This society has demonstrated its world-class intellectual vigour in highly respected areas. **Or by attacking the writer's own words:** Ronge's words 'in general' exposes the gross over-generalization and pessimistic view he has of our society.
He then provides the evidence:	**You can then provide evidence to support you statement:**
False academic qualifications, bogus passports, auctions of Matric exam papers . . .	South Africa has set the example for the world when it launched and successfully concluded the Truth and Reconciliation Commission's work . . .

You need to analyse an argument carefully and plan you counter argument by engaging with each element of the original **statement** and the **evidence** provided for it. It is usually easier to look for weak aspects of the evidence, introduce new evidence and then come to a **conclusion** that is in opposition to the original statement.

When answering an essay-type question which requires you to argue for or against something, keep the following in mind (also refer to the notes on argumentative writing in units 8 and 10):

- Plan your essay. Draw up a rough scheme in which you outline your argument.
- Remember to structure your answer into an introduction, body with subheadings and a conclusion.
- In the introduction you should state what you are going to be arguing about, so that you can place the reader in the context of the argument. If you do not know how to start your essay it may be a good idea to start with something like 'In this essay I [will] attempt to . . .'
- The body of your essay should consist of the main aspects of your argument. Remember that you should use different paragraphs for different main ideas and also use topic sentences and subheadings.
- Where possible, include support or authority in the form of case decisions and academic opinions.
- The conclusion or final paragraph of your essay is very important as it is here where you will summarise your argument. New ideas are not

203

usually included in a conclusion. Restate your position on the main argument but do not repeat your entire argument. Remember that your conclusion very often creates the final impression on which you will be evaluated.

Writing task:
Argue against the following statement:

> But when the laws themselves become immoral, and require the citizen to take part in an organised system of oppression — if only by his silence and apathy — then I believe that a higher duty arises.

Plan your essay carefully and make sure that it contains an introduction in which you place the reader in the context of your argument and a conclusion in which you consolidate your counter arguments.

2   STUDY NOTES

When writing a test or examination you should make sure that you know exactly what is being asked. Read through the question more than once to ascertain that you know what is expected of you.

A question usually has three elements; it tells you what to write, how to write it and for how many marks, for example

> Mention the requirements for the operation of estoppel (5).

All three aspects are extremely important and you should note carefully *how* you should answer:

- When you are asked to 'name', 'mention' or 'identify' something it means that you merely have to list or identify certain aspects.
- When you are asked to 'discuss' something you are required to do more than merely name or list certain aspects. You will need to expand fairly extensively upon that which you are required to discuss. Take note of the mark allocation so that you do not write more than necessary.
- When you are asked to 'compare' you need to say in what way two things differ and in what way they are the same. It is not sufficient to merely list the properties of each – you should rather attempt to illustrate how the two relate to each other, that is, how they are similar and how they are different.
- When you have to 'analyze' something you are required to examine minutely the different parts or sub-sections of something. When you

204

have to analyze a judgement in a case you will examine and discuss all the different aspects of that case.

Look at old test and examination papers and underline the words that tell you **how** to answer a question. When you find words and phrases that are not in the list above, discuss them with the relevant law lecturer so that you know what is expected of you in tests and examinations. Refer to unit 12 for more on this topic.

UNIT 12
LAW AND LITERATURE

In this unit we look at literary texts and the insights they can provide in the study of the law. You will read extracts from different sources and different types of text, including a literary text, in which we will discuss metaphorical and other types of language. In the language section we continue our discussion on the way in which various tenses fit together and we conclude with a few hints for tests and examinations.

A READING

Before you start reading think about the article you read in unit 10 where the use of plain language was discussed. We also talked about the perception that lawyers are deliberately obscure in an effort to win clients and, therefore, make money. Think back to your discussion about lawyers in unit 10. Are you familiar with the following stereotypes about lawyers?

- Lawyers are unscrupulous.
- Lawyers defend people whom they know to be guilty, get them acquitted on a technical point and then let these dangerous criminals loose on the public.
- Lawyers are just in it for the money.
- Only the very rich can afford a lawyer.

Do you think as a law student you should take such stereotypes seriously? How do these perceptions affect the noble idea that justice should not only be done, but should be seen to be done? Discuss these matters with your fellow students.

1 EXTRACT FROM *COLD STONE JUG* BY HERMAN CHARLES BOSMAN

Read the following extract from Herman Charles Bosman's *Cold Stone Jug*, an account of the time he spent in prison after being found guilty of murder.

A queer thing that I found among first offender convicts — and something that I thought very much to their credit — was the fact that they were all of them innocent. Every man jack of them. And without exception — bar one. Of all the convicts doing stretches in A-2 Section (the section occupied by the first offenders), I was the only one who was guilty. Among the old offenders there was also a pretty substantial proportion that was innocent (or that had been framed), but the percentage of innocent men was not nearly so high as among the first offenders. For that reason I respected the first offenders. But I felt very dismal there, all the same, as the only guilty man chucked in with a whole lot of innocent lambs, and guileless simpletons who were only trying to do somebody else a favour, and angels with large, white wings and plaster saints . . .

You have no idea what a source of distress this was to me. It gave me the most awful feeling of inferiority, after a while.

I would talk to a man in the first offenders' section. A stranger to me. But rather decent looking, somehow. I would go up to him on exercise, let us say, and I would introduce myself, and I would say I am in for murder, and I am doing ten years. How long are you doing, and what for?

And he would always begin his answer with the remark, "Well, of course, I didn't do it, but the judge gave me five years for arson." Or he would say, "I got two years for taking a cheque along to the bank, man, a cheque that I received in all good faith. It was only a cheque for nine thousand four hundred pounds. Imagine a man in my position doing anything so silly, and just for nine thousand four hundred pounds. Why, my good name alone is worth much more than that."

"Was," I would say. Or something to that effect.

"What do you mean, 'was'?" he would ask.

"Well, you good name isn't worth that amount any more, is it?" I would remark.

But you have no idea how inferior I felt. Every man in the first offenders' section I spoke to was innocent. And he would explain his innocence to me in such detail, and his countenance, as he spoke, would be lit up with so pure a radiance, so noble a refulgence, that I believed him implicitly, and I felt very sorry for him, and I wondered how he would bring himself, from the noble elevation of his guiltlessness, to hold converse with so sorry a worm as myself — I wondered how he could even talk with this shabby felon shuffling along by his side. And I would walk beside my new acquaintance, my shoulders drooping and my self-esteem in the dust, pondering on how lost a part of creation I must be. I was a member of some sub-pariah species. I was in prison, and, on top of everything else, guilty.

Answer the following questions by referring to the text.

1 How would you describe the author's **tone** in this extract: is it sincere, ironic, complaining or happy? Quote words from the extract that support your answer.
2 What kind of picture is painted of the justice system in general?
3 Although Bosman's story is autobiographical, he tells us something about all 'criminals' — what do you infer from his description of the 'innocent' inmates of the prison, especially among the old offenders?

4   Make a list of the words and phrases the author uses to describe the other criminals and then a separate list with the words and phrases he uses to describe himself. What do you think is the author's purpose with these two very different sets of descriptions?

Try to find out more about the South African system of law that was in effect when Herman Charles Bosman wrote this account of his stay in prison.

2   EXTRACT FROM *"SOMETHING AS STRANGE AS THE AFRICAN VELD": HERMAN CHARLES BOSMAN, STORYTELLING AND DEMOCRATIC CITIZENSHIP* BY WESSEL LE ROUX

In this extract the author describes a movement that began in the late 1970s in the USA, called Critical Legal Studies: "This movement was united, if at all, by a shared disillusionment with both the dominant liberal tradition (proclaiming the neutrality, objectivity and rationality of the law and the liberal social order) and the dominant Marxist tradition" (Le Roux 2000:14). One of the results of the Critical Legal Studies 'movement' was the rise of the *law and literature* movement, and the extracts that follow attempt to explain what this movement is and how it aids the study of the law.

> Attempts to combine law and literature have generated two broad categories of scholarship in recent years. The first, often termed *law-in-literature*, is explicitly concerned with the depiction of law and legal issues in novels, plays and movies.[5] (This is also the traditional understanding of law-and-literature.) The second, *law-as-literature*, comprises a broader range of theoretical investigations into questions of interpretation and takes literary theory, rather than the literary texts themselves, as the subject of investigation. Law-as-literature challenges the claim that the law should be regarded as a technical science of abstract rules. In this sense law-as-literature could be regarded as a postmodern reaction to the overly rationalistic claims of modern legal thought. It presents an attempt to re-introduce previously neglected or so-called "irrational" aspects like imagination, storytelling and good judgement into the law. The ideal of the literary or storyteller-judge slowly being developed in law-and-literature jurisprudence is one of the many postmodern alternatives to the legal formalism of modern, or classical, American legal thought.
>
> [5] See for example "Peter Robson 'Images of law in the fiction of John Grisham' in John Morrison and Christine Bell (eds) *Tall Stories? Reading law and literature* (1996) 201; Wessel le Roux 'And am I then reveng'd?': Freud's Hamlet and the Oedipal histories of law" 1998 (39) *Codicillus* 21.

The end of the story?

I suggested above that storytelling is an essential element of a democratic culture in which difference is celebrated as a positive virtue and a fruitful way of engaging life and law in a radically divided society.

In the light of what was said above, it seems strange that the courses in which Bosman, Dickens, Whitman, Kundera, and the many other brilliant exponents of the literary imagination (Nussbaum) and the genres of democracy (Rorty) were studied but a few years ago, had to make way in the LLB curriculum, ironically with the arrival of South Africa's new democracy, for legal courses in which the focus falls narrowly (still, and yet again) on rules ... either of law or language. Over the past five years the humanities component of the LLB has been all but eliminated and the one or two remaining language courses focus almost exclusively on grammatical aspects, to the exclusion of any literary component. It is a chilling thought, as *oom* Schalk might have said, that syntax has replaced narrative precisely at a time in South Africa's history when the need for storytellers and poet judges is at its greatest.

"Something as strange as the African veld": Herman Charles Bosman, Story telling and democractic citizenship. Le Roux 2000: 20, 21

Think back to the passage from *Cold Stone Jug* and answer the following questions.

5   Which of the following adjectives are more descriptive of the extract by Bosman and which are descriptive of the extract by Le Roux? (Be prepared to defend your choices!)

argumentative	descriptive	narrative
explanatory	emotional	linear
objective	metaphorical	factual

Check the answers with your lecturer and fellow students to see whether you agree. Once you've decided on a final division, you will have a list of words that, to a large extent, distinguishes a literary text (such as *Cold Stone Jug*) from an expository one (such as the article by Le Roux).

6   Do you think that literary texts can help your understanding of legal issues? For example, can a text like *Cold Stone Jug* provide clues regarding problems in the criminal justice system?
7   When you think of books like *A long walk to freedom* by NR Mandela, *Cry the beloved country* by A Paton: would a study of such texts improve

lawyers' understanding of how law impacts upon society? What about movies that deal with such issues, for example, the South African movie, *A reasonable man* or Australian movie like *The Castle*?

8   To what extent have your own expectations of law studies been shaped by the media? For example by television series like *LA Law* or media coverage of the Truth and Reconciliation Commission?

9   Discuss the distinction made by Le Roux between "rational law" and "irrational' aspects like imagination, storytelling and good judgment". Do you think that the law is always 'rational' and 'objective'?

WORDS AND THEIR MEANINGS

When you compare the extract from *Cold Stone Jug* to the extracts from textbooks and newspaper articles, you will agree that each represents a unique use of language: the literary, the academic and the popular. Each type of language has its own conventions and suits the purpose for which it is used. The metaphorical language of literature is sometimes used in academic and ordinary texts, for example, we often hear people say, 'A little knowledge is a dangerous thing', a line written by an English poet, Alexander Pope. Literary images like 'to kill two birds with one stone' and 'better the devil you know' have also passed into everyday use. There is a danger, though, that your language might become too literary or worse, flowery. If you are not sure about the use of an image or a metaphor, rather leave it out and use ordinary language.

Study the following examples of metaphorical language use gone wrong and try to improve the sentences.

1   The husband was in the deepest depths of despair and decided to return to his wife.
2   In this decision the court sank to new heights.
3   The doctor was a good person and one could always fall on him when the need arose.
4   The argument took the thunder out of the opposition's sails.
5   We can run this up the flagpole and see if it sticks.
6   You must decide whether you want to be a big fish in a frying pan or a small fish in a cesspit.

Can you improve the next two sentences (quoted by Block in her book *Effective legal writing*, 1992:119)?

7   'We are creating a monster that is bound to backfire.'

211

8   'The proof of the pie is in the pudding.'

The golden rule with any writing that you do, is to:

- write short sentences using simple language;
- use your dictionaries;
- avoid trite images.

B LANGUAGE FOCUS

In units 4 and 10 we discussed the way in which a longer piece of legal writing can switch from the past tense to the present depending on whether the writer expresses a general rule or reports on past events. In this unit we want to look at the way in which certain families of tenses interlock.

I   INTEGRATION OF TENSES: CONTINUOUS TENSES

Usually a writer tries to stick to a specific group of tenses, for example, if she presents an argument she will use mainly the present tenses (simple present, present continuous and present perfect – see underlining) with conditionals:

> Lawyers are regarded with much ambiguity in Western societies; on the one hand studies in law are more popular than ever before, on the other lawyers are the butt of jokes that are sometimes downright insulting. Anybody who has seen *Jurassic Park* remembers the scene where the Tyrannosaurus Rex grabs the lawyer and while he is shaking him so that his limbs fly in all directions the whole cinema erupts with laughter. Would they have done the same if the victim were a crippled preacher or even a female lawyer?

If the writer is narrating past events she would use mainly the past tenses (simple past, past continuous and past perfect – see underlining):

> While the family was sleeping, the kidnapper broke open the kitchen window and crept upstairs to the nursery. After he had drugged the baby, he carefully put the child into a sportsbag, left the ransom note in the crib and fled the same way he had entered.

These simple (non-legal) examples show that a switch from one tense to the next is made for very specific reasons. In units 4 and 10 we indicated that in law texts, a general rule is usually expressed in the present tense and the facts of the case are usually reported in the past tense. We can refine

212

this distinction even further. As you can see from the examples above the continuous tense (past and present) is used to indicate that some action continues over time (indicated with the continuous tenses) and another action occurs in the middle of it (indicated with the simple tenses), for example:

... while he *is shaking* ... the cinema *erupts* ...

and

While the family *was sleeping*, the kidnapper *broke* ...

Clearly some verbs are more capable of expressing continuous action than others, but the context of the sentence is also an indication of how continuous and simple tenses interlock. A word such as *while* would certainly prompt the use of a continuous tense.

a) Study the following letter by a student to her lecturer. Say where you think her use of the continuous tense is incorrect and try to improve on her letter. (Simply changing the tenses will not be enough.)

Dear Mr Webb

I am having problems with my assignments and I am feeling that I am needing extra guidance. I know that you are thinking this student is taking a chance, but I am really seeing great difficulties ahead if I don't get help now.

I am proposing that we meet next Thursday and I am including my latest assignment so that we can discuss my mistakes. Please let me know if you agree and I will 'phone again to check with you.

Yours sincerely

Jane Thorpe.

---

b) In the following exercise decide whether the simple present or past or the continuous tense should be used. Check your answers afterwards with your lecturer.

In a televised interview with a journalist a prominent lawyer discusses the negative image that the public has of the law in South Africa.

Journalist:	Mr B, why do you think this negative image should change now?
Mr B:	Look, we (live) in a very young and fragile democracy. It is imperative that the law is not seen as a privilege, but as a right. When the Apartheid era (end) we (not try) very hard to address this problem. I (think) lawyers in particular (suffer) from delayed shock and (try) to make sense of a new Constitution and the Bill of Rights and their effect on legal procedure. But now that things (settle) down we need to take positive steps towards redressing what I (call) our image problem.
Journalist:	You mean you want to engage a Public Relations firm to work out a new image for the law profession?
Mr B:	No, no, I (want) to do something far more radical. I would like firms of attorneys to employ and pay one or more lawyers to be fulltime *pro bono* practitioners, but in this case their payment should come from the firm itself.
Journalist:	You probably (go) to get a lot of opposition!
Mr B:	Initially I probably will, but I (hope) that firms will realize the marketing potential of my strategy. Can you imagine the goodwill such a firm will generate? In fact, I know of a Pretoria firm who (try) this out last year and the only reason they (not carry on) this year, is that they could not immediately replace the lawyer who (do) this work for them last year and who has since left the firm because he (build) up such a loyal clientele!
Journalist:	Mr B, thank you for your time.

There is a general rule that some verbs should not be used in the continuous tenses. As you probably saw in the exercises, forms such as *I am wanting* and *I am liking* are regarded as **incorrect**. The following verbs do not take the continuous tense, or take this tense very rarely. (These categories are based on and adapted from the book *Grammar troublespots* by Ann Raimes 1992:41.)

- Verbs of preference and desire: *like, need, prefer, want, love*
- Verbs that indicate a mental activity: *think*, wonder*, understand, believe, know*

214

- Verbs that describe the senses: *see, hear, smell, taste, feel**
- Verbs of possession: *have, own, belong, possess*
- Verbs of inclusion: *include, contain, comprise, hold**
- Verbs of appearance: *appear, seem, look**

Verbs indicated with an asterisk (*) can also be used in the continuous tense but only in specific circumstances, for example:

I am thinking of going overseas.
I was wondering how you would feel about accompanying me?
I'm not feeling too well.
He's holding the future of the country in his hands.
You're looking good!

2 INTEGRATION OF TENSES: PERFECT TENSES

As you know from your secondary school days, the perfect tenses also interact in a very specific way with the simple tenses. Look at the following extracts and say whether the verb should be in a simple or in a perfect tense.

c) 'The issue at hand (involve) an action against the Minister for unlawful arrest and detention. The plaintiff previously (be) arrested on charges of fraud and (be) subsequently released. … After the interim Constitution (come) into operation the plaintiff (apply) for an order to compel the defendant to make available the privileged documents.' (Adapted from a discussion of the case *Khala v Minister of Safety and Security* 1994 4 SA 218 WLD by Ehrenbeck 1995:72: see 5 *Study note*.)

d) 'The court *a quo* found on the facts that there was at least the reasonable possibility that the deceased (be) fatally injured only after the accused (leave) the scene, but nevertheless (convict) him of murder on the basis that he (not intend) to dissociate himself from the actions of the other perpetrators whose actions, in terms of the doctrine of common purpose, (be) regarded as his own.' (Adapted from a discussion of the case *S v Singo* 1993 1 SACR 226 (A) by Jordaan 1993:75.)

If you found that you had difficulty with this exercise, you should ask your lecturer to give you additional exercises or you should find additional exercises in a grammar book.

215

C INTEGRATED SKILLS

1 WRITING TESTS/ EXAMINATIONS

In previous units we discussed different types of questions and how you should go about answering them. For example, in unit 4 we discussed multiple-choice questions, in unit 6 problem-type questions and in units 8 and 11 the structuring of essay-type answers. Here we want to discuss more general issues with regard to test and examination writing.

Most residential educational institutions have a system whereby students accumulate a year mark by means of tests and assignments. At distance education institutions students also submit assignments but do not usually accumulate a year mark because of the difficulty of controlling whether the work is their own. Whatever the case, assignments and tests are meant to get students to apply themselves to smaller, more manageable sections of the work. It is always in your own best interests that you work as best you can for these tests and examinations because they make it much easier to study for the final examination. Particularly in those cases where a **year** mark is used with a **final examination** mark to determine your **pass** mark, a good year mark may drag you through a difficult examination, or at least give you a second chance in the form of a supplementary examination. Even at distance education institutions good marks for assignments could be taken into account if you are a borderline case. Students who study at distance education institutions should ask their lecturers about the policy in this regard.

Think back to your own study pattern as you described it in unit 1. You will probably follow this pattern when you prepare for the examination. By this time you should know whether your study habits are effective or not. Look at your responses under *1 Drawing up a schedule of work for the academic year* in unit I and decide whether you still agree with the study habits you described there.

2 PREPARATION FOR TESTS/ EXAMINATIONS

Most lecturers provide information about tests and examinations in a course outline. Study this document carefully and make sure that you know the following:

- Which work will be covered in the test/ examination? You need **specific** information: which chapters, which pages?
- What is the total number of marks for the paper?
- What is the length of the paper, that is, how much time do you have?
- What types of questions will be asked?

Different types of questions imply different study methods. For **multiple-choice questions** you need detailed, **receptive** knowledge. This means it will not be necessary for you to **produce** correct information, only to **recognize** it. Although this may sound easy, it might be a good idea to get hold of previous multiple-choice items set by a particular lecturer, so that you can get some idea of the type of detail on which she or he concentrates. It would be perfectly reasonable to ask the lecturer for two or three examples. (Usually lecturers expect you to return multiple-choice questions, so it will be difficult to get hold of them in old papers.)

For **problem-type questions** you need to know the problem cases in a particular section of the work. You will need to memorize:

- names of relevant cases;
- the facts, arguments and decisions in these cases;
- the applicable Latin phrases for the relevant rules (if this is required);
- the rules and requirements for specific acts to be legal or illegal (for example the requirements for a successful hire-purchase agreement, or the conditions whereby an immigrant can become a naturalized citizen, and so on);
- requirements for remedies, that is, requirements for specific applications or pleadings to succeed in court.

Problem questions will invariably sketch a tricky situation, so you need to know and **produce** the relevant position in the law. You need **productive** knowledge. Remember that the lecturer in family law will most probably not expect you to include information from, for example, Roman-Dutch law, or law of contract: focus on problems in the subject of the test. (Revise the work on problem questions in unit 6.)

To be able to answer essay questions you will probably also need to memorize certain cases, their facts and the rules that apply, but you will have to present a well-structured, logical argument as well. To prepare for such questions you should think up topics and try to compose answers. The idea is not to learn these off by heart, but rather to get into the habit of incorporating cases and decisions and legal rules into a coherent argument. (Revise units 8 to 11.) Previous examination papers could once again prove invaluable.

NOTE:

If you have built up a good relationship with a study group you could study with them. Just remember, in the examination hall **you are on your own**! You must know the work and you cannot depend on other (older) students to tell you what to study or how to study. People, their study methods and their emotional reactions to lecturers and subjects differ vastly. The last thing you need before a test or examination is a hysterical fellow student saying, 'I heard Ms Dube's multiple-choice questions are all set from the footnotes of the textbook!' If you passed examinations at school, the chances are good that you will manage at institutions of tertiary education. With each successful test you can trust your own study methods and abilities more. Have confidence in your own (successful!) study methods and do not fall for all kinds of weird advice!

3 DURING THE TEST/EXAMINATION

You need to take the following, presented in order of importance, to the examination room:

- **two** pens of which one is new;
- a watch of some description (preferably one that does **not** tick loudly);
- a ruler;
- your student card or some other form of identification.

Carry these in you hand rather than in a pencil case or bag; invigilators (people who supervise the writing of the examination) are very suspicious of bits of paper (including tissues and handkerchiefs!) and closed boxes and bags. It is better not to give them anything to complain about!

Decide how much time you have for each question and stick to it. In this regard you will have to rely on your own examination and test experience. You should adapt and experiment with the following rules of thumb:

- If your reading speed is average, you could allocate 1 to 2 minutes for a multiple-choice item or other short questions that count 1 or 2 marks.
- Problem questions of up to 15 marks would probably take you 25 minutes to figure out and write down. (Similarly, a 5-mark question could take 8–10 minutes, and a 10-mark question 15–18 minutes.)
- Essay questions of 30 marks would probably take 45 minutes or even an hour to prepare and write.

Questions that count for a lot of marks **should not**, in our experience, be left until the very end. If you leave multiple-choice questions until the end and you cannot manage, for example, the last five items, you will probably lose 5 marks. If you leave out a problem question you could lose up to 15 marks.

4 AFTER A TEST/ EXAMINATION

It is customary for lecturers to discuss tests and provide a general type of feedback on the test. If you still cannot work out where you went wrong, it is probably wise to make an appointment with the lecturer to discuss your problems. You should do this sooner rather than later. If you work in a good study group with fellow students that you trust, you could discuss your papers, compare them and see **where** the lecturer awarded marks and **why**.

Think back to your school days and past examinations. Think back to how you prepared for these tests and examinations, how much time you took for preparation, what happened in the examination room and how you felt afterwards. Write these things down and discuss them with your fellow students. Try to find out from them if they have specific strategies that might also help you. However, be sensible about the advice you take from others!

5 STUDY NOTE

The extracts from discussions of cases in questions (d) and (e) (under B LANGUAGE FOCUS) were taken from the journal Codicillus. As explained in unit 1, we use the referencing style appropriate to texts written in faculties of arts and education.

G.B. Trudeau. DOONESBURY

UNIT 13
FORMAL CORRESPONDENCE

In this unit we look at types of formal business communication in both spoken and written form. We introduce formal letters, office memorandums, faxes and electronic mail. The type of language used in business communication is discussed as well as the level of formality that is appropriate in everyday office communication.

A READING

Study the following types of written communication and say in each case who you think the writer is, what his or her status is in relation to the recipient of the communication and what the purpose of the communication is.

TEXT 1: LETTER

Yokomoto, Sanders, Mbali And Partners

Byrnes 1120, Suite 4
2456 Sunningdale
Tel +11345 0789
Fax + 11345 0788
Internet Yoksanmab-01@sunmail.com.za

Ms N Pieters
c/o Mr A Ndwambi
Dieprivier Hyperstore
2334 Dieprivier

20 June 2002

Dear Ms Pieters

YOUR CLAIM FROM WORKMEN'S COMPENSATION FUND (931WCF1023)

1. Your letter of 2 February has reference.
2. Information provided by sources to which you make mention in above-mentioned communication necessitates the following resolution:

   2.1 notwithstanding your demurral to the contrary and,
   2.2 notwithstanding Mr Lekalakala's letter of testimony,

   we hereby disclaim any further association with your representative and urge timeous settlement of outstanding balance as per agreement.

Yours sincerely

C. du Toit

pp   P Williams (Ass)
cc Mr J Sanders

TEXT 2: MEMORANDUM

Yokomoto Sanders Mbali
MEMORANDUM

TO: Mr J Sanders   FROM: P Williams
                                     Accounts Section

PIETERS FILE 93/WCF1023: 20 JUNE 1996

1. Please find attached a copy of final notification to Ms Pieters for your information.

2. Advise if further action is required.

Regards

Jay, hope
this is okay
P

Pam

223

TEXT 3: FAX

COVER PAGE FOR FAXES
YOKOMOTO, SANDERS, MBALI AND PARTNERS

DATE: *2/5*

PAGES: *6*

TO: *Hope University*

FAX NO: *(011) 322 4582*

FOR ATTENTION: *Dr R. Beneke*

FROM: Yokomoto, Sanders, Mbali And Partners
Barnes 1120, Suite 4
2456 Sunningdale
Tel +11345 0789
Fax + 11345 0788

IN CASE OF PROBLEMS WITH THIS FACSIMILE MESSAGE, PLEASE
TELEPHONE *K Mbali* IMMEDIATELY
AT THE ABOVEMENTIONED NUMBER.

MESSAGE:

Remi – the draft contract

for editing. Please take a

careful look! K.

Written communication always takes place within a specific context: before you even read the message you know something about the sender and nature of the message. A plain envelope with a transparent window and your name in typescript usually means official business, whereas a brightly coloured airmail envelope with your name in a familiar handwriting usually means a friendly letter. Once we read the message we can make more inferences by looking beyond the meaning of the words on the page.

Study Text 1 (the letter) again and answer the following questions.

1 What does the information contained in the addresses of the sender and the receiver in Letter 1 tell you about the material circumstances of the sender and receiver?
2 What kind of information would you expect to find in the subject line (the line in capitals just below 'Dear Ms Pieters)?
3 What is the subject line in this letter supposed to tell the receiver (Ms Pieters)?
4 What is the meaning of the first sentence below the subject line in Letter 1?
5 Why are there separate, numbered points in the letter?
6 What is the meaning of *cc* at the bottom of the letter?
7 What is the meaning of *pp* below the signature *C du Toit*?

Discuss with your fellow students the possible scenario that could have led to the writing of Letter 1 to Ms Pieters.

Do you think that formal features of the letter such as the subject line and the numbering of sentences and phrases provide more information and therefore make the letter easier for Ms Pieters to understand?

Study Text 2 (the memorandum) and answer the following questions.

8 What can you infer from the way in which the sender and receiver are identified after 'TO' and 'FROM'?
9 What kind of information would you expect to find in the *subject line* of such a memorandum?
10 What is the subject line in this memorandum supposed to tell the receiver (Mr Sanders)?
11 What is the function of separate, numbered points in the memorandum?
12 What does the handwritten note in the memorandum tell you about the sender and receiver of this communication?

225

Discuss with your fellow students the possible scenario that could have led to the writing of the memorandum.

What is the function of 'memos' (as they are called) in a law practice? Do you think that formal features of the memorandum such as the subject line and the numbering of sentences are justified? Where would you expect such formal features to be more functional: in the letter or in the memorandum?

Study Text 3 (the fax) and answer the following questions.

13 What do you think is the function of a cover page?
14 Why is the number of pages of the document specified?
15 Why does the cover page include a heading, 'FOR ATTENTION'?
16 Can you find (in Text 3) the word for which 'fax' is an abbreviation?
17 What is the purpose of a fax? In other words, under which circumstances would you send and expect to receive a fax?

In the above examples the format of different types of business communication is provided. The features of such communication are listed below, but the separate items are not complete. See if you can add more detail to this list on the basis of the examples you were given at the beginning of this unit.

A formal business letter:
- When the letter is printed or typed on a business letterhead, the sender needs only add ...
- The following details of the receiver must be included: *Name, address,*
- The salutation in English is always ... *Dear*
- A subject line which states ... must be typed in capitals just below the salutation. *Summaries topic*
- Usually the business of the letter is stated in a manner that is brief and to the point.
- One concludes the letter with ... *Sincerly*
- If copies of the letter are sent to other people, they should be listed at the end of the letter, prefaced by ... *cc*

An inter-office memorandum:
- Sender and receiver are identified mostly by name only and sometimes also by ... *Department*
- It is important to add the date.
- The salutation ...
- A subject line ...
- A memorandum can be less formal than a business letter because ... *Its between colleges*
- A memorandum is concluded by ... *regards & Thanks*

226

A fax:

- The following information must be included on the cover page: ...date, pages, company
- The person for whom the fax is meant is indicated by the words ...
- The number of pages of the document is indicated because ...

Ask your lecturer to show you examples of letterheads, memos and faxes of the institution where you study, or simply take a close look at the letters you received at the beginning of the year to confirm your registration as student. Take careful note of the information provided in the letterhead: what would you need to add if you were a secretary and had to write a letter to a student? Ask your lecturer about the format and style of formal letter-writing in the institution where you study.

B LANGUAGE FOCUS

1 PASSIVES AND AUXILIARIES

In units 7 and 8 we discussed the passive voice and the use of modal auxiliaries (could, would, should, and so on) in law texts. In formal letters these aspects of language are also used to make the letter more formal. In instances where specific legal phrases and words are used with passives and auxiliaries we can recognize such a letter as an expression of a specific *register*. The *register* of a text indicates the specific language use of a professional domain. For example, a report written by a radiologist on chest X-rays will be written in the register of the medical profession just as Text 1 (in A READING above) displays the register of law.

Study the following letters and try to make them more appropriate by using, among others, the passive voice and modal auxiliaries. You must also decide whether the information given in the letters is relevant. Take out what you think is unnecessary.

a) The secretary of a law firm is told by a senior partner in the firm that a client, whom the secretary knows, did not settle her account. The secretary is instructed to write a letter to the client on the law firm's letterhead, asking her to contact the firm about her account. This is what the secretary writes:

Dear Mary
Listen, the boss is hopping mad because you didn't pay last month's account. I think you'd better send him a cheque or, if you're in trouble, come and chat to him.
Bye
Sipho

227

b) A letter requesting more information about a specific client goes out to another law firm:

Dear Ms Ngongola

PLEASE SEND MORE INFORMATION ABOUT CLIENT MS PIETERS WITH REGARD TO HER PRESENT DOMICILE

Thank you for the fax about Ms Pieter's new address. However, we need to know more about this address. Is she living there permanently or do you think this is a trick to evade property tax? Send us more info about the owner of this place, whether Ms Pieters is renting and if so, whether she signed a contract with the owner.

Yours sincerely

J Collins

c) The following letter is addressed to a widow who is in the process of drawing up her will.

Dear Ms Singh

We studied your handwritten will very carefully and came to the conclusion that we cannot comply with some of your provisions. It is not acceptable to stipulate that your grandchild must divorce her husband before she can claim her inheritance. You can, however, add a clause stating that her inheritance does not form part of her husband's estate.

Contact us as soon as possible so that we can finalize this matter.

Yours sincerely

V. M. Moody

2 SUBJECT LINES

As explained under A READING, a subject line is a crucial part of a formal letter. Its purpose is to indicate to both sender and receiver the main business of the letter and often contains references to file numbers or a specific reference number that facilitates filing or computer search procedures. That is why, in unit 1, we emphasized the fact that you should give your student number in the subject line and state the main business of the letter.

It is in the nature of a subject line that it should be short and to the point. Did you notice that the subject line in letter (b) above is far too long?

Usually we leave out articles (*a* and *the*), prepositions (*with regard to* and *about*) and words such as *please* or pronouns such as *her*. Active voice is often made passive and the full form of the passive voice is also shortened, from, for example, *INFORMATION IS REQUIRED* to *INFORMATION REQUIRED*. One can also use a *colon* (:) to separate parts of a subject line, for example,
FINAL AGREEMENT: CASE 96/54/S127

The idea is to tell the reader the **subject** and **purpose** of the letter in as few words as possible.

Find suitable subject lines for letters (a) and (c) (above) and try to improve on the following subject lines.

d) THIS LETTER IS CONCERNED WITH YOUR CLIENT MR AHMED (FILE 24/A321) AND HIS CLAIM AGAINST OUR CLIENT MR VAN DER MERWE
e) WE REQUEST YOUR URGENT ATTENTION FOR THE MEETING WITH YOUR CLIENT MR VAN DER MERWE (FILE 25/A324) ON 23 JUNE 1996.
f) SEND US MORE INFORMATION ON YOUR CLIENT MR AHMED AND HIS PROPERTIES IN SUNNINGDALE.

If you found this a difficult exercise, do not despair — this is a skill that improves with practice. It is the same skill that you need to take short but sensible notes and to make meaningful summaries. You need to focus on essential elements which will leave enough clues so that you can reconstruct the full text (in the case of study material) or the full request (in the case of a letter).

C INTEGRATED SKILLS

Institutions like law firms, big business offices and universities often prescribe a specific style to be used by their employees. However, this style goes further than the basic format of letters and includes the **type** of language used in letters. In most firms one of the higher-ranking partners or a very experienced secretary would have the reputation that they are accomplished writers or that they know the rules of the language better than everybody else. Such people are valuable resources specifically when it comes to *formulaic expressions* (fixed phrases) and the *tone* (your written 'manners') of various types of letters. However, these fixed linguistic habits can also become old-fashioned or inappropriate and in such cases lead to stilted (unnatural) language use, especially when people use word processors to simply copy and adapt existing letters. The letter in *Text 1* (A READING) is an example of stilted language use that can be said to actually obscure the meaning of the letter.

Study this letter again and try to improve it by using simpler, more straightforward language. (Revise units 9 and 10 on Plain English.)

1   E-MAIL

In unit 1 we briefly touched upon the use of e-mail when you communicate with lecturers. Since e-mail is increasingly used in businesses and companies, it is important that you take note of the rapidly-developing conventions of e-mail communication and of the unique problems that may arise when you use this form of communication.

Most universities, colleges and technikons in South Africa have electronic mail and more and more companies and individuals are 'getting connected', that is, joining servers who, for a minimal fee, give individuals and companies access to electronic mail services and the internet. Just as with ordinary mail, institutions, firms, companies and individuals have their own addresses and these usually follow a specific pattern:

   yourname@institution.ac.za

E-mail addresses differ widely but they all have one thing in common, and that is the @ sign, which means **at**. In the above address, *za* is the international sign for South Africa and *ac* is short for *academic*, which immediately indicates that the addressee is connected with an educational institution. Some educational institutions use another 'path', like **edu** (for education) or **com** (for communication) to deliver their electronic post. It is extremely important that you note your own and other people's e-mail addresses with care, because spaces, full stops, hyphens and capitals are all meaningful and your message will be returned to you if you make errors which to you may seem insignificant.

In general, e-mail communication is quite informal but as companies use it increasingly to communicate with each other and with their clients, people tend to become more formal, depending on the receiver of the message. When you use e-mail for formal business, you need to take note of the following:

230

a) Your subject line must give a clear indication of the purpose of your message – the same guidelines apply as for written communication (see B2 *Subject lines* above).

b) If you don't know the receiver personally, rather stick to the customary form of address: *Dear Ms So-and-so*.

c) If the message is very important, you should try to go into the properties of your e-mail system and choose the option that will notify you when the message is received and opened on the other side.

d) When you attach files to your message, make quite sure that you give them explicit names that will help the receiver to link it to your name (see unit 1 for suggestions)

e) In e-mail communication the continuous use of capital letters is regarded as SHOUTING!

f) Be considerate of your colleagues' time: don't pass on jokes, pictures, photos and other kinds of 'junk' mail at random. Be careful what you forward to others – people do not have the same sense of humour. Keep this kind of communication for close friends.

g) E-mail is not private. Don't use it to gossip or discuss private matters with another colleague. Many employees have found themselves in trouble because of this. In the UK and employee was fined £10 000 for a racist and sexist remark. James Davies, chairman of the Employment Lawyers Association's working party on workplace privacy, said: 'This case reinforces the need for employees to know that their internal e-mail systems are a permanent record and should not be treated as if it is the same as something said in conversation.' (*The Independent* at **http://www.independent.co.uk/story.jsp?story=118594**)

NOTE:

It is important for students to realize that electronic mail can be an invaluable resource when studying at a distance education institution. Depending on the institution, you can contact your lecturer far more quickly, regularly, cheaply and reliably than through ordinary post. You could also build up a study group and discuss work without ever leaving your desk! Obviously students at residential educational institutions can also form study groups with students at other universities, although they usually have the choice to decide whether personal contact is not perhaps cheaper.

Today academics make extensive use of the internet and some academic journals exist in electronic format only. Academics from all over the world, who are interested in the same field of research, form discussion groups and professors and research assistants collaborate with each other from places as far away as Japan, Iceland, South Africa and Indonesia, in the comfort of their offices. If you want to find out more, your library is probably the best place to start. You should also try to find out if the institution where you study has a computer centre, because the people there usually have the latest information on access to electronic mail and the internet.

A word of warning: the internet can ruin your life! Some people get so engrossed by the seemingly unlimited information that is on offer, that they either run up a huge telephone bill or they get addicted and cannot stop 'surfing' the net.

Discuss the status of electronic mail and faxes with your fellow students and perhaps with one of your law professors. If a law firm sent your firm a message by electronic mail, confirming some or other arrangement, can this message be printed out and regarded as a valid agreement? Can you, for example, send a cheque by means of a fax?

DE MINIMIS NON CURAT LEX

UNIT 14
ADVANCED
RESEARCH IN LAW SUBJECTS

At some stage in your law studies you will be asked to write a dissertation or assignment on a topic of your own choice and for which you will need to do research. In this unit we discuss different types of research and some of the ways in which you should go about doing research. We can provide only the most basic of guidelines and you should realize right from the start that you need to work closely with the law lecturer in whose field you choose to do your research.

A READING: DECIDING ON A TOPIC

Look carefully at the following research proposals that students handed in to their law lecturers. Decide which one(s) you think are good proposals.

Proposal 1

Dear Prof Latha

I would like to find out whether one's right to privacy as regards electronic mail is the same as with ordinary mail. The way it is now, a server can read his or her clients' mail and I want to find out if one can make a case against a server when one's private affairs are somehow made known. I will look at the way in which the right to privacy is protected in our country and in the USA and make suggestions for South African legislation.

Benjamin Ndwambi

Student number 19430076

Proposal 2

DEPARTMENT OF COMMERCIAL LAW: PROF N WILLIAMS

PROPOSAL FOR PAPER ON CHEQUES AND POSTAL ORDERS:

J M MABULE: 19430088

Introduction

I.   The legal history of cheques and postal orders in South Africa.
     1.1 Earliest cases
     1.2 Current state of affairs
2.   South African cases dealing with cheques in the past ten years
3.   South African cases dealing with postal orders in the past ten years.
4.   Problems and the current state of affairs as decided by the courts.

Conclusion

References

234

Proposal 3

Dear Prof Van Niekerk

I want to work on the interaction between South Africa and the European Commission as far as the export of poisonous and dangerous atomic waste to Africa is concerned. I want to look at the history of European and American waste transport to so-called third-world countries, the role of Greenpeace and the systematic exploitation of Africa's weak, economic position by offering them money to safeguard the life-threatening leftovers of their capitalist, expansionist, industrialist and imperialist policies. I want to show to the world that Africa is not underdeveloped, but was underdeveloped by so-called first-world countries.

V N van der Merwe-Smith (Std no: 19323490)

Proposal 4

For Prof Moodley: I will work on the influence of the new constitution on the rights of gay people.

C Dlamini (19354399)

Which proposal impressed you the most? We list the most common errors that students make when they choose a topic for a research paper and you can decide which errors appear in the proposals above.

a) Some proposals do not address a **problem**: the student doesn't propose a specific problem that she would like to investigate. The study is merely a description of the *status quo* or of a specific concept or phenomenon.

b) In some proposals there is a problem, but it is so wide that it would probably take a whole team of professors to work on it for many years. The proposal is **too ambitious** and the student will quickly find that she took on more than can be handled by one person. The result is that the student then has to go back to the professor, discuss the topic again, decide which part she can reasonably deal with and start again.

c) Often the proposal is formulated in such **vague** terms that it is not possible to see what the problem is or what the scope of the work will be.

d) In some cases the student has already decided what the outcome of her investigations will be. The research problem is not open-ended anymore; the outcome is **pre-determined** and the student will look only for evidence to support this pre-determined conclusion.

235

e) Sometimes the student places **too much value** on the research paper. Students must be realistic about the role of a research paper in their studies. It is one of probably more than 10 other papers that they have to fit into a tight schedule. They will probably not be able to shake the world or right all its wrongs: science usually progresses in small steps — although the Einsteins of this world might not agree!

Can you see where the proposals given above go wrong? **Proposal 2** looks impressive, but contains no problem, **Proposal 3** implies years of research and the outcome is pre-determined. This student wants to do too much! **Proposal 4** is very vague and the topic may have been exhausted, in which case there are not too many problems left. **Proposal 1** seems the most promising: this student sees a problem and says how it will be approached. It may still be ambitious, but her supervisor will probably be able to guide the student to demarcate those areas which should be included for investigation.

> What is research? Most researchers will probably agree that the researcher sees problems, difficulties or possibilities and systematically tackles them according to the methods and in the context of a specific field or discipline.

Some researchers regard the problems identified in other fields and disciplines as insignificant or self-evident but this is often a sign of prejudice: there are no 'easy' fields of academic research. In the end, everybody works on her side of a puzzle that is changing all the time!

B TYPES OF RESEARCH

You can approach problems that you perceive in a specific field in a variety of ways. The following categories should not be seen as an exhaustive list, nor are they watertight compartments. There are studies in which all or some of the categories are simultaneously present. All types of research imply the ability to analyze and organize a large volume of material, to see connections, find a line of argument and counter argument and to maintain a logical argument in which other researchers' results are not merely listed, but integrated. We will say more about this under 4 below.

1 STUDIES THAT FOCUS STRICTLY ON THE LEGAL SYSTEM AND PRACTICE

In these studies researchers look at a problem in one or a combination of the following ways:

- A study of **current South Africa law** with theory and cases: conflicts are indicated, court decisions and the positions of other researchers are criticized and a well-argued conclusion is presented. The **purpose** is usually to suggest changes to current law.
- The **historical development** of a specific concept or practice is traced from its earliest appearance, through developments to current practice. Such studies often imply the ability to gain access to older texts or older sources from which South African law developed. The **purpose** of such studies is usually to de-mystify certain concepts and/ or to show that their current application does not fulfil their original intent, and so on.
- A specific practice and/or concept in South African law is **compared** to similar practices in other legal systems. Such studies usually imply a thorough knowledge of the other legal systems and students who know languages that are used outside South Africa are in an excellent position to write such studies. Their **purpose** is to find perspectives from other legal systems for problems that such systems may already have faced and solved.

As stated above, students can focus on one of these approaches or use all three, although that might be too ambitious! Look at the following examples:

- You perceive problems surrounding the lack of rights of access and guardianship of fathers of illegitimate children. The problem as it exists can be described in terms of current legislation and court cases. (This is usually enough material for a dissertation at LLB level.) However, you could also look at the historical development of the concept to explain why the problem arose (the **historical** perspective) and you can then look at the situation in other countries to see if they did not perhaps find a solution that can be applied in the South African system (the **comparative** perspective).
- You heard from one of your professors that people in Germany and the Netherlands are allowed to put stickers on their postboxes to say that they do not want junk mail. You want to **compare** the legislation in these countries to the situation in South Africa and make suggestions for future developments in South African law. (This is usually enough for a dissertation at LLB level.) You could go further by tracing the development of the idea that a person's post box is his/her private property (a **historical** perspective).

237

2   QUANTITATIVE OR QUALITATIVE CROSS-DISCIPLINARY STUDIES

Quantitative studies in human sciences usually emulate the methods of the natural sciences by using, among others, questionnaires, surveys and statistics to, for example, show why women who murder their husbands usually receive lighter sentences than men who murder their wives. (This is just an example – we do not claim that this is indeed the case!) Such studies are cross-disciplinary both in terms of the methods used and the sources from which data are obtained: students need to know something about creating questionnaires and interpreting statistics on the one hand, and on the other they need to be conversant with the literature in the fields of criminology, sociology and psychology. Students may also need access to court and police records! The **purpose** of such a study could be, for example, to make suggestions for rules of criminal procedure.

Qualitative studies depend on structured and unstructured group and individual interviews and on observation studies. In this case a student could do a study on the linguistic behaviour of lawyers towards clients with whom they do not share a language, that is, in situations where lawyers use interpreters during consultations with clients. The student would have to observe the interaction between client, lawyer and interpreter and conduct interviews with all these people afterwards (in as far as this is possible). Such a study is cross-disciplinary because the student should have a sound grounding in linguistics and knowledge of all the languages and qualitative research methods concerned. The **purpose** of such a study could be to make suggestions for the training of lawyers, court interpreters and judges to sensitize them to certain problematic issues of language use and translation.

3   MORE THEORETICAL, PHILOSOPHICAL STUDIES

Studies in this category are usually also cross-disciplinary because the researcher might draw on legal philosophy, or jurisprudence as it is also called, to study a phenomenon and its implications for law practice. Such a study could also include aspects mentioned under 1 (above), but the focus of the study would be wider. So-called 'hard law' or current legal practice might not even play a role in such studies. The following are examples of such studies:

- The student could analyze and criticize the education of law students by comparing the curricula that are followed at various universities and by conducting interviews to find out what law professors and law practitioners think should be the aim of law studies. The purpose of such a study would be to make suggestions (if necessary!) for the improvement of such courses.

238

- The role of the law and its 'image' in society could be investigated (by quantitative and qualitative methods) to determine how justice can be brought to even the poorest of citizens. The purpose of such a study could be to make suggestions for changes in the funding of law clinics and the training of public prosecutors and public defenders.
- The relationship between the law and the development of writing systems can be studied by investigating how oral legal systems were affected by the introduction of script and the process of 'fixing' a rule inflexibly in print. The (extremely brave) student who tackles such a project would have to be trained in both Latin and Greek and the history of law and, to make it really interesting, a few African languages and customary law as well! The purpose of such a study would be to provide insights in the development and 'transcription' of South African customary law.

The examples mentioned above form the smallest tip of an iceberg of extremely interesting topics that you could investigate!

C MATERIALS FOR RESEARCH IN LAW

Study the following extract from *Legal Research: materials and methods* by Campbell, Glasson, York and Sharpe (1988:271,272):

The Objective of Legal Research

Most legal research has as its objective *the collection of authoritative materials* relevant to the problem. What are authoritative materials? They comprise legislation in force and judicial decisions. Judicial decisions need to be sub-divided into (a) binding and (b) persuasive authorities. They are binding if they meet the following two conditions, namely:

1. They are decisions of a higher court or, sometimes, a court of co-ordinate authority in the same jurisdiction as that in which the action is being contemplated; and

2. The decision is directly relevant to the problem being re-searched. There are theoretical and practical difficulties in determining when a decision is directly relevant.

If either of these conditions is unsatisfied the decision is merely persuasive.

It may be objected that this statement of the basic objective of legal research places an undue emphasis on litigation and that the vast majority of situations in which a lawyer is consulted are situations in

---

239

which no litigation is contemplated and in which none occurs. Legal research is the foundation for good legal advice. Before advising a client a lawyer should be satisfied that, if the necessity arises, he or she will be able to persuade a court that there is a legal principle which, properly interpreted, governs the question in dispute. Poor legal research may result in advice which, at the least, is incomplete and inaccurate, and which at the worst, may be positively wrong. Quite apart from questions of professionalism, no responsible lawyer will want to compromise with mediocrity. If litigation arises unexpectedly it may be too late to remedy the miscalculations of the past. All legal advice should be given on the basis that litigation is an ever-present possibility.

What do the authors of this paragraph regard as the two major sources of *authoritative materials*? What do the authors state as the main purpose of legal research?

Now study the following extract from *Beginner's Guide for Law Students* by Kleyn and Viljoen (1995:302,303):

Legal research sounds like something very difficult and academic. But such research is required from students when resolving hypothetical problems or analysing sets of facts in assignments. In legal practice lawyers are confronted by problems rooted in reality. Often they will not have answers readily available. In many cases it will be necessary to do research in order to give an opinion, to prepare arguments or to ascertain the legal position.

A simplified step-by-step approach to legal research is now presented. It is based on the following example:

> A is divorcing her husband, B. The reason for the irretrievable breakdown of the marriage is that A has for some time been involved in a lesbian relationship with Ms C. Based on this, B claims custody of their two minor children (a son aged 9 and a daughter aged 6). B also wants to prevent A from having any contact with the children. A has approached you. She needs your advice on whether she has the right to retain custody and/or access to her children.

Would you agree that the main purpose of legal research according to Kleyn and Viljoen is the same as in the extract from Campbell and others? The research methods that are described in these two sources are focused on the type of research that you will need to do when and if you decide to become a practising lawyer. The type of research you may have to do while you study is of a different nature and has a different purpose.

A major part of **academic research** is concerned with demonstrating writing and language skills and the skillful application of academic conventions, such as the use of footnotes, a specific style of reference and a specific style of writing, called **academic writing**.

The discussion that follows will focus on those academic aspects that distinguish research at university level from research that aims at solving a real-life legal wrangle. Although the principles for research into legal problems are probably the same for students and practitioners, you should realize that academic research mostly implies a wider field of research material and far more trouble to get it down on paper!

The following materials are sources for your research paper. Depending on the topic and the type of research you need to do, these materials might feature more or less prominently in your research endeavours:

a) Sources that describe the current position in South African law: legislation, reports of cases and regulations in the *Government Gazette*.
b) Discussions and criticism of current South African law: law textbooks, law encyclopedias and law journals. Sometimes it might also be useful to look for publications that contain papers read at national and international conferences.
c) Unpublished research in the form of LLM dissertations and LLD theses. Find out if the law faculty where you are studying has its own collection of such research or whether these documents are kept in the library. The topics may not be directly applicable to your area of study, but the references and bibliographies in these studies are invaluable.
d) Publications on the law systems, legislation and court cases of other countries.
e) Historical and traditional oral sources that provide insight into the historical development of the law. These can range from current word-of-mouth reports by senior citizens to handwritten manuscripts copied by monks in medieval times. However, it is doubtful whether students at LLB level should be so bold as to venture into research that requires sources of this kind.
f) Material in newspapers, medical journals, police records and encyclo-pedias, depending on your topic. Your subject advisor in the library and law professors will probably be able to give you guidance in this regard.

Make full use of the library resources. If there is a subject advisor for law students in the library, talk to her/him about **inter-library loans**. Most libraries can order copies of articles or books if these materials are not available in your library. You need to start collecting your material early, because it takes time for the library to track it down.

Another valuable source could be CD ROM and the Internet (as mentioned in units 2 and 13).

D GETTING STARTED, KEEPING AT IT AND REVISING THE FINAL DOCUMENT

It is difficult to give general hints for the writing of a research paper because like study methods, research practices differ from one person to the next. Even experienced researchers will say that they 'always do it like that, but this new project of theirs is totally different'. So the methods and procedures change depending on the topic, the researcher, the materials available, the amount of guidance provided by the academic supervisor and so on. What follows should be seen as suggestions and hints, not rigid prescriptions.

STEP 1: ASK THE QUESTION

In 1 above we said that your topic should be formulated around a problem. One of the ways in which you can get yourself started is by formulating your topic as a question. If the problem seems too complex to be formulated as one question, you could try to break it down into smaller questions. This exercise will give you some idea of the point at which you should start. It will also make explicit the 'answers' or pre-determined solutions you may have in the back of your mind.

It is not wrong to have pre-determined solutions or preconceived ideas about the outcome of your research, as long as you are aware of these solutions and ideas and as long as you do not exclude any other possible solutions and ideas. It is dishonest to decide beforehand what your conclusions are going to be and to then look only for the evidence that proves your point. You will have ideas about the direction that your research should take but you should keep an open mind as to other points of view (and you should include them in your dissertation) and be prepared to change the direction in which you were going if the evidence dictates it.

Write down in full sentences what the problem of your research is and how you are going to tackle it. Use the first person (*I* will start by ...) and write in simple language — your purpose is not to write an academic essay at this stage. Once you have written down what you intend doing, you can break down the work into a manageable plan of action, for example:

In this paper I want to find out why attorneys seem to interrupt more often those witnesses whose language they don't understand and who communicate by means of interpreters. When our class attended a court hearing this seemed to me to be the case. I want to sit in on court proceedings at least once a week in the next month and keep count of the times that interpreters are needed, note the procedure that is used (who speaks first, when the interpreter speaks and when the witness speaks) and count the number of times that witnesses are interrupted, why and when they are interrupted and the role of the judge/ magistrate in this process. I will then look at sociolinguistic studies by Lakoff and Schlegoff and Sacks about the language of the courtroom and turn-taking in conversations. I will try to find an explanation for the interruptions (if any) by looking at the relative status of lawyer, witness and interpreter in the courtroom. Finally I will make suggestions as to how these insights could be incorporated in the training of law students and how they could affect South African rules of procedure.

(Please remember that this topic is entirely fictitious!)

By simply stating in active sentences what you intend doing, you have summarized both the content, method and organization of your study. You can now proceed to step 2.

STEP 2: DRAW UP A PROVISIONAL TABLE OF CONTENTS

Writing a dissertation is not like writing an essay — you need sub-headings to guide your writing and to move the main argument forward. There are very few people who can sit down and write coherently for pages and pages without headings. Your ideal should be to have a heading for each paragraph. You can always take out some of these headings and streamline your writing later on.

In her book *Effective legal writing* Block (1992:215) suggests the following, very basic outline for students' research papers:

Sample Outline

1. Introduction
   A. Why you chose this subject
   B. What you intend to do with this subject
II. History
   A. The genesis of your subject
   B. The changes that have occurred during its development
   C. Why it has developed into its present state

243

II. Status quo
   A. Its advantages
   B. Its defects
   C. Why it cannot (should not) continue
IV. Changes suggested (attempted) by others
   A. Advantages
   B. Defects
V. Your ideas for change
   A. Advantages
   B. Defects
VI. Conclusion
   A. Predictions
   B. Summary of ideas presented in paper

Depending on your topic, this outline can be adapted to most types of research in law subjects. You need to make the outline specific to your topic. You should also make a point of studying LLM dissertations and LLD theses so that you can see the types of headings used in these research documents. Quite often you might find that there is a heading which looks at comparable legislation or case law in other countries. Such a heading would probably fit in between III and IV of the outline above.

You can also see how Block's outline will be useful for the more traditional types of law research where you have to discuss the *status quo* in terms of existing legislation and current cases and the changes suggested or attempted (IV) would probably come from textbooks and law journals.

Study the topic on the interruption of witnesses' testimony in court above. Block's outline could be made specific like this:

I Introduction
   A Preliminary observations on courtroom behaviour.
   B Why do lawyers interrupt witnesses and interpreters?
II History
   A The role and purpose of interpreters in court
   B Language ability of lawyers and interpreters
   C Courtroom procedures and turn-taking
III Status quo
   A The role of the current constitution and language rights
   B Current aspects of linguistic behaviour included in law curricula
   C Observations of courtroom behaviour
IV Changes suggested (attempted) by others
   A Analysis of courtroom behaviour by Lakoff
   B Attempts to redress imbalances in State of California courts (USA)
   C The right to justice in the mother tongue in Australia.

244

V Suggestions for change in South African courts
   A Applicability of Californian model
   B Applicability of Australian model
   C Words of warning regarding extra-national models
VI Conclusion
   A Suggestions for changes to South African procedural rules.
   B Suggestions for changes in the training of law students.
   C Summary of the main argument.

STEP 3: KEEP AT IT
OR
A RESEARCH PAPER IS NOT WRITTEN IN AN EVENING

Some of the most common mistakes that you should avoid when you have to write a research paper are the following:

- **Do not** start a week before the closing date.
- **Do not** tell yourself that you first have to read all the material before you can start writing. You need to do some reading, some writing, a little reading again, adapt existing writing and add to it, do more reading, and so on.
- **Do not** write a bit and then leave the paper for a week or two. If you look at the paper and work on it regularly, the main argument remains in your head and your subconscious will work on it. If you leave it, you not only forget what it was actually about, you'll also become anxious because it's lying there gathering dust ...
- **Do not** think that you need to start at the beginning and continue towards the end. You can write the different sections in random order and then link them to make a coherent whole during the final editing stages.
- **Do not** leave the references or bibliography until the end. Note the details of the different types of sources: books, contributions to books, journal articles, legislation and court cases must all be included in a list of references. You might have to list court cases and statutes separately — ask your lecturer how this should be done. Try to keep a full record of all the sources you use the minute you start reading them. There is nothing more frustrating than having to rush around the library looking for a book that somebody else took out, or trying to find a source with only the surname of one of the writers or only part of the title.

STEP 4: EDITING AND PROOFREADING

If you are writing your paper in a language that is not your own, you should plan to have the paper edited either by a fellow student who is good at this sort of thing or perhaps by a professional editor. Some educational institutions offer such services to staff members and students. Remember that a first-language speaker is not necessarily the best person for this job; you need somebody with experience of editing.

Before and after you give the paper to an editor, you should edit and review it extensively:

- **While** you are writing, you should re-read the text and work on clarity of expression and logical organization. Decide on a specific numbering system **and stick to it**. Check for consistency of style, headings and referencing. Make a point to re-read and edit the whole text whenever you continue with your writing. Remember, **writing is rewriting**!
- **After** you have written a first draft you should check for obvious aspects like spelling, punctuation, footnotes and referencing. Check, in particular, that you have the full details of all the sources that you use in the text. Once again, check consistency.
- **After** the editor has made changes you should read the whole text again to see whether you agree with those changes.

Proofreading is a skill that only a few people develop. Even fewer people can successfully proofread their own writing. If you work on a computer you can do a spellcheck which should remove the most obvious errors. However, the programme will not pick up instances where you used *there* instead of *their* or *witch* instead of *which*.

The problem with proofreading your own work is that you know what it is supposed to say, so you focus on the meaning and do not pick up small typing errors. You could arrange with one of your friends to swop your papers and proofread each other's work.

Whatever technique you use, it is vital that you do proofread your work. Lecturers allocate marks for the technical aspects (footnotes, referencing) of research papers as well as their presentation. It is not enough to have brilliant ideas: they must also be packaged neatly and legibly!

E   A FINAL WORD ON REFERENCING

It is common knowledge that you must refer to or acknowledge the sources that you use in your research paper. You should ask the law lecturer who will be your research supervisor to give you a style sheet or guidelines which describe the referencing style that she prefers. As a general rule it can be said that law texts use mainly **footnotes** and sometimes **endnotes** to acknowledge the sources referred to in the text. You should check with your lecturer whether there is a prescribed style you should follow. Check your referencing system against LLM dissertations and LLD theses that were completed in the faculty where you study.

Study the text on the next page and the way in which footnotes are used. The format below is generally used in footnotes. The numbers in this list correspond to numbers written in the margin of the extract provided below the list. (From Van Wyk 1991:72.)

- Cases are referred to by their full title.
- Articles in journals are usually referred to by giving the author, the title of the article, the date of publication, the name of the journal with its volume and number, the specific page being referred to and the first (and sometimes last page number) of the article. (See 1.)
- Books are referred to by giving the author, the title of the book, the year of publication and, where a specific point is referred to, the page number where it is made. (See 2.)
- Sections of statutes are referred to by the abbreviation 'sec'. (See 3 and refer to unit 7 in this regard.)

Footnotes in law texts do not act only as a referencing system but also provide authoritative support to an argument. Therefore the author might write in the footnote: 'See ...' or 'See also ...' and list many sources that support her argument. Similarly the author might point out counter arguments in a footnote by writing: 'See, however, ...'. Some authors also use footnotes to mention a matter that has no direct bearing on the main line of argument, but should be taken into account for some or other reason. (See 4 in the margin of the text on the next page.)

Many authors make use of Latin words such as the following:

- *op. cit. (opera citandi)* which means that the work has been referred to previously and the current reference is the same;
- *idem* which means 'the same source referred to previously';
- *ibid (ibidem)* means 'at the same point in the same work referred to previously';
- *Supra* which means 'referred to above'.

However, these Latin terms do not appear very often anymore.

Check with your lecturer which style she prefers and make sure that you use it *consistently*. Most supervisors do not mind that you follow a style slightly different from the one they prefer, as long as you use it consistently.

247

All the early planning measures concentrated on town planning, which is concerned with the urban environment and ignores the greater physical environment. This fact was not recognized until 1947, when the Natural Resources Development Council was established to

plan and promote the better and more effectively coordinated exploitation, development and use of the natural resources of South Africa.[6]

This initiative was followed by the introduction of guide plans in 1971[7] and the publication of the National Physical Development Plan in 1975,[8] neither of which has been entirely successful.[9]

Although statutory planning provisions and particularly town planning measures have been in existence in South Africa for some sixty years, the acknowledgment of a planning law discipline has only recently come to the fore. Very little has been published on it, and since it is not generally taught as a separate subject in law schools, and no general principles exist, it can be accepted that the law relating to planning in South Africa is still very much in its infancy.

2 A definition of planning law

As with most young disciplines, the first aspect requiring attention is a definition or description. It is no easy task to provide a definition where boundaries have not been clearly drawn,[10] a problem which has beset many new disciplines, the most notable of which is environmental law.[11]

Planning law at the national, regional and local levels has as its purpose the creation of an environment which is conducive to the health, safety and welfare of society as a whole.[12]

---

[6] This council was established in terms of the Natural Resources Development Act 51 of 1947. Sec 3 provides for the objectives of the council.

[7] Initially the guide plans operated by way of ministerial and cabinet authority only. The Physical Planning and Utilization of Resources Amendment Act 73 of 1975 provided a statutory basis for the provision of guide plans. See further JJ van Tonder 'The guide plan and its application in practice' 1978 *IMIESA* 12–15; SC Jaspan 'A critical evaluation of the guide plan procedure' 1979 *Municipal Engineer* 9–11; Page and Rabie (1983) 445 473–475.

[8] For more detail on the plan and its provisions see WF Visagie 'The place of the NPDP in national planning' 1976 *Beplanning* 29–36; Page and Rabie (1983) 445 447–458.

[9] The National Physical Development Plan was not practically feasible and the guide plan procedure has been halted by the introduction of the new Physical Planning bill GN 77 GG 12280 of 1990-02-09.

[10] This has occurred not only in South Africa, for, in the Introduction to *Planning law in Western Europe* (2ed 1986) 1 JF Garner and NP Gravells (eds) state that "the principal difficulty which appears at the commencement of any discussion on planning law, is to ascertain a definition of the term 'planning'."

[11] MA Rabie *South African environmental legislation* (1976) 3; DV Cowen 'Toward distinctive principles of South African environmental law: some jurisprudential perspectives and a role for legislation' 1989 *THRHR* 3–30.

[12] See the purpose of town planning as set out in the ordinances, namely the Town Planning Ordinance 27 1949 (N) sec 40(1); the Townships Ordinance 9 of 1969 (O) sec 25(1); the Land Use Planning Ordinance 15 of 1985 (C) sec 5(1) and the Town-planning and Townships Ordinance 15 of 1986 (T) sec 19. See also JB Wadley 'The emerging social function context for land use planning in the United States' 1988 *Washburn Law Journal* 22 25.

REVISION UNIT 1

The purpose of this unit is to help you to revise the work you did in units 1–6. Because this unit is structured in the form of a test, you should try to duplicate test conditions when attempting it. You should not take longer than one hour to complete the exercises. All the exercises are based on the work you did in previous units. Refer to unit 12 and skimread the hints on the writing of tests and examinations before you start.

Remember the following:

- Skimread the test and decide how much time you need to complete the various sections, then stick to that time allocation.
- Look carefully at the mark allocation so that you do not write more than is necessary on each question.
- Read the instructions with care.

QUESTION 1: READING COMPREHENSION

Read the following extract from *South African Family Law* by Cronjé and Heaton (1999: 49–54) and then attempt to answer the questions which follow.

VOID AND VOIDABLE MARRIAGES

The distinction between void and voidable marriages
A void marriage is one which has simply never come into existence and the position is thus exactly as it would have been had the "marriage" never been contracted.[1] A voidable marriage remains   5
in force and has all the normal legal consequences of a valid marriage until is dissolved by a court order[2].

1 Sinclair assisted by Heaton 396; Lee and Honoré par 48 (i).
2 Sinclair assisted by Heaton 401; Lee and Honoré par 48(iii).

249

A marriage that is void *ab initio* (since its inception) does not have the legal consequences of a valid marriage and does not affect the status of the parties because they are not legally married to each other and thus retain the status of unmarried persons.[3] Although a court order is not required to declare such a marriage void, it is desirable from the point of view of legal certainty that such a marriage is formally declared void, and declaratory orders are usually applied for.[4]

10

15

By deciding that a marriage has been void since its inception, the court merely confirms the existing position and thus its ruling is merely declaratory. The court does not exercise any discretion whatsoever in this connection.[5] .

The principle that a void marriage has none of the consequences of a valid marriage is subject to certain statutory and common-law qualifications. Lee and Honoré[6] therefore correctly point out that the distinction between void and voidable marriages should not be exaggerated. The statutory qualifications to the principle of voidness are contained in the Marriage Act 25 of 1961.

20

25

Firstly, as was pointed out above,[7] a marriage solemnised by a person who was not a competent marriage officer is null and void, but in terms of section 6 the Minister of Home Affairs may ratify the marriage in which case it is validated.

Secondly, section 26(1) of the Marriage Act provides that a boy under the age of 18 years and a girl under the age of 15 years cannot enter into a valid marriage without the permission of the Minister of Home Affairs. A marriage concluded without the minister's consent is null and void but section 26(2) empowers the minister to ratify the marriage subsequently, in which case it will be valid.

30

35

---

3 The result of this is eg that no joint estate exists, the reciprocal duty of support does not apply, the parties will not inherit intestate from each other, children born of the marriage are illegitimate, the spouses are free to enter into another marriage, and so on. The innocent party to a void marriage may, however, have an action for satisfaction against the other party. See eg *Arendse v Rhode* 1989 1 SA 763 (C) where the defendant had told the plaintiff before their "marriage" that he was a divorced man while in actual fact he was still married to someone else. The plaintiff was successful in her claim for satisfaction. See also *Cronjé and Heaton Casebook on Family Law* 6-1-66.

4 Lee and Honoré par 48(i).

5 "[T]he decree is merely declaratory of, and does not alter the existing status of the parties. The object of the decree, however, is to place on record by means of a judgment *in rem* the fact that the marriage entered into by the parties was void *ab initio* and gave rise to no legal consequences": per Searle J in *Ex parte Oxton* 1948 1 SA 1011 (C) 1015.

6 Par 48(ii). See also De Waal and Van Heerden 1987 *TSAR* 255.

The common-law qualification relates to the putative marriage. In the case of a putative marriage the marriage is still void but it has certain of the consequences of a valid marriage.[8]

A voidable marriage is a valid marriage although grounds are present either before, or at the time of concluding the marriage, on the basis of which the court can be requested to dissolve the marriage. A voidable marriage thus does affect the status of the parties because they are legally married. For example, the parties have equal capacity in respect of the joint estate if they are married in community of property and the children born or conceived during the course of the marriage are legitimate. 35

40

The effect of a decree of annulment of a voidable marriage is retroactive, which means that all the consequences of the marriage are extinguished as from its solemnisation.[9] The status of the parties changes so that they are in the same position as if the marriage never took place. Formerly it was uncertain whether the children born of a voidable marriage were retroactively made extra-marital. [10] The Children's Status Act 82 of 1987 has now brought certainty in this respect. Section 6 of this Act provides that the status of a child conceived or born of a voidable marriage is not affected by the annulment of the marriage. In section 7 it is further provided that a voidable marriage shall not be annulled until the court concerned has enquired into and considered the safeguarding of the interests of any minor or dependent child of that marriage. Furthermore the provisions of section 6 of the Divorce Act 70 of 1979[11] and of section 4 of the Mediation in Certain Divorce Matters Act 24 of 1987[12] apply *mutatis mutandis* in respect of any such child as if the proceedings in question were proceedings in a divorce action and the administration of the marriage was the granting of a decree of divorce. 45

50

55

60

---

7 See ch 3 above.

8 See 55-56 below.

9 Lee and Honoré par 48(iii); Sinclair assisted by Heaton 402.

10 See Van der Vyver and Joubert 518; Sinclair assisted by Heaton 403; Lee and Honoré par 48 (iii), but see also Rabie 1965 *THRHR* 46.

11 In terms of the Divorce Act s 6 the court will not grant a divorce unless it is satisfied that the provisions made or contemplated with regard to the welfare of any minor or dependent children of the marriage are satisfactory or the best that can be effected in the circumstances: see ch 10 below.

12 In terms of the Mediation in Certain Divorce Matters Act s 4 a family advocate may be appointed in divorce proceedings to institute an enquiry to enable her to furnish the court with a report and recommendations on any matter concerning the welfare of a minor or dependent child of the marriage.

The provisions of sections 8(l) and (2) of the Divorce Act in regard to the rescission, suspension or variation of maintenance orders or an order relating the custody or guardianship of, or access to, a child, also apply to the annulment of a voidable marriage.   65 A reference in any law to such orders or their rescission, suspension or variation under the Divorce Act, shall be construed as a reference also to such orders in respect of the annulment of a voidable marriage.[18]

Although the effect of a decree of annulment of a voidable   70 marriage is retroactive, transactions which the married parties entered into with third parties before the annulment will not after annulment be regarded as though the parties were unmarried when the transactions were entered into. This is so because the annulment of a voidable marriage should not affect the interests of third   75 parties.[14]   75

It is important to distinguish clearly between annulment of a voidable marriage and granting a divorce. As has already been indicated, a marriage is voidable on the strength of circumstances which were present before or at the time of contracting the marriage. A divorce, on the other hand, is granted on the strength of   80 circumstances that developed during the marriage. As the Divorce Act 70 of 1979 does not apply to the annulment of a voidable marriage, the court cannot make an order for maintenance in respect of one of the parties, forfeiture of patrimonial benefits, or a redistribution of the assets of the spouses married out of community of property.[15]   85

Grounds for voidness of a marriage

The court is empowered to declare a marriage null and void on the following grounds:[16]

13 Children's Status Act 82 of 1987 ss 7 (2) and (3).

14 In this regard reference may be made to the remarks of Steyn CJ in *Van Zyl v Credit Corporatiom of SA Ltd* 1960 4 SA 582 (A) 590 in connection with the setting aside of a voidable contract. "Dat partye teruggeplaas word in die stand van sake voordat die betrokke regshandeling aangegaan is, asof dit nie aangegaan was nie, beteken nie sonder meer dat die handeling regtens altyd nietig was of nooit met enige regsgevolg bestaan het nie." (Where parties are returned to the position they were in before a transaction was entered into, as if the transaction was never concluded, it does not mean that the transaction was void or never had any legal consequences.) The chief justice's observation was made in connection with a voidable contract, but it is a universal truth which doubtless also holds good for the voidable marriage. The court further held that the interests acquired by a bona fide third party before the cancellation of a voidable *contract*, are not upset by the setting aside of the contract.

15 See ch 10 below.

16 The nullity of the marriage is absolute, in other words either of the parties or an interested third party can raise it even after the death of one of the parties: Sinclair assisted by Heaton 397.

1 Non-compliance with the formal requirements for a valid marriage[17]

The following situations could, for example, arise:
  (a) The parties did not submit their identity documents or the prescribed affidavit to the marriage officer.   90
  (b) The marriage was solemnised by a person who was not a competent marriage officer.
  (c) A girl under 15 years of age or a boy under 18 years of age married without having obtained the written consent of the Minister of Home Affairs.   95
  (d) No witnesses were present at the marriage.

2 Non-compliance with the material requirements for a valid marriage

The material requirements for a valid marriage were discussed in chapter 3. Here the following situations could, for example, arise: 100
  (a) Both parties are of the same sex.
  (b) One of the parties is already married to someone else.
  (c) The parties are related to each other within the prohibited degrees of blood relationship (consanguinity) or affinity.
  (d) One of the parties has not yet reached the age of puberty. 105
  (e) One of the parties was mentally ill at the time of contracting the marriage.

Grounds for the voidability of a marriage

A marriage can be voidable owing to the presence of one or more of the following circumstances: 110

1 Minority

This issue is discussed fully in chapter 3 and is only mentioned here for the sake of completeness.

2 *Stuprum* (sexual intercourse before marriage)

Extra-marital intercourse with a third party before the marriage   115
normally does not affect the validity of the marriage.[18] Even where an extra-marital child was born as a result of *stuprum* before the

---

17 The formal requirements for a valid marriage are discussed in ch 3 above. Lee and Honore par 50 fn argue convincingly that the courts ought to interpret the formal requirements *in favorem matrimonii* and ought only to find that a marriage is void when a "material" formal requirement is not met. Material formalities concern the identification of the parties to the marriage, the existence of *consensus* between the parties and the participation of the state and community in the establishment of the marriage, but not those provisions which only ensure that an orderly and dignified marriage ceremony takes place. See also *Ex parte Dow* 1987 3 SA 829 (D).
18 *Gabergas v Gabergas* 1921 EDL 279; *Reyneke v Reyneke* 1927 OPD 130.

marriage, the validity of the marriage is not affected.[19] It is
only if the wife was at the time of marriage, unknown to her
husband, pregnant with another man's child that her husband   120
can apply for the annulment of the marriage.[20] There obviously is
a vast difference between the birth of an extra-marital child before
marriage and pregnancy at the time of marriage, because in the
latter case the presumption *Pater est quem nuptiae demonstrant*
comes into operation, with the result that the husband can be   125
held responsible for maintenance of another man's child.

The fact that the husband himself had intercourse with his wife
before the marriage does not affect his right to have the marriage
annulled, as long as he did not know at the time of contracting
the marriage that his wife was pregnant as a result of having had   130
intercourse with another man.[21]

If the husband accepts the wife's pregnancy, and condones her
actions, he loses the remedy.[22, 23]

If the husband cannot discharge the onus of proving pre-nuptial
stuprum, or if his action may possibly be defeated by knowledge   135
or acquiescence, he can, instead of suing for annulment, sue for
divorce on the ground of irretrievable breakdown of the marriage.
It may be easier to prove irretrievable breakdown and to obtain
a divorce, but he then runs the risk of being ordered to pay
maintenance to his wife and an order for forfeiture of benefits   140
under section 9 of the Divorce Act 70 of 1979 may be made
against him.[24] Despite the fact that her pregnancy was the cause
for the breakdown of the marriage, the wife can also institute
an action for divorce on the ground of irretrievable
breakdown.   145

3 Material misrepresentation

The effect of a material misrepretation on the validity of a marriage
was discussed in chapter 3 and is only mentioned here for the
sake of completeness.

19 *Stander v Stander* 1929 AD 349; *Cronjé and Heaton Casebook on Family Law*
    66-67. See also Sinclair assisted by Heaton 394 and Lee and Honoré par 55.
20 *Smith v Smith* 1936 CPD 125.
21 *Reyneke v Aynehe* 1927 CPD 130; *Smith v Smith* 1936 CPD 125.
22 *Kilian v Kilian* 1908 EDC 377.
23 It has been argued that the remedy is based on fraud (Sinclair assisted by Heaton
    395) but it is perhaps better to say that it is based on mistake (error). The error
    refers to a fundamental feature of marriage, namely that the wife should not be
    pregnant by another man. If the remedy is based on misrepresentation/fraud it
    would mean that the husband could not rely on it if the wife herself did not know
    of the pregnancy, and according to Lee and Honoré par 55 fn this is not the
    position.

4 Impotence

Impotence is the inability to have sexual intercourse. The marriage is voidable when one spouse proves that the other was impotent before the marriage and remains impotent, and that she was unaware of the impotence at the time of entering into the marriage.[25] The 150 plaintiff cannot succeed if she was aware of the impotence[26] or condoned it,[27] or if the impotence is temporary or probably curable.[28]

The impotent spouse may apply for the annulment of the marriage on the basis of his own impotence, provided that he 155 was unaware of the impotence at the time of contracting the marriage.[29]

5 Sterility

Sterility must be distinguished from impotence. When a person is able to have intercourse but cannot procreate children and is 160 thus infertile, that person is sterile.

In *Venter v Venter*[30] it was held that if one of the parties at the time of marriage fraudulently concealed that she was sterile, the other party may have the marriage annulled. In this case the wife knew that she was sterile due to an operation she had undergone, 165 but she concealed this fact from her husband. The husband's action to have the marriage rescinded was rejected because he did not allege in his pleadings that his wife had fraudulently concealed her sterility. In other words, the court held that the action rests not on the mere presence of sterility but on the 170 fraudulent concealment thereof.

In *Van Niekerk v Van Niekerk*,[31] on the other hand, it was held that the mere fact of sterility renders the marriage voidable, regardless of whether or not it was fraudulently concealed. This at least holds good where the procreation of children was 175 an express or implicit aim of the marriage.

24 Sinclair assisted by Heaton 411 and see ch 10 below.
25 *Wells v Dean-Willcocks* 1924 CPD 89; *Smith v Smith* 1961 3 SA 359 (SR); *Joshua v Joshua* 1961 1 SA 455 (GW); *B v B* 1964 1 SA 717 (T); *D v D* 1964 3 SA 598 (E).
26 *Smith v Smith* 19613 SA 359 (SR).
27 *Wells v Dean-Willcocks* I924 CPD 89.
28 Sinclair assisted by Heaton 390.
29 *W v W* 1959 4 SA 183 (C); Cronjé and Heaton *Casebook on Family Law* 68-71. Usually the impotent spouse will have little difficulty in convincing the court that the marriage has broken down irretrievably as a result of his impotence and he would thus succeed in a divorce action. A divorce will also be granted if the marriage has broken down irretrievably as a result of impotence which developed during the course of the marriage.
30 1949 4 SA 123 (W); Cronjé and Heaton *Casebook on Family Law* 72-75.
31 1959 4 SA 658 (GW); Cronjé and Heaton *Casebook on Family Law* 75-80.

> The approach adopted in *Venter's* case is preferred to that in *Van Niekerk's* case:[32] it is not the mere fact of sterility, but the fraudulent concealment thereof which should found the action.[33]
>
> 32 Although our common-law writers did not distinguish clearly between impotence and sterility, *Venter's* case accords with the position at common law: see Scholtens 1961 *SALJ* 159 347; Van der Walt 1960 *THRHR* 220. Lee and Honoré par 54 fn 2 submit that *Van Niekerk's* case should not be followed because it is not based on authority, and also for policy considerations. Where childlessness has rendered a marriage unhappy, the marriage has usually irretrievably broken down and an action for divorce is the obvious remedy.
>
> 33 However, one can also raise valid objections to acceptance of fraudulent concealment of sterility as a ground for the annulment of a marriage. Hunt 1963 *SALJ* 107 puts it clearly: "Why should fraud turn the scales? It is true that this concealment seems particularly dishonest, but is it any more dishonest or shocking than fraudulent concealment of cancer, insanity or previous prostitution?" See also Lee and Honoré par 54 fn 2.

a) What would you guess the extract to be about when looking at its title? Use your own words.   (2)

b) What is the purpose of the reference to the Marriage Act in line 25?   (2)

c) Name two grounds for voidness of a marriage.   (3)

d) Explain the difference between void and voidable marriages.   (2)

e) Give three examples of marriages where the marriage is void because of the parties' non-compliance with the formal requirements of a valid marriage.   (2)

f) Distinguish between the cases of *Venter v Venter* and *Van Niekerk v Van Niekerk* regarding the concealment of sterility.   (3)

g) What is the essential difference between the annulment of a marriage and the granting of a divorce?   (1)

h) Study lines 175–179 carefully. What is the writer's point of view regarding the question whether the mere fact of sterility renders the marriage voidable? Are we given the reason why the writer holds this point of view? Explain.   (3)

Now read the following extract from the same textbook (Cronjé and Heaton 1999: 57–61):

256

THE INVARIABLE CONSEQUENCES OF MARRIAGE

Marriage has far-reaching consequences regarding the person and property of the spouses. Some consequences come into being automatically by operation of law and cannot be excluded by the parties. They are generally referred to as the invariable consequences 5 of marriage. Other consequences can however be agreed upon by the parties (usually beforehand in an antenuptial contract), and these are known as the variable consequences of marriage. The variable consequences mainly affect the estates of the spouses and their control in this regard, while the invariable consequences 10 of the marriage mainly concern the person of the spouses.[1] This chapter discusses the invariable consequences of marriage.

Status of spouses

Upon marrying, the parties gain the status of "being married". This entails *inter alia* the following: 15

(a) Neither spouse is allowed to marry anyone else while the marriage subsists.

(b) New impediments to marriage, which continue after the dissolution of the marriage, arise as a result of the relationships by affinity which are created by marriage.[3] 20

(c) A right of intestate succession is created between the spouses.[4]

(d) Extra-marital children born of the parties before the marriage are legitimated as a result of the marriage.[5]

(e) Both parents become the guardians of the legitimate children born of the marriage.[6] 25

(f) The parties' capacity to act may be affected.[7]

(g) The wife can take the husband's family name, (surname) or add it to her own surname should she want to.[8]

---

1 The reciprocal duty of support between spouses, which comes into existence when the marriage is concluded, is an example of an invariable patrimonial consequence of marriage.

2 See ch 3 above.

3 Ch 3 above.

4 Intestate Succession Act 81 of 1987 s 1 (1) (a) and (c).

5 Children's Status Act 82 of 1987 s 4.

6 Ch 11 below and the Guardianship Act 192 of 1993 s 1(1).

7 If the spouses are married out of community of property the marriage does not affect their capacity to act. On the effect of the Matrimonial Property Act 88 of 1984 on the capacity of spouses who are married in community of property see ch 7 below.

8 The wife is not obliged to adopt the surname of her husband — Births and Deaths Registration Act 51 of 1992 s 26. See further below 80.

Attaining majority

A spouse who is a minor at the time of marriage attains majority   30
through the marriage and consequently acquires full capacity to act.[9]
   Should the marriage be dissolved by death or divorce before
the spouse turns 21, the capacity to act bestowed by marriage is
retained. For example, neither the husband nor the wife will
require parental consent to enter into a second marriage.[10]   35

Consortium omnis vitae

Marriage creates a *consortium omnis vitae* between the spouses.[11]
The concept *consortium* does not lend itself to a precise definition.
One of the most acceptable legal descriptions of *consortium* can
be found in *Grobbelaar v Havenga*[12] where it was said that the   40
consortium between husband and wife is "an abstraction
comprising the totality of a number of rights, duties and
advantages accruing to the spouses of a marriage". This totality
comprises *inter alia* "[c]ompanionship, love, affection, comfort,
mutual services, sexual intercourse[13] – all of which belong to   45
marriage. In *Peter v Minister of Law and Order*[14] it was said that
the word "*consortium*" is used "as an umbrella word for all the
legal rights of one spouse to the company, affection, services and
support of the other".[15] It is clear that one cannot formulate an
exhaustive list of objects of the rights emanating from marriage.   50
All the objects of all the rights emanating from a marriage can
be collectively grouped under the concept *consortium*. These
include not only the right to "comfort, society and services"
but also rights such as those to maintenance, care of the
household, and so on. Material as well as immaterial things   55
can therefore be part of the objects grouped under *consortium*.[16]

---

9 On the difference between the Afrikaans concepts "mondigheid" and
   "meerderjarigheid" ("majority") see *Meyer v The Master* 1935 SWA 3.

10 Act 25 of 1961 s 24(2).

11 The concept originated in D 23.2.1. Generally on the meaning of the concept
   consortium see Church 1979 *THRHR* 376. See also Robinson 1991 *THRHR* 508.

12 1964 3 SA 522 (N) per Harcourt J at 525; see also Cronjé and Heaton *Casebook
   on Family Law* 97-100.

13 At 525E where the court quotes from *Best v Samuel Box Co Ltd* 1957 2 KB 639
   665.

14 1990 4 SA 6 (E).

15 9F. See also *Rattigan v Chief Immigration Officer, Zimbabwe* 1995 2 SA 182 (ZSQ
   (also reported in 1995 1 BUR I (ZS)).

16 See eg *King v King* 1947 2 SA 517 (D); *Bruwer v Joubert* 1966 3 SA 334 (A); *Peter v
   Minister* (A) *Law and Order* 1990 4 SA 6 (E).

Perhaps *consortium* should be described as a number of legal objects of the same kind rather than as rights, duties and benefits. The *consortium* is thus a collection of a number of legal objects of a particular type of right.[17]   60

The *consortium* between the spouses is primarily protected in an indirect manner by the threat of divorce. In other words, spouses are not entitled to enforce companionship, "togetherness", and so on by means of a court order, but they have recourse to a divorce action as a remedy when the marital relationship is no longer   65 normal due to the absence of these aspects of the *consortium*, and there is no reasonable prospect of the restoration of a normal marital relationship.[18]

However, a divorce action protects not only a spouse's rights regarding the objects of the *consortium*, but also other rights.   70 Thus for example, physical or mental abuse[19] indicates that the marital relationship is no longer normal. In first place, the abuse is an infringement on the right of physical integrity of the injured spouse which can render the violent spouse liable in terms of criminal law and/or private law. The violent spouse may for example be charged 75 with assault, or be sued in delict for damages, or the injured spouse may invoke the provisions of the Prevention of Family Violence Act 133 of 1993 to obtain an interdict against him or her.[20] Secondly, one can argue that the same conduct also infringes the right to *consortium*. Abuse is in conflict with the duty of 'comfort,   80 society and services'. By committing abuse a spouse in fact destroys the *consortium*.

The personality rights of a spouse must be distinguished from the right to *consortium*. When a third party infringes the *consortium* by adultery, enticement or harbouring, a claim for satisfaction   85

17 *Contra* Sonnekus 239, but see PJJ Olivier *Huldigingsbundel, Daniel Pont* 272 *et seq* as well as Hahlo and Kahn *Legal System* 78-79.
18 Divorce Act 70 of 1979 s 4; see further ch 10 below.
19 *Holland v Holland* 1975 3 SA 553 (A) is an example of a case of mental cruelty. The wife made life unbearable for her husband after she had joined the Jehovah's Witnesses.
20 Because of criticism of the Prevention of Family Violence Act, the Domestic Violence Act 116 of 1998, which is wider in scope and protects more victims of domestic violence, was promulgated. It is hoped that this Act will soon come into operation. It should further be noted that, at common law, rape of a wife by her husband was not recognised as a crime. The Prevention of Family Violence Act s 5 now provides that a husband may be convicted of raping his wife. The new Domestic Violence Act retains this provision.

against that third party can be instituted on the ground of *iniuria*.[21]
As far as the position of the spouses *inter se* is concerned, it must be
pointed out that the normal delictual actions cannot be instituted
by a spouse[22] on the ground that his or her right to *consortium*
has been violated by the other spouse. A spouse can also not   90
obtain an interdict to prevent the other spouse from committing
adultery.[23]

To summarise, *consortium* can be legally expressed as the
objects of rights. The rights perhaps do not precisely fit the
traditional classification of rights.[24] However, it would be   95
unscientific to deny the existence of a right simply because it
did not exactly fit the traditional classification of rights according
to their objects. Hahlo and Kahn[25] classify these rights as so-called
rights to 'domestic relations'. The uncertainty about the category

21 *Mulock-Bentley v Curtoys* 1935 OPD 8. In *Potgieter v Potgieter* 1959 1 SA 194 (W);
    Strydom v Saayman 1949 2 SA 736 (T) and *Viviers v Kilian* 1927 AD 449 the courts
    refused to grant any satisfaction for injury to the feelings arising from interference
    in the *consortium*, in circumstances where the *consortium* had not been
    terminated. In these cases sight was lost of the fact that the plaintiff does indeed
    suffer an infringement of his or her personality right to his or her feelings and that
    two separate rights are in fact involved. In *Van der Westhuizen v Van der
    Westhuizen* 1996 2 SA 850 (C) a woman sued her husband for divorce and also
    instituted an action for damages against the woman with whom her husband had
    committed adultery. King said: "Marriage remains the cornerstone, the basic
    structure of our society ... I regard this as a disgraceful case of conscious and
    deliberate desecration of the marriage relationship, necessitating an award of
    damages (I intend to award one lump sum) which will reflect the serious nature of
    the ... misconduct" (852J–853A). The judge then awarded the relatively large
    amount of R20 000 "as damages for adultery, alienation of affection, loss of
    consortium and *contumelia*. . ." (853B).
22 Our case law on this point is clear: see Ex parte *AB* 1910 TPD 1332; *Currie v Currie*
    1942 NPD 362; *Lamprecht v Lamprecht* 1948 4 SA 416 (N); *Asinovsky v Asinovsky*
    1943 CPD 131. *Contra* P I Olivier Huldigingsbundel, Daniel Pont 272; Sonnekus I
    fn I and 311 *et seq*, MAD 1943 SALJ 222. These authors argue that an ordinary
    delictual action should lie between spouses if one of them eg commits adultery.
23 *Wassenaar v Jameson* 1969 2 SA 349 (W); *Amra v Amra* 1971 4 SA 409 (D); *Osman
    v Osman* 1983 2 SA 706 (D); Cronjé and Heaton *Casebook on Family Law* 100-104.
    In *Wassenaar's* case the court questioned whether an interdict is available against
    a third party who commits or intends to commit adultery with one of the spouses.
    In his discussion of the case in 1969 *SALJ* 267, Hahlo points out that, on policy
    considerations, the actions for satisfaction and damages provide better remedies
    than would an attempt to prevent a third party by interdict from committing
    adultery.
24 See Cronjé and Heaton *Persons* ch 1.
25 *Legal System* 78-79.

in which these rights should be placed does not detract from   100
their existence. It is clear that our case law recognises a group of
rights which emanates from marriage and that these rights are
legally protected in several ways, such as by means of an action
for maintenance, actions against third parties on the grounds of
adultery, enticement and harbouring, and, most importantly, the   105
divorce action.

Protection of the marriage relationship against interference by third parties

Our law makes provision for three actions which may be instituted
in situations where a third party interferes with the marriage   110
relationship: the action on the ground of adultery, the action
on the ground of enticement and the action on the ground of
harbouring.

The action on the ground of adultery can be instituted in the event
of a third person committing adultery with one of the spouses.   115
By committing adultery the third party commits a delict and
infringes the other spouse's rights. Our case law recognises that the
other spouse can claim both damages and satisfaction from the
third party.[26]

The action on the ground of enticement can be instituted   120
where a third party intentionally persuades one spouse to leave
the other, and by so doing deprives the latter of *consortium*.[27] In
order to succeed in such an action the plaintiff must prove that
the actions of the third party were indeed the cause of the spouse's
desertion. In terms of the ruling in *Van den Berg v Jooste*,[28] the   125
plaintiff must prove that the defendant enticed, persuaded and
incited the spouse to leave the plaintiff, with the result that this
alienated her affection for him.[29]

The action on the ground of harbouring can be instituted where
a third party provides accommodation to a married person with   130
the deliberate intention of thereby severing the marital
relationship and depriving one spouse of the other's *consortium*.

26 *Bester v Calitz* 1982 3 SA 864 (0).
27 *Woodiwiss v Woodiwiss* 1958 3 SA 609 (D).
28 1960 3 SA 71 (W).
29 See also *Wassenaar v Jameson* 1969 2 SA 349 (W); *Grobbelaar v Havenga* 1964 3
SA 522 (N); Cronjé and Heaton *Casebook on Family Law* 97 *et seq.*

261

The continued existence of the action on the ground of adultery, and even more so the actions on the ground of enticement and harbouring, has rightly been questioned in modern times in view   135 of the fact that adultery is no longer regarded as a ground for divorce but merely is a factor that may indicate that a marriage has broken down irretrievably.[30] All these actions may also be challenged on the ground that they violate the third party's constitutional right to freedom of association.[31]   140

A

30 Divorce Act 70 of 1979 s 4; Van Heerden *LAWSA* vol 16 Marriage par 56.
31 Constitution of the Republic of South Africa 108 of 1996 s 18. See further Heaton *Bill of Rights Compendium* par 3C 14.

i) Look carefully at the section of the text immediately under the heading 'Consortium omnis vitae' (lines 36–40).
    Identify the topic sentence and the main idea of this section of the text.   (4)

j) Write down the main idea of each of the following three paragraphs under the heading mentioned in question (i).   (6)

Carefully study the section of the text marked 'A' in the extract printed above.

k) What is being questioned by the writer in this section of the text? (2)

1) What is the writer's position on the fact that the question is being posed? Quote to substantiate your answer.   (1)

m) What support does the writer give for her point of view?   (2)

n) Do you agree with the writer? Formulate your opinion in your own words.   (1)

WORDS AND THEIR MEANINGS

o) Find the negative forms of the following words in the extracts printed above:

compliance	included
competent	variable
legitimate	normal

(3)

p) Find one word in the second extract which means the same as:
blood relationship   where there is no will
relationship by marriage made to be legitimate   (2)

Sub-total: 40

QUESTION 2: LANGUAGE FOCUS

a) The following two sentences are incorrect in some way. State
what is wrong with them and attempt to improve both sentences.
   i) Hoping that the court will annul their marriage.
   ii) The capacity to marry.   (3)

b) Give the correct form of the words in brackets:
   i)   They are blood (related) and therefore may not get married.
   ii) There is no (prohibit) on your marrying your second cousin.
   iii) To marry your ward you need the (require) consent once he
        is of marriageable age.
   iv) The (controversial) in Roman Dutch law was about
        whether a man could marry his stepmother.   (4)

c) In the following sentence the relative clause has been used
incorrectly. State why you think it is wrong and correct it.

   The woman that I married is my cousin.   (1)

d) In the next sentence, the apostrophe has been used incorrectly.
Correct this error.

   Theyr'e not legally married.   (1)

e) Why have the following sentences been written in the past tense?

   'The position in Roman-Dutch law was controversial. Some of
   the text writers, following Roman law, considered that such a
   marriage was not permitted.'   (1)

Sub-total: 10

QUESTION 3: INTEGRATED SKILLS

You received an incorrect statement of your student account from the
university. Write a letter to the relevant person, drawing his or her
attention to the error.

Sub-total: 10

TOTAL: 60

263

REVISION UNIT 2

The purpose of this unit is to revise the work you did in units 7–13. The revision is in the form of a test and you should duplicate test conditions when you attempt it: clear your table and time yourself. You should not take more than one hour. The questions in this unit are similar to the ones you did in the previous units. Go back to unit 12 and skim-read the hints on test and examination writing before you start.

Remember the following:

- Skim-read the test and decide how much time you need to spend on the various sections, then stick to that time allocation!
- Do not write more than is necessary for the mark allocation.
- Read instructions with extreme care.

QUESTION 1:   READING COMPREHENSION

Read the following extract from *The Bill of Rights Handbook* by De Waal, Currie and Erasmus.

(a) The idea of equality

Equality is a difficult and deeply controversial social ideal. At its most basic and abstract, the idea of equality is a moral idea that people who are similarly situated in relevant ways should be treated similarly. Its logical correlative is the idea that people who are not similarly situated should not be treated alike. For example, it is generally thought wrong to deny women the vote. This is because, when it comes to voting, men and women are in the same position; they are equally capable of exercising political choices. So, if men and women are alike, they should be treated alike. At the same time, it is generally not thought wrong to deny children the vote. This is because children and adults are not in the same position when it comes to their ability to exercise political choices. Because adults and children are not alike, a law restricting the franchise to adults is therefore usually thought to be justifiable.

(b) *The stages of enquiry*

In *Harksen v Lane NO*, the Constitutional Court tabulated the stages of an enquiry into a violation of the equality clause as follows:

(a) Does the provision differentiate between people or categories of people? If so, does the differentiation bear a rational connection to a legitimate government purpose? If it does not, then there is a violation of s 9(1). Even if it does bear a rational connection, it might nevertheless amount to discrimination.

(b) Does the differentiation amount to unfair discrimination? This requires a two-stage analysis:

   (i) Firstly, does the differentiation amount to 'discrimination'. If it is on a specified ground, then discrimination will have been established. If it is not on a specified ground, then whether or not there is discrimination will depend upon whether, objectively, the ground is based on attributes and characteristics which have the potential to impair the fundamental human dignity of persons as human beings or to affect them adversely in a comparably serious manner.

   (ii) If the differentiation amounts to 'discrimination', does it amount to 'unfair discrimination'? If it has been found to have been on a specified ground, then unfairness will be presumed. If on an unspecified ground, unfairness will have to be established by the complainant. The test of unfairness focuses primarily on the impact of the discrimination on the complainant and others in his or her situation.

   If, at the end of this stage of the enquiry, the differentiation is found not to be unfair, then there will be no violation of s 9(3) and (4).

(c) If the discrimination is found to be unfair then a determination will have to be made as to whether the provision can be justified under the limitation clause.

Basically, this means that there is a preliminary enquiry as to whether the impugned provision or conduct differentiates between people or categories of people. This is a threshold test: if there is no differentiation then there can be no question of a violation of any part of s 9. If a provision or conduct does differentiate then a two-stage analysis must be applied. The first stage ((a) above) concerns the right to equal treatment and equality before the law in s 9(1). It tests whether the law or conduct has a rational basis: is there a rational connection between the differentiation in question and a legitimate governmental purpose that it is designed to further or achieve? If the answer is no, then the impugned law or conduct violates s 9(1) and it fails at the first stage. If however, the differentiation is shown to be rational, then the second stage of the enquiry ((b) above) is activated. A differentiation that is rational may nevertheless constitute an unfair discrimination under s 9(3) or (4).

In principle, both unfair discrimination and differentiation without a rational basis can then be justified as limitations of the right to equality in terms of s 36. However, as we will argue below, it is a matter of considerable conceptual difficulty to justify unfairness and irrationality in an 'open and democratic society based on human dignity, equality and freedom'.

Answer the following questions.

1.1 What is the role of government purpose in the first stage of enquiry into the violation of the equality clause? (2)

1.2 What two questions form the basis of the two-stage analysis in stage (b) of the enquiry? Start each question with the words 'Is the differentiation …?' (2)

1.3 In b(i) discrimination can be identified for two reasons: describe them in your own words. (3)

1.4 Why are the stages of enquiry described as 'a threshold test'? (2)

1.5 What is the role played by *rationality* as described in the last paragraph of this extract? (4)

1.6 What is the difference between *differentiation* and *discrimination*? (2)

1.7 What is the difference between *violation* and *limitation*? (2)

1.8 Provide an example of a government purpose. (2)

1.9 Quote a sentence that indicates the problematic nature of finding reasons for unjustified limitations to the right to equality. (1)

WORDS AND THEIR MEANINGS

1.10 Write down the verb form of the following words:
Violation
Complainant
Analysis (3)

1.11 Write down the negative forms of the following words:
Equal
Rational (2)

SUBTOTAL: 35

266

QUESTION 2: LANGUAGE FOCUS

2.1 Read the following (adapted) paragraph and give the correct form of the words in brackets. Give only the number and your answer.

'However, the Constitutional Court (1. hold) that it (2. is/was) neither desirable nor feasible to divide the equal treatment and non-discrimination components of s 9 into watertight compartments: the equality right (3. is/was) a composite right. Moreover, in *National Coalition for Gay and Lesbian Equality v Minister of Justice*, the Constitutional Court (4. hold) that a court need not 'inevitably' perform both stages of the enquiry ... In other words, in those cases in which a court (5. find) that a law or conduct injustifiably (6. infringe) s 9(3) or (4), there (7. is/was) no need to first consider whether the law or conduct (8. is/ was) a violation of s 9(1). In *Harksen v Lane NO* the Constitutional Court (9. state) that the limitation analysis (10. involve) 'a weighing of the purpose and effect of the provision in question'.'

SUBTOTAL: 10

QUESTION 3: INTEGRATED SKILLS

Study the following extract on the historical context of the equality clause in the Constitution and write a summary of no more than 20 lines or 250 words. (15)

TOTAL: 50

(b) The historical context

The importance of the equality right to the post-apartheid constitutional order is obvious. The apartheid social and legal system was squarely based on inequality and discrimination. As the Constitutional Court has pointed out, apartheid systematically discriminated against black people in all aspects of social life. Black people were prevented from becoming owners of property or even residing in areas classified as 'white', which constituted nearly 90 per cent of the land mass of South Africa; senior jobs and access to established schools and universities were denied to them; civic amenities, including transport systems, public parks, libraries and many shops were also closed to black people. Instead, separate and inferior facilities were provided. The deep scars of this appalling programme are still visible in our society.

267

The 'deep scars' of decades of systematic racial discrimination can be seen in all the key measures of quality of life in South Africa. White South Africans are significantly healthier and better nourished than their black fellow-citizens. They enjoy relatively high standards of literacy and education. Infant mortality rates and life expectancy among black South Africans are equivalent to those of the poorest nations of the world. Wealth and poverty are notoriously unequally distributed.

The legacy of inequality inherited from the past means that the constitutional commitment to equality cannot simply be understood as a commitment to formal equality. It is not sufficient simply to remove racist law books and to ensure that similar laws cannot be enacted in the future. This will result in the society that is formally equal but that is radically unequal in every other way. The need to confront this legacy is recognised in the equality clause, particularly in s 9(2) which permits measures 'designed to protect or advance persons, or categories of persons disadvantaged by unfair discrimination'. In addition, the Constitution protects a list of socio-economic rights which require the state to implement progressive measures to achieve a minimum level of basic goods such as education for all, the right not to be refused emergency medical treatment, and the right of a child to basic nutrition, shelter, basic health care services and social services.

PROGRESSION OF SKILLS

1 NOTE-MAKING

Unit 1:   Note-making skills: staying organized
Unit 2:   Note-making skills: developing a system of abbreviations
Unit 3:   Note-making skills: listening and making notes
Unit 4:   Note-making skills: using the textbook
Unit 5:   Note-making skills: listening and reading notes, using diagrams to represent complex texts.

2 SUMMARIZING

(Summarizing is often linked with note-making and extended writing skills):

Unit 2:   Identifying main & supporting ideas. Diagrammatic representations of a text
Unit 3:   Main ideas in a case
Unit 4:   Use of symbols when producing a summary for study purposes, using writer's summary to make own summary
Unit 5:   Use of headings, main ideas and topic sentences, mindmaps
Unit 7:   Summarizing the gist of an act: identifying key words, breaking up sentences, using headings to predict content and then using answers to write a summary
Unit 8:   Summarizing of newspaper article, linking title and contents, identifying headings in an act
Unit 9:   Breaking up complicated sentences, simplification of language
Unit 10:   Re-arranging jumbled summary of magazine text
Unit 11:   Identifying structure of newspaper article, tracing an argument
Unit 12:   Abbreviated style of subject lines (in letters) and application of this skill in summarizing

3 EXTENDED WRITING SKILLS

Unit 1:   Semi-formal letters and faxes to the University
Unit 2:   Formation of paragraphs
Units 3,
4 and 5:   Identifying main lines of argument and writing them down

269

Unit 6:   Answering problem questions
Unit 7:   Integrating references to statutes in writing
Unit 8:   Drafting and planning argumentative writing
Unit 10:   Supporting and expressing opinions in argumentative writing;
            use of reported speech in discussions of cases
Unit 11:   Planning and writing an argumentative essay
Unit 13:   Improving formal, business letters
Unit 14:   Hints on writing a research paper

4 READING SKILLS

Most reading texts are introduced by pre-reading exercises to focus readers'
attention.

Units 1
and 2:   Overview reading:
            Understanding conventions such as bold print, arrows in the
            text
            Making sense of diagrams that provide an overview
Unit 3:   Reading a court case
Unit 4:   Reading from a subject-specific textbook
Unit 5:   Reading complex texts (1)
Unit 6:   Reading complex texts (2), dealing with footnotes
Unit 7:   Reading an act (1)
Unit 8:   Reading an act (2) and relating this to a newspaper article
Unit 9:   Comparing complex and plain language using extracts from
            constitutions
Unit 10:   Reading from the popular press (1): identifying facts and
            opinions
Unit 11:   Reading from the popular press (2): tracing an argument
Unit 12:   Reading literary texts: comparing different genres
Unit 13:   Identifying the register of communication in a law office
Unit 14:   Academic writing: the difference between academic research
            and solving problems of a legal nature

5 STUDY SKILLS

Unit 1:   Drawing up a schedule of work
Unit 2:   Using the library
Unit 3:   Finding a court case in the library
Unit 4:   Multiple-choice questions
Unit 5:   Mindmaps
Unit 6:   Problem-type questions
Unit 7:   Referring to an act in writing

Unit 8:   Planning, drafting and revising argumentative writing
Unit 9:   Simplifying legal texts
Unit 10:   Integrating quotations from textbooks and cases in extended writing
Unit 11:   Dealing with test and examination questions
Unit 12:   Writing examinations and tests
Unit 13:   Electronic mail
Unit 14:   The whole unit is about doing research

6 LANGUAGE FOCUS

Unit 1:   Parts of speech: verb, adverb, noun, adjective; word formation: negative forms of adjectives, adjective build-up, nominalization
Unit 2:   Parts of speech: articles, pronouns, prepositions, participles; complete and incomplete sentences, asking questions and making requests
Unit 3:   Breaking down complex sentences, relative clauses, connectors
Unit 4:   Pronouns; conditionals
Unit 5:   Sequence of tenses: simple and perfect; apostrophe
Unit 6:   Sequence of tenses in discussion of cases
Unit 7:   Passives
Unit 8:   Modals: degrees of certainty and uncertainty
Unit 9:   Articles and prepositions
Unit 10:   Modals (in expression of opinion); reported speech
Unit 11:   Structures of contrast, reason and purpose
Unit 12:   Sequence of tenses, avoidance of continuous tense; interaction past and past perfect tenses
Unit 13:   Passives and modal auxiliaries

BIBLIOGRAPHY AND RECOMMENDED READING

In the list below sources indicated with an asterisk are recommended for lecturers who would like to elaborate on the exercises in this book or who would like to read more about the language of the law.

* BHATIA, V.K. 1993. *Analysing genre: language use in professional settings.* London: Longman.

BLOCK, G. 1992. *Effective legal writing for law students and lawyers.* Westbury, New York: The Foundation Press, Inc.

BOSMAN, H.C., 1999. *Cold Stone Jug.* Cape Town: Human & Rousseau.

BUTTERWORTHS FORMS AND PRECEDENTS 2 1994. *Marriage and settlement contracts.* Durban: Butterworths.

CAMPBELL, E., GLASSON, E.J., YORK, L.P. and SHARPE, J.M. 1988. *Legal research: materials and methods.* Sydney: The law book company.

DAVEL, C.J. and JORDAAN, R.A. 2000. *Law of persons: Student's handbook.* Cape Town: Juta.

DE WAAL, M.J., CURRIE, I and ERASMUS, G. 2001 *The Bill of Rights Handbook.* Cape Town: Juta

DE WAAL, M.J., SCHOEMAN, M.C. and WIECHERS, N.J. 1996. *Law of succession: Student's handbook.* Kenwyn: Juta.

CRONJÉ and HEATON, 1999. *South African Family Law.*

EHRENBECK, M. 1995. Constitutional Law — Human Rights — Right of access to state Information — Police docket — *Khala v Minister of Safety and Security* 1994 4 SA 218 WLD. *Codicillus* 36(1):72-73.

FLANZ, G.H. (ed.) 1996. *Constitutions of the countries of the world.* New York: Oceana Publications.

* HASHEMI, L. with MURPHY, R. 1995. *English grammar in use: Supplementary exercises with answers.* Cambridge: Cambridge University Press.

JORDAAN, L. 1993. *Mens rea* — common purpose — dissociation from — *S v Singo* 1993 1 SACR 226 (A). *Codicillus* 34(2):75-76.

KLEYN, D. and VILJOEN, F. 1995. *Beginner's guide for law students.* Cape Town: Juta.

* KOK, A, NIENABER, A, VILJOEN, F. 2002 *Skills workbook for law students* Kenwyn: Juta

LE ROUX, W. 2000. "Something as strange as the African veld": Herman Charles Bosman, storytelling and democratic citizenship. *Codicillus* 41(2): 7–21.

NAUDÉ, J.P. 1994. *Butterworths forms and precedents* (6):2: Marriage and settlement contracts, mining and mineral contracts. Durban: Butterworths.

NAUDÉ, J.P. 1994. *Butterworths forms and precedents* (6): 1: Leases. Durban: Butterworths.

PRESIDENTIAL PRIVACY. 1996. *Mail and Guardian* 12:12, March 22–28.

RAIMES, A. 1992. (2nd ed.) *Grammar troublespots: an editing guide for students.* New York: St Martin's Press.

* RILEY, A. 1994. *English for law.* Ismaning: Max Hueber.

RONGE, B. 2000 Filthy Lucre. *Sunday Times Magazine* of 2000.

ROOS, A. 1994. Law of Delict — Defamation — Defences — Onus of proof — Neethling v Du Preez and Others; *Neethling v The Weekly Mail and Others* 1994 1 SA 708 (A). *Codicillus* 35(2):102–104.

SINCLAIR, J.D. 1996 *The Law of Marriage.* Kenwyn: Juta.

SMITH, A.S. 1995. The legislated double bluff: How our democratic rights are undermined by the language of the new constitution. *Proceedings of the 15th Annual Conference of the Southern African Applied Linguistics Association,* Stellenbosch, 10–12 July. 532–554.

STRAUSS, S.A. 1991. *Doctor, patient and the law.* Pretoria: Van Schaik.

USHER, D. 1995. Plain Words. *Fair Lady,* 17 May 1995.

VAN DER WALT, A.J. and PIENAAR, G. 1997. *Introduction to the law of property.* Cape Town: Juta.

* VAN DER WALT, C. 1992. Teaching a foreign language, the language of the law. *Tydskrif vir Hedendaagse Rorneins-Hollandse Reg* 55(l):94–102.

* VAN DER WALT, C. and NIENABER, A.G. 1996. The language needs of undergraduate law students: A report on empirical investigations. *De Jure* 29(l):71–88.

VAN WYK, A.M.A. 1991. Into the 21st century with the reform of planning law. In VAN DER WALT, A.J. (ed.) *Land reforrn and the future of landownership in South Africa.* Juta: Cape Town. 69–79.

WATERS, M. and WATERS, A. 1995. *Study tasks in English.* Cambridge: Cambridge University Press.

LIST OF CASES

Tshabalala v Natal Law Society 1996 4 SA 150 (N)

Van der Westhuizen v Van der Westhuizen and Another 1996 2 SA 850 (C)

The State v Bram Fischer Transvaal Provincial Division, 28 March 1966 (Unpublished Court Records)

LIST OF STATUTES

Admission of Advocates Act 74 of 1964

Approved Revised Draft of the Constitution of the Republic of Liberia

Drugs and Drug Trafficking Act 140 of 1992

Constitution of the Republic of South Africa Act 200 of 1993

Constitution of South Africa Act 108 of 1996

Criminal Procedure Act 51 of 1977

The Simplified version of the Approved Revised Draft Constitution of the Republic of Liberia